Barcode in back

D1569388

Digital Publics

Today we often hear academics, commentators, pundits and politicians telling us that new media has transformed activism, providing an array of networks for ordinary people to become creatively involved in a multitude of social and political practices.

But what exactly is the ideology lurking behind these positive claims made about digital publics?

By recourse to various critical thinkers, including Marx, Bakhtin, Deleuze and Guattari, and Gramsci, *Digital Publics* systematically unpacks this ideology. It explains how a number of influential social theorists and management gurus have consistently argued that we now live in new informational times based in global digital systems and new financial networks, which create new sbjectivities and power relations in societies.

Digital Publics traces the historical roots of this thinking, demonstrates its flaws and offers up an alternative Marxist-inspired theory of the public sphere, cultural political economy and financialisation.

The book will appeal to scholars and students of cultural studies, critical management studies, political science and sociology.

John Michael Roberts is Senior Lecturer in Sociology and Communications at Brunel University. He has taught the sociology of new media at undergraduate and postgraduate levels at Brunel for ten years. His publications include *New Media and Public Activism: Neoliberalism, the State and Radical Protest in the Public Sphere* (Policy Press, 2014), *The Competent Public Sphere: Global Political Economy, Dialogue, and the Contemporary Workplace* (Palgrave, 2009) and *The Aesthetics of Free Speech: Rethinking the Public Sphere* (Palgrave, 2003). His research interests include cultural and social theory, new media activism, the public sphere, free speech, state theory and global political economy.

Routledge Advances in Sociology

Digital Publics

Cultural political economy, financialisation and creative organisational politics

John Michael Roberts

Routledge
Taylor & Francis Group

LONDON AND NEW YORK

First published 2015
by Routledge
711 Third Avenue, New York, NY 10017

and by Routledge
2 Park Square, Milton Park, Abingdon, Oxon OX14 4RN

Routledge is an imprint of the Taylor & Francis Group, an informa business

British Library Cataloguing-in-Publication Data
A catalogue record for this book is available from the British Library

Library of Congress Cataloging in Publication Data
Roberts, John Michael
Digital publics: cultural political economy, financialisation and creative
organisational politics / by John Roberts.
pages cm. -- (Routledge advances in sociology)
1. Information society. 2. Digital media. 3. Public spaces. I. Title.
HM851.R627 2014
302.23'1--dc23
2014020220

ISBN: 978-0-415-64125-8 (hbk)
ISBN: 978-0-203-08213-3 (ebk)

Typeset in Times New Roman
by Integra Software Services Pvt. Ltd.

Contents

Acknowledgements

I would like to thank my colleagues in Sociology and Communications at Brunel University, Monica Degen, Sharon Lockyer, Sarita Malik, Sanjay Sharma and Peter Wilkin, for providing a supportive environment in the workplace. I would also like to thank Joseph Ibrahim at Leeds Metropolitan University for sustained friendship over many years.

Brunel University allowed me to go on research leave for one term during 2012, which enabled me to start work on the book. I am grateful to them for this time away from normal admin and teaching duties.

I am also thankful for the excellent guidance of Gerhard Boomgaarden, Emily Briggs, Emily Davies and Alyson Claffey at Routledge, all of whom have been extremely supportive while I have been writing the book.

My mother and sister have as always provided me with loads of encouragement throughout the writing process. Lucy has provided constant love and support throughout the writing process and beyond. I dedicate this book to all three of them.

1 Introduction

Digital publics and cultural political economy

Introduction

It is common for many social commentators to argue that at least since the 1980s there has been a gradual shift towards the 'aestheticization of everyday life'. Usually this is taken to imply that capitalism is now overwhelmed by images and signs associated with a proliferation in advertising, brands, media spectacles, reality TV, smart digital technology and so on. We live in an age of excessive consumption where the exchange value of goods has overtaken the use value so that life no longer has any 'depth' but has itself collapsed into an array of images (Featherstone 1990: 66–67). Culture and communication media now saturate society to such an extent that we can finally talk about a 'cultural circuit of capital' that has taken hold in society. Culture is said to have moved beyond the consumption of goods to encompass a whole range of social spheres. Today, so some argue, culture circulates through consumption, production, identity, representation and regulation (see du Gay 1997).

Some in business and management broadly agree with these sentiments. Popular management texts, for instance, often herald the onset of network 'fluid' organisational formations based primarily around the ascendancy of information and knowledge. Under these circumstances, organisations are called upon to foster a cultural outlook in their respective workforce attuned to the need to be responsive and flexible in order to capture and take advantage of the rapid turnover and transformation of global information and knowledge. What were once thought to be stable social structures have thus increasingly given way to fluid and messy social processes. Business guru Alec Reed (2003: 4–8) is typical of those from the management community who suggest that the nation-state has lost its powers to create wealth and regulate a country's labour markets. Indeed, suggests Reed in a manner that evokes some contemporary socio-logical insights, the social structures once associated with the welfare state are disappearing, to be replaced by the likes of 'fluid' temporary job markets (Reed 2003: 14). Meanwhile, Davis and Meyer (1998) employ the metaphor of 'blur' to describe what's novel about the 'new' global economy.

> In the BLUR world, products and services are merging. Buyers sell and sellers buy. Neat value chains are messy economic webs. Homes are

offices. No longer is there a clear line between structure and process, owning and using, knowing and learning, real and virtual. Less and less separates employee and employer. In the world of capital – itself as much a liability as an asset – value moves so fast you can't tell stock from flow. On every front, opposites are blurring.

(Davis and Meyer 1998: 7)

Others, however, adopt a different and arguably more critical approach towards the informational economy. Jessop (2005) situates the rise of the informational economy within the structural contradictions and strategic dilemmas of contemporary capitalism. In particular, he is interested in how specific 'economic imaginaries' become established through semiotic material and discursive narratives, and aim to legitimise new or existing socio-economic hegemonic projects, such as that of neoliberalism. In this respect he makes a distinction between the contradictions and strategic dilemmas evident in 'real' socio-economic projects and how the economy is 'imaginatively narrated (as a) more or less coherent subset of these activities' (Jessop 2005: 145; see also Sum 2009). Of course, the two are closely connected because narratives must be attached to socio-economic relations in order to prove convincing, while narratives likewise serve to naturalise socio-economic activities if accepted as being common sense by enough people. Nevertheless, where Jessop also differs from the other informational perspectives described is in his belief that the discursive and non-discursive realms are closely connected but do not collapse into one another. For these reasons, Jessop is critical of many informational perspectives because he thinks they often become part of hegemonic and discursive projects that naturalise and mystify specific contradictions in society.

This book takes some of the theoretical insights develop by Jessop and other critical theorists of cultural political economy, and applies and develops them to investigate what is sometimes referred to as the digital public sphere, or just 'digital publics'. By recourse to a Marxist approach to cultural political economy, the book therefore unpacks some of the empirical and theoretical assumptions deeply embedded within digital publics in order to ascertain exactly what might constitute a meaningful type of political engagement in today's new media public spheres. This is a worthwhile project if for no other reason than the fact that some of what is claimed or said about the capacity for digital publics to make a political impact in society is often rather moderate in a sense of containing political aspirations within existing liberal institutions. Alternatively, much of what is written about digital publics by left-liberals and political radicals often makes assertions that are far too general to be useful. Most commonly, they argue we have entered a qualitative new period in history in which political activism has changed beyond all recognition from previous periods, and that digital technology now socially constructs knowledge about our world around us. The current book seeks to criticise both viewpoints, although it concentrates more on the second school of thought because the book shares many of this school's empirical and theoretical beliefs. Before we map out the content of this book in more detail, it is worth, first, examining some of the assertions made about the changing nature of the public sphere in relation to digital technology.

Digital publics and mobile communications

Arising as a way to understand the nature, shape and form of how people might become involved in democracy and participation, the term 'public sphere' directs one's attention to the different mechanisms and ways of getting people to engage in debate and discussion with one another. To this extent, Somers provides a neat definition of the public sphere as being

> a contested participatory site in which actors with overlapping identities as legal subjects, citizens, economic actors, and family and community members, form a public body and emerge in negotiations and contestations over political and social life.
>
> (Somers 1993: 589)

Drache (2008) adds that because of its contested participatory nature it is often difficult to know where to draw the line for rights and responsibilities between private interests and public purposes. Globalisation gives this issue a further dimension, says Drache, because it compels nation-states to look at their traditional conceptions of rights for their citizens within a context of rapidly porous boundaries between countries. 'Societies need rules, and when political power is no longer contained within the nation-state, finding new ways to address transnational issues, from poverty eradication to climate change, becomes a primary focus point for publics' (Drache 2008: 8).

The rise of global and digital societies has also prompted some to argue that the boundaries of the public sphere have fundamentally altered in form and content. Digital technology naturally lends itself to circulating debates, documents, information, images, video footage and so forth, across the globe. The very fact that all of these modes of communication are transformed into zeroes and ones indicates how information can be compressed and transferred across technological formats, such as credit cards, iPads, laptops, library cards, phones and TV. This convergence of media formats means that information is now interchangeable across digital networks and through a wide variety of technological arrangements and formats (Miller 2011: 73–74).

But the effects that digital media has on society is also part of a broader set of assertions made about contemporary societies. Many believe, for example, that we live in digital networked times in which 'normal' boundaries associated with 'modern' societies have become blurred and liquid-like. Urban space has become more complex, with different spatial scales, nodes and networks criss-crossing one another in new ways. Computer networks, airports, roads, mobile phones and so on are both moored to specific spaces such as an office and they are free of these moorings to move across other connected nodes and bring to life new spatial relations with other human and non-human bodies and objects. Consumption has therefore inescapably become grounded in everyday representations. Globalisation, for example, is portrayed to us through the likes of everyday consumer products (e.g. coca-cola cans), iconic figures (e.g. Nelson Mandela) and global communities (e.g. the Olympic Games). As a result, the 'private' consumption of everyday goods is irrevocably connected with a global public (Szerszynski and Urry 2006). Internet technology is an exemplary symbol of these developments. People now gain everyday public information sitting in their private spaces at home, while data transforms people into 'bits' of information to be reassembled elsewhere in numerous databases into non-private virtual selves (Hannam *et al.* 2006; Sheller and Urry 2003).

Mobility is likewise palpable in the way in which the temporal rhythms of the normal working week have changed. Laguerre (2004) observes that while it is still possible to delineate what he terms is the 'civil week' comprised by a linear notion of time – working from the morning until the evening for example – he also notes that we have become immersed in a 'cyberweek'. This latter temporal movement is a continual non-linear 168-hour week. These days, therefore, a week is both linear and non-linear and gives us the choice and freedom of how to structure our day. 'Because the cyberweek has no fixed beginning or end, it does not follow the logic of any of these other weeks. It may start or end at any time' (Laguerre 2004: 230). Different temporalities can therefore be noted based around the fluid interrelationships of a civil week and a cyberweek. Both flow into one another, thus creating a situation in which cyberweek and civil week feed off from one another and instigate new temporal hybrids. Other consequences follow these changing coordinates of time. Work time can now be compressed into fewer, albeit longer, working days, which in turn alters leisure time.

Arguably, one of the best illustrations of how digital media has reconfigured the public–private divide comes in the guise of mobile phones. While the first venture into commercial mobile telephony arose in the USA just two years after the Second World War, it was in 1979 that the so-called 'first generation' (1G) commercial cellular network system was established in Tokyo. Increasing digitalisation of mobile phones during the 1980s and 1990s meant that they could be devised with greater features such as address books and an alarm setting. It is during this period that mobiles started becoming a ubiquitous element of life. But these 'second generation' (2G) mobile phones were soon being eclipsed by 'third generation' phones throughout the early 2000s. Equipped with more interactive elements, mobile phones entered an era that saw them converge their design with other media devices and formats such as computer databases, the Internet, movies, satellite images and so on (see Green and Haddon 2009; Lacohée *et al.* 2003). In a relatively short space of time, then, the form and content of mobile phones have obviously made some dramatic changes but they have also visibly changed social behaviour along with the relationship between public space and private space.

Personalisation is also evident in the use of mobile phones. Think momentarily about communities. According to Wellman (2001), whereas people once lived in close-knit communities based on face-to-face interaction, this was slowly being merged by place-to-place interaction throughout the twentieth century. Cars, for example, enabled people to move around locations beyond where they lived and this meant that they could socialise beyond immediate communities. With the rise of mobile technology and cyberspace communities we have now moved into the era of person-to-person interaction. People no longer have to be physically present to the person they want to communicate and interact with. At the same time, though, new modes of digital communication encourage individuals to stay in regular contact with others. Personalised community networks, Wellman further observes, thus encourage greater socialising between individual people in a manner no longer restricted by physical boundaries. Far from fragmenting society, mobile phones can therefore serve to reconfigure public and private spaces in ways that strengthen friendship and family ties. On one level, at least it is possible to say that mobile technologies therefore at a minimum give people a sense of being permanently connected to other people and other spaces (Sloop and Gunn 2010).

Other research finds that mobiles bring families together in new, meaningful ways. Devitt and Roker (2009) discovered that mobile phones helped families manage their lives in a generally positive way. Mobiles are a convenient technological tool for family members to speak to one another. Moreover, parents told Devitt and Roker that mobiles offered security and safety for their children, while children generally felt that some functions of a mobile phone such as text messaging offered them new avenues to discuss potentially difficult subjects, say, being bullied at school, in an alternative environments that they considered to be 'safer'. In these instances, mobile phones have helped to con-solidate particular social ties. Geser (2006) nevertheless insists that mobile phones do not necessarily develop new social ties but tend instead to strengthen existing social ties (e.g. family social ties). In this way, mobile phones reinforce close-knit social ties in an almost pre-modern, traditional manner in the sense that mobiles contribute towards making one dependent on a narrow range of 'significant others'. Increasingly we 'keep in touch' with significant others and in the process strengthen divisions and boundaries between others and ourselves.

Schroeder (2010) adds an important caveat here by arguing that while similarities can be noted across societies there are also important cultural differences between countries in the use of mobiles. For example, in Sweden and the USA people use the Internet to send emails more so than in Japan and Korea. One of the reasons for this is that in Japan and Korea there is generally no limit to the amount of information one can place on a text message, and so these are used like traditional emails. What follows from this is that the changing boundaries between public and private will no doubt also be distinct in different countries. Others point out that mobile phones often serve to disrupt social interaction between people rather than strengthen social contact. Rettie (2009) draws on the work of Erving Goffman to distinguish between synchronous interactions, which are located in the same time but not necessarily in the same place (e.g. phone conversations), and asynchronous media, which are located in different times and places (e.g. letter writing or sending a text message). Synchronous interactions therefore have a 'co-presence', as when two people communicate and cooperate through shared experiences in real time. Rettie discovered in her qualitative study of 32 individuals that co-presence through mobile phones operates in different ways that regularly disrupt communication. For instance, two people in face-to-face conversation might have their talk disrupted by a mobile phone, which in turn leads to a decline in focused interaction between both. Text messages also do not necessarily give people a shared definition of cooperative practices and ongoing intersubjective experience. Some of Rettie's respondents for example saw texts as being based on 'distance' from the other.

Researchers are equally interested in how mobile phones capture an aesthetic moment in how public and private spheres are negotiated. Katz and Sugiyama (2006) develop the term 'apparatgeist' as a means to understand how people use mobile technologies as symbolic technological tools in relation to the body and social identity. For example, people will frequently choose a mobile phone by how it publicly represents them in terms of fashion. Mobiles thus demonstrate how people can be part of communicative interest to others and be desired in some way or another. Mobile phones are therefore not merely used only for instrumental reasons such as talking to others, but are also used for more symbolic modes of communication. Katz and Sugiyama also found that heavy users of mobiles were more fashion-sensitive than light users. In fact, heavy users favoured style over battery use. Therefore, they did not have a functional attitude towards mobile phones.

Camera phones can also be thought of as a symbolic object. In fact, according to Lee (2009), camera phones enable people to engage in a form of self-disclosure and self-exhibitionism by blurring the public–private boundary. While mobile phones give people the opportunity to create their own social space as they travel around public spheres, camera phones have the potential to transform every event in public space into an object of personal photography. This means that everyday and often intimate images, images that are frequently disregarded by traditional photography because they are perceived as being just too banal, now find a place in the public sphere. Camera phones capture conversations, self-expressions and display social relationships. In other words, they 'aestheticise' the everyday; or, suggests Lee, camera phones render visible those micro-activities of everyday experiences of street life that might usually go unnoticed. More precisely, they have the potential to capture those moments in between private and public and in the process capture the mobility and constant shifting boundaries between both. There is also a learning curve at work here. People become skilled at recognising what photos might prove attractive to particular online groups or particular websites. A specific online group might consider some photos more newsworthy, others might be considered more humorous, while other images might be thought of as being artistic, and so on. In the words of Green and Haddon: 'Hence the choice of pictures taken is not just an individual decision but reflects a collective sense of what is appropriate to share' (Green and Haddon 2009: 134).

Social networking sites of course provide a good illustration of the shifting boundaries between public and private spheres. YouTube is one amongst numerous social media sites that has achieved this blurring of the edges between public and private. According to Lange (2007), YouTube users disclose private incidents and events to their friends. Indeed, the 'friends only' option means that one can limit who will view a particular uploaded clip. We also know that hundreds, sometimes millions, of strangers watch many clips, and will develop their own opinions and views about what they see. Think for a moment about the famous clip of a man walking with his dog, Fenton, in Richmond Park, London. Somebody else walking nearby captured the moment when Fenton escaped from his owner to chase after some deer who had until then been quietly grazing. The next few seconds of the clip, watched by millions on YouTube, showed the owner running after Fenton, shouting his dog's name with an exasperated tone. Fenton meanwhile was seen running off into the sunset after the extremely scared deer. Who would have thought that such a short clip would have been viewed by so many across the world, many of whom had their own beliefs and thoughts about this private event between a dog owner and his dog. But like many social media sites, YouTube also enables its users to hide their real identity, so that their private selves are masked in this public setting. What Lange conveys is the reworking of not only public–private boundaries but also presence–absence boundaries as well as the distinction between patterned and random interactions. In all of these instances, public–private boundaries are remade in new ways, which also facilitate unpredictable patterns of behaviour to emerge across countries (Lange 2007).

These characteristics of digital publics are complemented by a new emphasis on democracy. People now sit in the privacy of their homes and yet still engage in public debates and discussions through a whole number of digital devices. Moreover, politicians and policy-makers have increasingly experimented with digital technology as a means to get more people actively engaged in the decision-making process. In an age in which different communities are being constantly consulted about various policy initiatives, new media presents policy-makers with innovative possibilities to enhance these consultative forums. For example, digital media has the capacity to distribute questionnaires to constituents, reduce costs in gathering information and circulate reports to local residents.

A cursory glance at social networking sites demonstrates the potential of this deliberative model. Often, social networking sites such as a Facebook page are set up to capture support for a particular social or political cause. Local citizens concerned with, say, planning permission being granted to a superstore chain in their vicinity can create a Facebook page as part of an ongoing campaign against such a development. Not only can the site have normal e-democracy tools at its disposal such as a petition for people to sign, but it can also be part of other networks of activism, both online and offline. In other words, social networking sites have quickly become an everyday aspect of a variety of strategies adopted in social and political campaigns designed to raise awareness and to stimulate public deliberation around a specific issue (Anderson *et al.* 2010; Chadwick 2009; Evans-Cowley and Hollander 2010; Hague and Loader 1999). According to Coleman, these types of consultations represent potentials to move outside formal parliamentary politics and they provide spaces to experiment with more engaging forms of participation beyond peer-generated chat rooms that often generate 'prejudiced and banal political arguments' (Coleman 2004: 6).

Digital publics have other functions however, some of which might actually take us away from being politically and socially active in our communities. After all, as Dahlgren (2009: 152) observes, the Internet and social media have given people a sense that they can engage in a large variety of social participation in society. Amateur musicians post up their latest recording onto YouTube, others vote online to keep their favourite contestant on a reality TV show, while a multitude of people debate and discuss a whole range of issues with others across the globe on numerous online chat forums. But this 'feeling' of empowerment, in which ordinary people are encouraged to contribute to an array of public discussions through the likes of Internet chat forums, might simply be exactly that, namely a 'feeling' rather than real democratic discussion. Perhaps Dean is therefore right to be sceptical of much that goes under digital democracy. Perhaps she is correct to say that we live in an age where messages have been disarticulated from their real context so that they become instead part of a never-ending circulating stream of information through new media outlets (Dean 2005). The labour of producing messages is thus lost to its circulation. Empowerment through democratic participation is then empowerment only for those prepared to fit a pre-defined model of participation: one can contribute to digital publics by voicing one's opinions online, but just don't expect that you'll receive an answer or get your hands dirty in 'real' activism (Charles 2012: 52).

Many others enter this debate by claiming we have entered a qualitative new phase in capitalism. According to Thrift (2005: 6), capitalism is today mediated through a cultural discursive circuit made up of the likes of 'business schools, management consultants, management gurus and the media'. There are now more consumer products that can be bought online that also require our active input into producing the good in question, with online digital games being a prime example as they rely on the consumer actively creating online games' characters. Social life has moreover become arbitrated by 'media events' whereby most bits of public information have become *media*-ted and the 'social world' is now totally media saturated (Lash 2002). We thus live in a world of immediacy. Castells similarly argues that we exist in a time of 'real virtuality':

It is a system in which reality itself ... is entirely captured, fully immersed in a virtual image setting, in the world of make believe, in which appearances are not just on the screen through which experience is communicated, but they become the experience.

(Castells 2000: 404)

In making these claims, however, these social theorists argue that we live in 'new times' that are qualitatively different to previous phases of capitalism. They thus misrecognise how capitalism still in fact operates through the same basic contradictions and processes as it has always done and that the nation-state, culture and continuing inherent contradictions of capitalism operate together to create hegemonic projects that benefit certain groups in society against the vast majority. But if this is indeed the case then we require a different set of theoretical tools to understand the complexities of contemporary capitalism and digital publics. These can be found in a Marxist-inspired cultural political economy (CPE) approach.

Cultural political economy

Marxist-inspired CPE takes seriously the need to incorporate a semiotic approach to help explain and understand how specific socio-economic projects gain hegemony and legitimacy in civil society (Jones 2008: 384). CPE therefore draws on critical discourse analysis, critical semiotic analysis, Gramscian theory and elements of post-structuralism to address this issue in Marxist theory. Critical discourse analysis explores how some texts help to justify certain ideological and unequal power relations (Fairclough 2010: 3–10). Semiotics is part of a critical discourse approach and investigates a whole array of cultural communication and meaning that includes written documents and texts, hermeneutics, rhetoric and identity-formation. By incorporating Gramscian theory and elements of neo-Foucauldian theory (see Sum 2009), Marxist-inspired CPE scholars are interested in how discursive and semiotic practices engage in an ongoing process to help (re)make the social relations and narratives of specific ideological socio-economic projects and in so doing include some groups in its hegemonic narrative while excluding others. Those who are excluded from a hegemonic project will nevertheless often develop their own alternative identities, narratives, discourses and so on, which may disrupt the hegemonic formation of a socio-economic project in various ways (Jessop 2004: 161).

What is usually referred to as 'the economy' is of course an immensely complex and chaotic system, which can never be regulated in its full complexity. What is required, according to CPE theorists, is that selective elements of the economy are chosen as sites for regulation by those aiming to win support for a socio-economic project. In this respect, a key moment for CPE's analysis is the application of three evolutionary mechanisms – variation, selection and retention – to the analysis of economic imaginaries. Variation explores how economic imaginaries operate at a number of levels of complexity and at different sites and scales. How and why a particular economic narrative emerges at any one site can often be contingent, but as soon as it starts to be created in a particular site and/or scale it tends to reduce variation of economic alternatives to particular issues or problems (Jessop 2012: 61). Once particular forces – governments, think tanks, particular global governance bodies, business associations, trade unions and so on – start to strategically manipulate and define the discursive parameters of a socio-economic project at a meso-level, semiotic material is selected by these forces and groups to justify their respective socio-economic project.

Such semiotic material must of course resonate with the lived experience of at least some groups in civil society if it is to gain hegemonic potential. Famously, for example, during the 1980s Mrs Thatcher's government chose to focus its reforming zeal on nationalised sectors of the UK economy in order to win support for its privatisation agenda. To this extent, the Conservative Party employed a variety of semiotic materials to justify its ideological position. These included policy documents from neoliberal think tanks and quango bodies, media images from the right-wing press and the use of financial data with the aim to promote the interests of the financial sector above that of manufacturing (Hall 1988; Jessop *et al.* 1988). The Conservatives also engaged in emotional dialogue with selective publics in British civil society by claiming that only neoliberal policies, such as the monetary desire to tackle inflation, could save Britain from past political mistakes and thereby overcome the 'pathologies' of decline associated with the likes of public ownership. In addition, they had to win the hearts and minds of leading civil servants, selective elements of the financial markets and some working in the nationalised industries themselves (Foster 1992: 109; Tomlinson 2012: 67). Global governance bodies also lent credence to Thatcher's neoliberal privatisation crusade. During the 1990s and early 2000s, for instance, the OECD circulated policy documents that set out the benefits for governments if they embraced knowledge-based economies, the financial sector, and service sector. Along all of these points OECD policy researchers produced indicators, numbers, texts and new utterances (e.g. 'innovation'), all of which sought to lend discursive and semiotic weight to the idea that the global economy was moving in the direction of free markets and an information economy (Godin 2006: 19–20; Warhurst 2008: 73–75).

As moments of hegemonic projects, Jessop argues that discursive and semiotic materials are strategically selective insofar that they are chosen and promoted to the extent that they support and articulate the aims of a hegemonic project in civil society. 'All narratives are selective, appropriate some arguments rather than others and combine them in specific ways. So we must also consider what goes unsaid or silent, repressed or suppressed, in specific discourses' (Jessop 2012: 26). Once these discursive and semiotic materials have been selected they then need to be extended and retained across a number of sites in civil society in order to become part of everyday common sense. Only then do they become embedded in a wide variety of organisational routines, institutional rules, material technologies, architectural designs and everyday utterances. At the same time, there is the selective recruitment of specific groups and organisations, all of whom will be brought on board to help articulate the economic imaginary to others (Jessop 2004: 164). In being selective, an economic project will distance itself from particular voices in the public sphere. As a result, these alternative voices will often mount a challenge to the discursive material of socio-economic projects, especially if they believe their interests are not being included in the hegemonic narrative (Bristow 2010: 157).

Unlike many of those who defend an alternative informational approach, Jessop (2012) is unambiguous in his insistence that capitalism is still held hostage to deeply rooted contradictions embedded in the value relations identified by Marx along with conjunctural strategic dilemmas. Still, he also maintains that if a crisis breaks out in capitalism then specific discursive selectivities, along with other hegemonic factors such as the media and intellectuals in public discourse, can start to narrate the crisis in particular ways in favour of economic, political and social hegemonic projects. Once constructed and after having gained some hegemonic potency in civil society, these discourses remain relatively coherent. Elsewhere, for example, Jessop (2005) argues that some social theorists and some business and management theorists construct a narrative that suggests we have made a wholesale transition from an industrial society to a knowledge-based informational society. We have already noted a number of perspectives in and around this discourse in respect to the work of Castells, Lash and several management thinkers. Such is the potency of this discourse that Jessop describes it as:

> (a) master economic narrative in many accumulation strategies, state projects and hegemonic visions ... (that) has not only been 'selected' from among the many competing discourses about the post-Fordist future but is now subject to 'retention' through a complex and heterogeneous network of practices across a wide range of systems and over many scales of action.
>
> (Jessop 2005: 152–53)

The aim of this book is to draw on a Marxist-inspired cultural political approach in order to criticise a specific element of this 'master' narrative. Specifically, the book takes aim at those theorists who argue that a transition from industrial to informational societies has now taken place. Culture and digital technology are therefore currently thought to constitute and socially construct the world. The claim, then, is that the 'new' global economy is made up of information and signs that are both 'de-centred' and come to us through global 'flows' based on 'ideas, images, technologies and capital' (Lash and Urry 1994: 321). This perspective further suggests that digital technology and digital publics are the most important source of mediation in the global world. Lash and Urry, for instance, also observe: 'There is indeed a structural basis for today's reflexive individuals. And that this is not social structures, but increasingly the pervasion of *information and communication structures*'

(Lash and Urry: 1994: 6; original emphasis). Here, digital technology overrides what is perceived to be an older, industrial form of life that sought to govern and regulate society through the nation-state and through the likes of mass media based within the borders of a country. But life has now changed. Today's societies are dominated by digital codes mediated through Web 2.0 technology that stretches across the borders of different countries. 'Most important is the ubiquity of code, of mediatic code pervading more and more regions of beings' (Lash 2007: 70). Accordingly, these theorists tell us that a transition has also occurred in the way in which the public sphere is socially constructed through digital technology, how people discuss matters in this new public sphere and the way in which issues are represented in digital publics.

For a large part of the book, I will concentrate on this perspective concerning digital publics in order to analyse it from an alternative Marxist perspective. By so doing, the book will not only demonstrate the continuing relevance of Marxist theory to make sense of the contemporary capitalist world, but will also reveal the limits of various wilder claims about digital publics made by some social theorists as well as management theorists. At the same time, the book will also construct an alternative Marxist account of the form that digital publics take in our financialised neoliberal world. That is to say, the book will not only criticise some contemporary accounts and approaches of digital publics but, more positively, it will also more accurately construct the ideological form of digital publics as this relates to what has become known as the financialisation of everyday life in relationship to a neoliberal state.

Outline of chapters

The next two chapters start this analysis by first mapping out some of the arguments that we have indeed made a transition to an informational society mediated through digital publics. In Chapter 2, I set out some early arguments made by social and management theorists from the 1950s up until the 1980s that asserted that industrial societies had been surpassed by post-industrial societies. We will then consider how, by the 1990s, these arguments were slowly surpassed by some new declarations made by various management and social theorists, which, all in their own way, maintained that advanced capitalist societies were now in fact in the midst of an informational revolution mediated through 'fluid' social relations. Both sets of thinkers thus agreed that capitalism has adopted a number of new traits since the 1980s, which has prompted it to undergo a qualitative transformation from an industrial *form* to a network *form* based on fluidity, flows and informational social media.

Naturally, in highlighting such similarities between social theorists and management gurus, one is not saying that social theorists are themselves management gurus. Indeed, differences in *content* often separate both from one another. For example, some social theorists draw on poststructuralist ideas such as Gilles Deleuze's theory of affects and intensity to make sense of what is perceived to be some of the leading traits of informational capitalism (e.g. Lash 2011). Yet, Deleuzian ideas find no place in the work of management gurus. However, what I will argue is that many ideas espoused by social theorists about 'new' informational capitalism are often 'guru-like' in their insistence that the shape and appearance of capitalism has now morphed into a complex, chaotic, fluid and informational global network form. As we will see, it is these types of arguments that point towards a convergence between social theorists and management gurus on the form which contemporary capitalism is now said to assume.

Chapter 3 then continues this exploration by looking further at some themes around the contention that global capitalism is now powered through informational communication networks that operate through complex configurations and patterns. As with the previous chapter, I suggest that further similarities exist between some business and management gurus and some social theorists in how each employs new discursive utterances to help describe the form of digital publics in informational societies. Two prominent utterances in this respect are 'complexity' and 'networks', which are employed to show how global contingency has now surpassed that of older ways of seeing the world in terms of structure, territorially bounded objects, hierarchy and order and so on. The chapter then looks more closely at some of their arguments that assert this new configuration has also provided a space for digital publics to flourish and, in some instances, pose a social and political challenge of sorts to dominant power relations across the world.

Following these two chapters, Chapter 4 begins to outline a critical response. To begin with, we map out some industrial themes in more detail. These themes are developed by various social theorists to describe the societies that have now been eclipsed by informational organisations. They usually advance a corresponding argument, which insists that while Marxism still has much to teach the world about the exploitative dynamics about the world, its main theoretical categories were unfortunately developed under industrial societies. As industrial societies have now disappeared, it is high time to reject some of Marx's main theoretical categories in favour of new ones more suited to explaining informational and digital societies. We will see, however, that those who argue these points are wrong to do so. I suggest, first, that their common critique of the 'industrial world' moves them instead to become fixated with the logic of flows and the complexity of surface, or 'flat', networked relations. More specifically, I contend that these theorists confuse different levels of analysis at which Marx works. When Marx outlined some of his main critical categories, such as that of surplus value, he did so not to understand actual industrial factories but to grasp the contradictory tendencies of capital irrespective of the actual context in which capital operates. By recourse to other social theorists such as Mikhail Bakhtin and Deleuze and Guattari, the chapter maintains that some contemporary theorists construct ideal-typical myths about industrial societies and, in the process, mistake what Marx says about *industrial capital* with that of *industrial capitalism*.

Chapter 5 continues this critical line of analysis by looking at how some of these very same theorists also explore the relationship between financial capital, information technology and the public sphere. Again, through a Marxist viewpoint, their insights on financial publics are criticised for not taking account of how capital refracts its more abstract contradictions into everyday finance, and how finance is mediated through digital information. This point is extended into a critical exploration of how these theorists explain the power of global finance in the world today since the 2008 crisis. This latter example is especially pertinent since both business and management gurus and social theorists have utilised their new metaphors such as 'fluidity' and 'networks' to write about the changing nature of global finance. Moreover, I further argue that some current approaches to finance and digital public spheres articulate a rather managerial way of exploring finance that is ideologically loaded. They also regularly over-identify with the concrete networks they claim are now dominant in the world, and they sometimes engage in a type of technological determinism when making their arguments. This then opens up a space to suggest that contrary to what some social theorists claim (e.g. Lash 2002: 205), it is in fact the logic of flows that is better explained by the logic of structures.

Chapters 6 and 7 present an alternative account of finance and digital publics. Chapter 6 argues that a robust account of digital publics must also incorporate an account of hegemonic state projects. This chapter therefore shows how the neoliberal state project in particular is a vital mechanism for financialisation to gain hegemony in civil society. The neoliberal state has sought to do achieve hegemony through the public sphere in order to persuade some ordinary people that it is in their best interests to become individual subjects of finance. How information is selectively applied, used and circulated in the public sphere, especially through digital channels, is subsequently vital in understanding the neoliberal and financial hegemonic project.

Chapter 7 continues this theme by arguing that hegemonic projects are contradictory because they refract in their own way the underlying contradictions of capital. This means that a hegemonic project is never entirely stable, but opens up gaps and fissures for alternative publics to pose a challenge of sorts to a dominant hegemonic project. I then explore this issue in more depth by outlining how these contradictions operate in the workplace by sustaining deskilling, Taylorist and lean management techniques, as well as equipping workers with new communicative capacities. These contradictions and the strategic dilemmas they usher in also provide dialogic spaces for workers to build creative public spheres in and against some themes of neoliberalism. Chapter 8 makes some concluding observations about cultural political economy.

2 From post-industrial societies to informational societies

Introduction

Published originally in German in 1957 and then substantially revised in English in 1959, Ralph Dahrendorf's *Class and Class Conflict in Industrial Societies* was one of the first notable books to argue that profound social changes had occurred in advanced industrial societies. Far from workers becoming progressively unskilled and locked into permanent struggle with owners and controllers of the means of production, capitalist societies had moved toward a new set of industrial structures. Dahrendorf argued that the working class had split into unskilled, semi-skilled and skilled technological occupations, while the extension of democratic mechanisms – voting rights, greater trade union recognition and so on – meant that workers could solve their grievances through collective means. Middle-class occupations had also widened to include salaried employees in the tertiary sector, which included shops, restaurants, cinemas and commercial firms, along with new bureaucratic occupations in the enlarged decision-making public body of welfare states.

As the years rolled on, other leading thinkers similarly began to put forward comparable views. In 1971 Ronald Inglehart published a seminal study in which he argued there had been a substantial increase in 'post-bourgeois' values among a generation of the middle-classes in Western Europe born after 1945. Post-bourgeois values were said to be 'expressive' values, typical examples being freedom of speech and participative political activity in civil society. These stood opposed to 'acquisitive' values, such as economic security and domestic order. Generally, what Inglehart noticed was that a sizable number of people across Western Europe had started to express political ideals associated with a new sense of identity. He found that those who expressed 'post-bourgeois' values also often voiced a need for belongingness gained by being a member of a social or political single-issue campaigns associated with cultural or humanitarian issues. In addition, they appreciated self-esteem, self-actualisation and the fulfilment of intellectual and aesthetic potential by being involved politically with these causes. In effect, Inglehart was presenting evidence that a transition was underway based on the growing importance of new social movements, which itself reflected 'a broad shift in emphasis from economic issues to life-style issues' (Inglehart 1971: 1012) evident in what became known as 'post-industrial societies'.

The wider context for making these claims was the belief that advanced capitalist societies had left behind their industrial past for one powered through new technologies and the service industries. Service sector jobs started to grow rapidly by the 1960s, while a consumer revolution driven by the likes of television and electronics provided new occupations for those employed to operate and manage the latest technology in the workplace (Rifkin 1995: 32). By the 1970s, then, industrial ideals and processes, such as assembly-line production managed through strict hierarchies between workers and management, had started to decline, to be gradually replaced by informational societies. The success of these societies was and is founded on their ability to maintain a flexible economy, which can also respond quickly to changing consumer tastes. One of the most efficient ways to achieve this is to establish decentralised, networked organisational formations that rely on the rapid coming together of people and technology in order to work on products when the need arises (Lash and Urry 1994).

What can we make of these claims? Kumar (1978: 192–200) asserts that since their inception after the Second World War such ideas and theorises about the decline of industrial societies and the rise of post-industrialism have articulated a number of key themes that have gone on to create a specific image of society. We are moving towards a 'knowledge society', so we are told, based on theoretical knowledge as well new scientific and technical discoveries. Through these innovations, society will be able to move away from scarcity and produce new goods that cater for everyone's personal tastes. At the same time, service jobs and a service economy are seen to be increasingly important not only for socio-economic growth but also for the identities that people gain in their everyday lives. 'Caring' and 'therapeutic' professions in particular flourish, and these professions focus on autonomous, individual, personal, psychological modes of consumption that transcend homogeneous habits of purchasing goods. The image bequeathed to us by these themes is one in which homogenous, rigid social identities attached to all-encompassing industrial class identities and bureaucratic organisations have given way to more cultural and fluid identities associated with an array of lifestyles based in part on new consumption habits and occupations rooted in and around new knowledge-based routines. The themes that comprise the wider narrative about the birth of post-industrialism and informational societies are thereby significant because they provide the basis for further claims made about digital publics. Indeed, and as we will see in later chapters, the idea that advanced capitalist societies have now left their industrial past is key to the arguments that new modes of communication have arisen that open up innovative spaces in society for public spheres to flourish within. Many public sphere theorists writing today often make these assumptions and thereby endorse the claim that we have made a transition from industrial to post-industrial and informational societies.

This chapter therefore begins by first setting out some of the key ideas of early social theorists of post-industrial societies, particularly those associated with Dahrendorf, Alain Touraine and Daniel Bell. We then chart similar themes in the rise of new management theory after 1945. The focus of attention here are some of the knowledge-based arguments put forward by the most well-known management gurus of the post-war era, those of Peter Drucker. Having established similar themes on the nature of post-industrialism between some social theorists and some post-war management thinking, we start to map out the ideas of a later generation of social and management theorists. These thinkers develop the original post-industrial thesis but do so by moving beyond what they feel are some of its more 'productivist' claims, such as reading off wider social changes from socio-economic relations. Of particular importance in this respect is the claim that societies are now characterised by various 'informational' themes that are associated with but also move beyond industrial or post-industrial socio-economic life.

As is evident from the description so far presented, one remit of the chapter is also to explore some of the overlapping narratives between management gurus and some contemporary social theorists, particularly around the view that the world has shifted from an industrial age to one characterised by networks and flows. More specifically, by demonstrating how some business and management gurus and some social theorists share, and indeed reproduce, remarkably similar beliefs about the changing form of the global economy, this chapter also adds some originality to ongoing debates in these areas. For example, for all of their innovative theorising about this new managerial paradigm, Boltanski and Chiapello never ask whether some contemporary social theorists reproduce managerial discourse in their own respective work. Both Collins (2000) and Parker (2002) likewise provide superb accounts of management discourse, and they relate some of their observations to some sociological debates, but they do not systematically highlight similarities between the well-known contemporary theorists explored in our paper and arguments made by management gurus. Frankel (1987), however, critically examines a selection of post-industrial theorists, but their relationship to emerging ideas in the business community is never given the same in-depth treatment. What seems to be the case, then, is that many critical social scientists tend to explore either new management discourse or the ideas of post-industrial/ new economy social theorists, but rarely, if ever, are they both critically examined together. The current chapter attempts to do this. We start, though, once again, with Ralf Dahrendorf.

Post-industrial social theory

By the end of the 1950s, Dahrendorf was arguing that Western societies were entering what he termed a 'post-capitalist' age grounded in new social structures and new aspirations and ideals. Social class provided him with an insight into these emerging trends. Working class groups, for example, 'have neither property nor authority, yet they display many social characteristics that are quite unlike those of the old working class' (Dahrendorf 1967: 56–57). One of these characteristics was the belief that social mobility could be achieved through the education system, while growing legal and social equality between individuals had helped to 'level' social differences in society (Dahrendorf 1967:50–63). Conflicts in post-capitalist societies no longer occurred, therefore, between 'two hostile camps', but were instead defined through battles 'confined to goals in which only these (hostile camps) are "interested" by virtue of their occupational and, more specifically, authority roles' (Dahrendorf 1967: 274). Industrial conflict was no longer predicated on the resolution of social and political problems, instead it revolved around single-issue claims such as job evaluation, shortening working hours, paid vacation and so on. On this estimation, trade unions were single economic interest groups while socialist parties became strictly political interest groups appealing to the mass voter rather than a specialised section of society such as the working class (Dahrendorf 1967: 275). Both no longer campaigned for holistic transformations of society along economic *and* political lines, but worked through single-issue campaigns.

By the late 1960s, other writers had transformed some of the post-capitalist industrial themes identified by Dahrendorf into a thesis about the rise of *post-industrial* societies. In terms of social and sociological theory, arguably the publication of Alain Touraine's *The Post-Industrial Society* in 1969 proved to be a watershed moment in these debates. According to Touraine, the conflict between a wage-earning class and capitalists had been overtaken by conflicts between new social classes. At the heart of these changes lay a transformation of industrial societies from that based on the accumulation of capital to that of 'programming' (Touraine 1974: 45). A programming society was not one based primarily on private investment in the guise of industrial conglomerates, but was instead founded on knowledge in the guise of factors such as education and science. In turn, this emphasised the importance of new occupations and social groups, such as salaried professionals, students, research technicians and maintenance workers. This was a tertiary and service society and as a result social conflict coalesced around how new knowledge-based areas of investment developed and how they would further people's desire to consume goods. Whereas the chief contradiction in nineteenth-century industrial societies was between exchange-value and use-value, by the late 1960s Touraine insisted it was between development and consumption.

In this new order, technocrats and elite bureaucrats assumed a growing significance. Although comprised by various fractions, this group could come together to champion both economic innovation and public consumption. For example, technocrats working in state administrations as managers of particular enterprises often took on board this twin role of pushing economic innovation and public consumption. As Touraine (1974: 53) noted: 'The technocracy is a social category because it is defined by its management of the massive economic and political structures which direct development.'

Importantly, this dominant technocratic class was no longer demarcated by property. Knowledge and education instead became its benchmarks to success (Touraine 1974: 51). Dominated classes thus no longer comprised only wage earners, but were also identified by their 'dependence on the mechanisms of engineered change and hence on the instruments of social and cultural integration' (Touraine 1974: 54). Alongside the technocratic management class, Touraine recognised another social group made up of the likes of technical workers, designers, higher office workers and technical assistants. Many of these worked inside bureaucratic state apparatuses and any grievances they had were directed towards their bureaucratic employment conditions as well as a defence of their employment status and careers (Touraine 1974: 58–59). Generally, though, such developments again demonstrated that the principle opposition in a post-industrial society 'comes about because the dominant classes dispose of knowledge and control *information*' (Touraine 1974: 61; original emphasis).

Class conflict subsequently lost ground to conflicts around the likes of self-identity and individualism. This is the reason why access to information became so crucial to one's sense of self-worth. For example, 'seeking information is an expression of an active social politics. Lack of information (hence of participation in the systems of decision and organisation) defined alienation' (Touraine 1974: 63). Subsequently, the alienated individual was now thought to be one who lost their identity to that of being a cog in systems of exchange and organisation. Revolt, Touraine believed, would thus be a revolt against power in all of its guises rather than revolution against the bourgeois state. It would be a revolt against consumption and its culture as well as a revolt against the penetration of the state into all aspects of civil society, and it would be a revolt against the monopoly of information by technocrats and elite bureaucrats. Centres of resistance would emanate from salaried professionals, students, research technicians and maintenance workers (Touraine 1974: 69–74). This was less a society based on exploitation as it was based on alienation.

In 1973, the futurologist and sociologist Daniel Bell observed that 'major orders ... of societies can best be studied by trying to identify *axial* institutions or principles, which are the major lines around which other institutions are draped, and which pose the major problems of solutions for the society' (Bell 1999: 115). According to Bell, one vital axial principle in the early 1970s was that of 'post-industrialism'. For Bell, a crucial ingredient for a post-industrial society was the service sector that housed a professional class equipped with the requisite education and training to maintain services. After 1945, Bell argued, the service sector grew in strength. Public utilities and transportation, a growing non-manufacturing blue-collar workforce, the growth in insurance, housing market, finance and white-collar employment, and the rapid growth of a 'third sector', made up of personal services such as restaurants, hotels, travel, entertainment, sports and so on, became increasingly important. White-collar work thus replaced blue-collar manufacturing work (Bell 1999: 127–34). Information and knowledge in turn ushered in a new ethos of cooperative relations among and between people and provided greater avenues for participation in public affairs by constructing innovative means for people to gather information about public issues (Bell 1999: 128–29).

While Bell suggested that many people will be employed in the professional class of the information and service sectors he nevertheless argued that 'scientific personnel' located in industry, government, universities, production, research and teaching would be the 'chief resource of the post-industrial society' (Bell 1999: 22; see also 216). The reason for saying this is that for Bell, scientific personnel were intimately related to advanced technology, which is the motor of post-industrial societies. Indeed, technology had helped to bring about post-industrial societies in five key ways. First, it ensured that goods could be produced for less and thereby it helped to raise living standards. Second, technology created a new class made up of the likes of engineers and technicians. Third, technology ushered in a new type of rationality based on efficiency, optimisation and utilisation of resources with relatively low costs and effort. Fourth, technology built better communication and transport systems that helped to produce 'new networks of social relationships' along with 'new economic interdependencies and new social interactions' (Bell 1999: 189). Finally, technological advancements changed people's perceptions of space and time. New notions of speed and height, for example, provided 'a different standard of assessing a landscape or cityscape' (Bell 1999: 189). Technology and knowledge consequently formed an intimate relationship in post-industrial societies. Innovations, including technological innovations, were gained from research and development (Bell 1999: 212), while technological discoveries quickened commercial uses in equally less time than in previous periods (Bell 1999: 209).

However, social theorists writing during this period did not operate in a vacuum but gained sustenance from academics, policy makers and writers from a number of backgrounds. One influential and important group of analysts were a number of management gurus who made comparable claims about the changing nature of society through a number of populist management texts. Emerging during the 1950s, especially in the United States, management gurus started to write texts that purported, and indeed still purport, to set out 'visions' that businesses must adopt if they wish to be successful. Importantly, these texts were and are written by management 'gurus' who come in a variety of guises – some are academics, some are consultants, some are managers who now write books to pass on their wisdom to others (Huczynski 2006: 68–69). We now briefly explore some of the early ideas of arguably the most famous management guru: Peter Drucker.

Management gurus and post-industrialism: Peter Drucker

Generally, a 'guru' is one who is almost like a spiritual leader and so is also somebody who not only solves problems for others by providing answers and solutions to those seeking salvation, but does so through an overarching 'vision' of a better life (Collins 2000: 4–10). Management gurus, then, are those individuals who impart a business vision to those willing to learn greater management wisdom. At the heart of this vision is the idea that the global economy has fundamentally changed since an industrial time and now encompasses a contingent network 'fluid' formation based around the pre-eminence of information and knowledge. As a result, 'culture' and 'value systems' are more important for business than in the past for capturing and taking advantage of information and knowledge than formal commands and rules (Huczynski 2006: 62). Accompanying this vision, therefore, are a number of 'soft' buzzwords and prescriptions. Typically, businesses are advised to set sail on a voyage of 'innovation' and 'teamwork' to take advantage of networks of global knowledge, employees should participate in decision-making activities, bureaucracies need to be 'flattened out' and opened up to a bit of 'chaos' and employees should be 'empowered' in how they work (see also Micklethwaite and Wooldridge 1997). Like social theorists, then, management gurus have also developed new metaphors to explain and understand the formation of knowledge-based organisations. These metaphors are employed to argue that the global world has become more contingent in how it operates and thereby subject less to being bound by organisational bureaucratic structures, regulation and measurement, hierarchy and order, cause and effect and so on (see Roberts and Joseph 2014).

One of the leading public figures in pushing forward this new managerial view of the world has been Peter Drucker. Indeed, as early as 1954, Drucker announced that the age of industry was being surpassed by a new socio-economic formation. He notably claimed that 'we no longer talk of "capital" and "labour"; we talk of "management" and "labour"' (Drucker 1993a: 3). For Drucker, then, business, or at least American business, had undergone a profound shift. This did not mean that the US economy had moved into a 'post-industrial' phase; during this period, Drucker still believed that America was an industrial economy (see Drucker 1993a: 8). However, Drucker was nevertheless adamant that American business could no longer be shackled by the then-prevalent management ideas. He had three management ideas in mind that he found to be particularly troublesome. First, he found fault with personnel administration theory; among other things, this argues that management is a specialist task in an organisation that devotes itself to managing employees' day-to-day dislike of work. Second, Drucker was critical of elements of human relations theory, which rests on the principle that employees should be guided by positive motivations. Finally, he had problems with areas of Taylorist scientific management, particularly its emphasis on the analysis of work into its simplest tasks in order to scientifically improve the output of individual workers (Drucker 1993a: 271–86).

Drucker broadly believed that each school of thought was not well suited for helping to nurture a competitive post-war business environment in America. For example, scientific management assumed that human beings were machine tools. It thus committed the further error of assuming that work is improved to the extent that an employer improved the manner by which individual operations are performed. Yet, 'this is not even true of a machine tool; to assert it of human beings is nonsense. The human being does individual motions poorly; viewed as a machine tool, he is badly designed' (Drucker 1993a: 283). Drucker added that workers each possessed a 'will' comprised by 'personality, emotions, appetites and soul' (Drucker 1993a: 283) and that any job must make use of these 'specific qualities' (Drucker 1993a: 284). In addition, scientific management separated the planning of job tasks from actually performing them. This was a mistake, however, because, observed Drucker, 'planning and doing are separate parts of the same job ... One cannot, above all, do only; without a trace of planning his job, the worker does not have the control he needs even for the most mechanical and repetitive routine chore' (Drucker 1993a: 284). This being the case, people should not be encouraged to 'work mechanically' but should instead aim to work in a 'community of individuals' where they 'build personal relationships over and above the work relationship'. In other words, managers should recognise that employees are individuals who gained pride in themselves and with others by working in a 'cohesive social unit' (Drucker 1993a: 298).

But why exactly did Drucker believe that organisations should move away from management systems such as Taylorism? In a manner strangely reminiscent of some post-industrial theorists, Drucker suggests that a process he names 'Automation' will ensure that:

> The worker ... will no longer do the repetitive routine chores of machine feeding and materials handling. Instead, he will build, maintain and control machines that do the repetitive routine work. To do this he must be able to do many operations, must have the largest rather than the smallest content to his job, must be able to co-ordinate.
>
> (Drucker 1993a: 286)

According to Drucker, Automation 'consists largely of people trained both in skill and theoretical understanding' (Drucker 1993a: 106) grounded in professional and technically skilled workers. Unlike repetitive routine work found in mass production, in which a worker concentrates their energies on one repetitive chore, Automation encouraged a worker to do many operations in his or her working day. New technological advancements also meant that each worker enjoyed a degree of planning over his or her work tasks. Under these conditions, the division between planning and doing had started to dissolve.

> (T)he new technology demands that the least production worker be capable of a good deal of planning. The more planning he can do, the more he can take responsibility for what he does, the more productive worker he will be ... To maintain the equipment, to program it, to set it and to control it, all demand of the worker in the new technology knowledge, responsibility and decision-making – that is, planning.
>
> (Drucker 1993a: 287)

Automation thus referred not merely to narrow technical advancements but also to a whole social process, 'which it sees as an integrated and harmonious whole' (Drucker 1993a: 19). Associated with producing a variety of goods in a stable fashion, Automation also saw its task as reducing cost and labour effort. Control of the production was maintained through equilibrium between output and effort achieved by simply rejecting those elements that a process could not handle. In addition, feedback mechanisms enabled results of a process to be relayed into an earlier cycle to maintain continuous production (Drucker 1993a: 20).

Elsewhere, Drucker (1970: 51–52) claimed that technological innovation had been transformed into a professional and specialised occupation. Inventors worked in increasingly narrow areas but also in institutionalised research laboratories. As such, technological work was turning into a team effort, 'in which the knowledge of a large number of specialists in the laboratory is brought to bear on a common problem and directed towards a joint technological result' (Drucker 1970: 52). Thus, the modern research laboratory was different from past scientific endeavours in the sense that it was exclusively concerned with research, discovery and innovation. In addition, different types of knowledge from different scientific disciplines were brought together, applying science to technology. These endeavours helped researchers to look at production as a system, 'which sees a host of formerly unrelated activities and processes as all parts of a larger, integrated whole ... ' (Drucker 1970: 61). Indeed, according to Drucker, a virtuous circle could be noted between technological innovation and systems approach to facilitate Automation (1970: 61).

To succeed, however, Automation had be combined with a business enterprise that understood the competitive gains to be made from the twin functions of marketing and innovation. Through these two functions, business action could set about creating unique customers for a specific product (Drucker 1993a: 37). Moreover, the motor of these processes was 'brain formation' – 'the rate at which a country produces people with imagination and vision, education, theoretical and analytical skill' (Drucker 1993a: 42). A successful business enterprise needed to consider all factors of productive effort and not just labour such as working on machines. As such, managing a business could not be set in stone. Instead, managers should draw on both tangible (machines and labour) and intangible (e.g. emotions and knowledge) resources in order to be creative in how one manages. Managers are creative when they reject a passive and bureaucratic acceptance of policies and instead adapt an entrepreneurial spirit alive to risks and uncertainty (Drucker 1993a: 46–47).

The rise of informational societies

There is little doubt that the ideas set forth by early pioneers of the post-industrial society thesis, such as those associated with Bell and Drucker, had a tremendous impact on subsequent debates concerning the transformation of capitalist societies. One need only glance at how the muses of a later generation of social theorists, along with business and management intellectuals, seemed to replicate earlier thinkers. During the 1980s, for example, various authors involved in the left-wing British magazine *Marxism Today* were proclaiming the importance of innovative technological forces in helping to foster new social relations. Such was the belief in this technological determinism that *Marxism Today* collected together a batch of articles that it believed best expressed and explained the processes already underway. *New Times* made it abundantly clear that at the forefront of restructuring the 'old' Fordist industrial paradigm was information technology and the microelectronics revolution. The book's introduction announced:

> New technology allows more intensive automation and its extension from large to smaller companies, pulling together the shopfloor and the office, the design loft and the showroom. It allows production to be more flexible, automated and integrated.
>
> ('Manifesto for New Times' 1989: 33)

New technology was thus thought to be reordering work by tearing apart traditional industrial distinctions between blue-collar and white-collar work, and between skilled and unskilled labour. What would replace these would be smaller working units along with new social divisions.

> In future, work in manufacturing will be about flexible team-working within much smaller, more skilled workforces. Services will continue to provide the main source of new jobs ... There will be more professional, highly-skilled technicians' jobs, but also more low-wage, low-technology jobs. The economy will be marked by a division between core full-time workers in large companies and the growing number of part-timers in small subcontractors, between those in employment and the long-term unemployed.
>
> ('Manifesto for New Times' 1989: 33)

Some in the business community also heralded this transition to a qualitatively new paradigm. In the same year that *Marxism Today* launched its 'Manifesto for New Times', one business theorist was proclaiming the arrival of 'just-in-time' system of management. According to Oakland, new technology and knowledge such as 'continuous flow production' had empowered businesses to install cost-effective production and delivery of goods or services to their destination as required and in the correct quantity. The advantages of introducing just-in-time production included 'increased flexibility (particularly the workforce), reduction in stock and work-in-progress, and the space it occupies, (and) simplification of products and processes' (Oakland 1989: 89).

Yet by the 1990s, the sociological terrain had shifted once again. According to some, a new socio-economic paradigm was coming into being that was different to the earlier post-industrial society thesis. A leading light in this new paradigm was and still is Manuel Castells. During the 1990s, Castells stated that his intention was to shift the analytical focus from post-industrialism to 'informationalism'. His reason for doing so was relatively simple, based as it was on the belief that the post-industrial paradigm was built on an industrial manufacturing structure that has become obsolete and outdated (Castells 2000: 219). In *Economies and Signs and Space*, Lash and Urry (1994: 60–61) similarly claimed that earlier terms devised to understand the transition to a qualitatively new period had reached their sell by date. 'Flexibility analysis', such as 'flexible specialisation', was now deemed to be too 'productionist' and thus failed to capture the manner in which culture had become fully integrated into the production and consumption of goods. For these reasons, Lash and Urry argued that a new theoretical framework more able to investigate the themes of informational societies must replace the post-industrial thesis. In particular, one requires new categories and metaphors to understand how the economy now hinges on the primacy of information and knowledge, and how social life has become embedded in aesthetic and cultural forms. The next section looks at these points in more depth.

Informational societies

Some social theorists suggest that flexibility in the economy now revolves around the primacy of information and knowledge. A new informational perspective is therefore required.

> In this perspective, societies will be informational, not because they fit into a particular social structure, but because they organize their production system around the principles of maximizing knowledge-based productivity through the development and diffusion of information technologies.
>
> (Castells 2000: 219–20)

Lash similarly argues that social structures associated with a manufacturing society have now been displaced by informational and communication flows (Lash 2002: 205). Manufacturing has thus given way to the logic of information underpinned by the accumulation of abstract finance capital, intellectual property, the prototype and brand (Lash 2002: 194).

Lash and Urry further argue that these new forms of knowledge and information are organised through collective, practical and discursive forms of 'reflexive accumulation'. This refers to the predominance of decentralised information-intensive practices in a business organisation. For example, some research and development processes have been devolved to the shop floor in some new media organisations (Lash and Urry 1994: 75). Again, Castells (2000: 208) broadly agrees with this position to the extent that he also suggests that even multinationals are beholden to 'internal differentiation in decentralized networks' as well as being reliant on ever-changing external interlocked networks. Indeed, the idea that bureaucratic organisations have altered their structure is a point that is integral to Castells's argument. As he observes, one fundamental process stands out with respect to the changing fortunes of organisational structure, and that is the general crisis of the old 'rigid model associated with the large, vertical corporation, and with oligopolistic control over markets' (Castells 2000: 179). Leading the way in helping to implement these networked formations are microelectronic and digitally-processed information communication technologies (ICTs) that gain a degree of flexibility to adapt and reconfigure themselves to suit new conditions (Castells 2010: 23–25).

Unlike their earlier work on disorganised capitalism, which explored the relationship between culture and production through new middle class identities, Lash and Urry now argue that the whole of socio-economic life 'is itself becoming cultural and aestheticised'. This latter point is noticeable in the rise of cultural and creative industries and the importance of brands. No longer is it the case, insist Lash and Urry, that popular music or movies are marketed solely for their 'product'. Instead, a company will market and sell the brand of an artist, author, musician or director. In this way the 'company's role comes more in "packaging" ... It sells not itself as a brand, but another product as brand' (Lash and Urry 1994: 137). Moreover, the music industry is no longer built on 'social structures', such as social class, but is maintained through communication images. In turn, these are transformed into aestheticised objects. Obviously, such processes have been around at least since the 1950s with the rise of mass youth culture. Today, however, the ascendancy of digital technology implies that the modernist aesthetic subject has finally given way to aesthetic image objects in a manner unimaginable in the 1950s or 1960s (Lash and Urry 1994: 131–34).

Michel Callon likewise argues that one revolutionary transformation of the new economy has been the ability of advanced technology to objectify different products into packages, or 'things', in order for them to be branded, personalised and valued in unique ways (Çaliskan and Callon 2010: 7). For example, new media technology has empowered the way that businesses attach, detach and re-attach the *cognitive* and *reflexive* potentials of a consumer's system of action and intellectual capabilities onto the singular qualities of a specific product (Callon *et al.* 2005: 40).

> With information renewed on the screen, with links and cross-references, and with scroll menus that multiply options from which users can and must choose, the Internet is a machinery that is *entirely* oriented towards the singularization of products.
>
> (Callon *et al.* 2005: 42; emphasis added)

In other words, and along similar lines set out by Lash and Urry, many companies are aesthetically branding a product through personalisation.

In *The Rise of the Creative Class*, Richard Florida likewise argues that capitalism has moved away from its industrial Fordist past and towards a 'knowledge-intensive' and informational form capitalism structured around 'learning regions'. In these regions, there exists a synthesis of intellectual and physical labour (innovation-mediated production), high-tech industries and venture capital. Indeed, according to Florida, venture capitalists are drawn to creative people and industries (Florida 2002: 50–51). For their part, learning regions encourage the growth of creative industries that include fashion, IT, cultural heritage, art galleries, museums, events, architecture, film, music, performing arts, advertising, services industry, homes and so on. A creative learning economy thus encourages different employees to work in 'teams' in knowledge and intelligence clusters. Important in this respect is the ability of these clusters to attract foreign direct investment. To achieve this, creative clusters not only look to the nation state for support but also and perhaps more importantly seek to build region-states based in creativity. Region-states build competitive advantage to the extent that they mobilise ideas – continuous knowledge creation and knowledge workers. This 'new economy' ideally facilitates communication networks that link together people, information, R&D (research and development), goods and services on a global basis so that knowledge will replace physical labour as the main source of value.

Interestingly, these viewpoints, or at least some of its main terms, are also eagerly endorsed and celebrated by many business and management theorists. Indeed, the content of what some sociologists take to be 'new' about the global economy is almost repeated verbatim in popular business and management literature. The next section will therefore explore how a number of business and management writers also endorse the informational narrative.

Business and management thinking on informational societies

The idea that flexibility in the economy hinges on the primacy of information and knowledge mediated through new technology is a theme found in management ideas for some time now. Originally published in 1978 in France, Nora and Minc (1980: 63) stressed the increasing importance of automation associated with digital networks and satellite communications that bring about the convergence of media formats and acceleration in the transfer of data and information across global networks (Nora and Minc 1980: Chapter 2). The social forecaster and business advisor John Naisbitt announced just two years later that we are witnessing a move not from an industrial to post-industrial society, but from an industrial society to an *information society*. Drawing on earlier analyses, such as Porat's delineation of the economy into primary information sectors that are relatively easy to calculate and quantify (e.g. clerks, librarians, and system analysts) and secondary information sectors that are less tangible (e.g. research and development), Naisbitt (1982: 19) argued that the new information society is premised on the speed that new technology communicates with one another. More precisely, Naisbitt was clear that an information network society is being formed (Naisbitt 1982: 194) through the sharing of knowledge and information between points, or what others today call 'nodes' (Naisbitt 1982: 192–94). Like many contemporary social theorists, then, Naisbitt insisted that an information society is so-called not just because knowledge and information are key, but also because information has the potential to create new informational 'activities, processes, and products' (Naisbitt 1982: 19).

The eminent management guru Tom Peters argued that advances in computer electronics and telecommunications could constantly gather information about changing consumer habits and generate different partnership networks across the globe. There was also 'a blurring of service/product distinctions ... by "software" services and the "intelligence-added" features provided courtesy of the microprocessor' (Peters 1987: 10). These developments prompted Peters to announce that one of the most powerful 'liberating forces' for contemporary business practices was that of the 'sharing of information' (Peters 1987: 506). Indeed, sharing quality information between businesses was now 'a must' because it confirmed that all employees were partners in business ventures. It also quickened problem solving among partners as well as demonstrating that organisations operated along flattened out structures (Peters 1987: 507–8). Besides, information sharing generated business networks such as word of mouth interpersonal marketing networks (Peters 1987: 240–41). Thus, Peters endorsed the point that information is a key ingredient in the 'new' technologically sophisticated economy.

Today, this general viewpoint concerning the transition to a new knowledge-based economy is one broadly accepted by the business community. As populist managerial gurus Ridderstråle and Nordström (2008) suggest, networks of knowledge powered by ICTs have all but eclipsed the old manufacturing indus-trial base. Knowledge and intangibility therefore represent the 'new battlefield for countries, corporations and individuals' (Ridderstråle and Nordström 2008: 12). Informational networks obtain this degree of flexibility because they are increasingly maintained by intelligence (Green 2010). New digital software allows networks to converge seamlessly. TerreStar, a company specialising in satellite and telecommunications, recently launched a satellite system that supports wireless phone communications. The rationale for this is eventually to allow users to seamlessly move between different communication networks without interrupting their communication experience (Green 2010: 35). In turn, such progress enhances the smart capacity of communication networks.

New media and business guru Nicholas Negroponte further argues that digital technology unleashes a 'post-information' order that empowers machines to 'personalise' information to the unit of one, namely 'me'. 'True personalisation' is about 'machines understanding individuals with the same degree of subtlety (or more than) we can expect from other human beings ... ' (Negroponte 1995: 165). What this does is to explode demographics based on statistical subsets. This way of measuring is no longer required when machines via digital technology can *learn* to automatically respond to and indeed pre-empt and influence our changing tastes over time. In a similar vein, the business advisor Alan Burton-Jones (1999) supports the by-now familiar distinction between data, information and knowledge. The first, data, can be defined as signals sent by an originator to a recipient. Information is data intelligible to a recipient. Knowledge is therefore the growing amount of information and skills gained in order for a recipient to increase its capabilities and competencies. Knowledge acquisition is thus acquired through learning, creation and innovation (Burton-Jones 1999: 5–6). Practically, this means that a business organisation must tap into and develop its intellectual capital such as that of human capital in its workforce or in the demands and preferences of its customers (Burton-Jones 1999: 6).

The generalisation of ICTs across organisational forms implies that complex types of knowledge can also be replicated more widely within and between businesses, aided in part by the declining costs of circulating such knowledge through global digital networks (McKeown 2009: 15). This has the added advantage of making business organisations more flexible in adapting to new circumstances and opportunities. Numerous management thinkers subsequently see a knowledge-based global economy as providing chances for businesses to operate along 'reflexive' decentralised lines (see Peters and Waterman 1982: 15–29). Many in management thus believe in implementing so-called 'post-bureaucratic' decision-making as the best strategy for a business to transform itself into a learning organisation (see also Johnson 2007). After all, competitive advantage for an organisation is often discovered by establishing project-based work and 'entrepreneurial cells'. It therefore makes perfect sense to encourage this type of decentralised formation (Scase 2007: 42; see also Chapter 7).

All of which brings us to the argument that we have moved towards a new economic formation, which of course is the claim that economic life 'is itself becoming cultural and aestheticized'. Unsurprisingly, elements of this argument are already present in earlier business and management theory. Before the Second World War and after, organisational and management theorists were already emphasising the importance of cultural and soft traits such as cooperation, involvement, openness and participation as ways to overcome alienating and routine work practices (Anthony 1994: 18–19). Today, argues Scase, the brand and culture of a company should connote 'excitement … creativity and non-conformism' (Scase 2007: 41) in order to attract and keep the best intellectual and knowledgeable workers. In addition to these benefits of brand culture, a leading textbook on brand management originally published in 1992 observes that new forms of communication, packaging and advertising enable businesses to create a brand in such a way that its values – its cultural and aesthetic presence – can be extended across a whole range of physical products to capture new consumers. 'Bic is not simply a brand name for pens: it is to be seen as simplifying utilitarian objects, as expressed by the "disposable" characteristic. It therefore went from the ball-point pen to the lighter and the razor … ' (Kapferer 2000: 233). In other words, those from the world of business would no doubt agree with social theorists that ICTs allow for new and complex brand images, representations and styles.

Conclusion

The importance of the theories of post-industrialism and informationalism is that they establish the foundations for a theory of digital publics to be developed more substantially by later theorists. Think for example of Florida's claim that the transformations he writes about also change the very nature of class relations and social identities. This is not just a socio-economic paradigm of development, but also an artistic and cultural one too. Creative industries include lifestyle and cultural institutions associated with the likes of fashion and new musical genres. A creative region also 'facilitates cross-fertilization between and among these forms, as is evident through history in the rise of creative-content industries from publishing and music to film and video games' (Florida 2002: 55). These developments have helped to produce a new creative class who 'add economic value through their creativity' (Florida 2002: 68). At the same time, such changes have unleashed decentralised digital communication forms into civil society that open up new opportunities for *public* collaboration between ordinary consumers. When one thinks of the Internet it soon becomes clear that collaborative projects and peer-to-peer communities have been made possible among a multitude of communities and digital publics across the world through networks thrown up by the Internet. Content can be uploaded and downloaded through these networks and ordinary people have the opportunity to now make money themselves from these ventures in ways unimaginable in previous decades.

For these reasons, Bruns suggests that production and consumption come together through digital networks. This is formed through a 'hive mind' in which activity among different individuals, groups and communities is coordinated through networks across space and time. Central authority is thereby rejected in favour of shared information and knowledge among 'nodes' in the network about consumer products, which serve to codify protocols of communal coordination. Emergent patterns of behaviour arise from these networks. Digital networks make it possible for users to use a collaborative logic and draw resources from communities to design and develop content for a digital product that they can use at the same time (Bruns 2008: 19). Communal digital projects therefore rely on a degree of sharing among a community of users – the sharing of knowledge for example – and they require a degree of flexibility and fluidity in completing tasks around a collaborative project. Value chains are no longer beholden to distinctions between production, distribution and consumption, but are instead built on 'endless string of users acting incrementally as content producers by gradually extending and improving the information present in the information commons … ' (Bruns 2008: 21).

What Bruns and indeed Florida and a whole host of other like-minded theorists allude to in their respective analyses is the importance of networks in conveying information to different groups and organisations about new consumer products. More precisely, these networks communicate not only information about new products, but also information about political issues across localities, regions and countries to distinct groups. However, these networked publics do not operate in a linear fashion that stipulates that knowledge should flow from point A to point B. Instead, they are said to operate in nonlinear and often unpredictable routes through digital communication channels.

Nevertheless, the idea about the nonlinear nature of networks was also present in earlier theories of post-industrial societies. Bell for example rejects a linear definition of the growth of this type of knowledge. In its place, he prefers a 'branching' theory of knowledge; the idea that 'new and numerous subdivisions of specialities within fields' of knowledge are created 'rather than just growth' (Bell 1999: 186). Bell thus favours something akin to a nonlinear theory of knowledge whereby 'each advance' in knowledge 'opens up, sometimes rapidly, sometimes slowly, new fields which, in turn, sprout their own branches' (Bell 1999: 186). A new discovery might therefore suddenly generate 'a series of new "spurts"' in discovering new knowledge (Bell 1999: 186). Bell seems to be alluding to something similar to that put forward by a number of complexity theorists. He considers new discoveries in knowledge as being contingent affairs based not merely on an 'immanent logic', but often on small random discoveries that then give rise 'to branching in several different directions' (Bell 1999: 187). The next chapter starts to develop these points on networks and nonlinear knowledge and to expand on some of the themes associated with informational societies in order to gain a more complete picture of networked digital publics.

3 Complex, networked digital publics

Introduction

In *The New Spirit of Capitalism*, Boltanski and Chiapello (2003: 104) observe that the concept of 'network' makes a relatively recent appearance in academic and management texts. Before the 1990s 'networks' were usually associated with distributional technical networks, such as water supplies, or with 'secret' organisations, such as resistance movements or the Freemasons. Since the 1990s, the 'network' concept has grown in importance and is now used by a whole array of academics, commentators, organisations, management theorists, politicians and 'ordinary' people, to *justify* new social relations. Important in this respect, continue Boltanski and Chiapello, is how the 'network' discourse gains justification by being closely aligned to another discourse, which they term the 'projective city'. Narratives that construct the image of a projective city are concerned with demonstrating the benefits of different people joining up in a network for a short amount of time to complete a particular project. Networks conjoin individuals to come together through the choice to work with others temporarily for the good of a project.

> In a reticular world, social life is composed of a proliferation of encounters and temporary, but reactivatable connections with various groups, operated at potentially considerable social, professional, geographical and cultural distance. The *project* is the occasion and reason for this connection.
> (Boltanski and Chiapello 2003: 104; original emphasis)

This is a moment that emphasises a degree of mobility individuals must possess in order to slide in and out of networks (Boltanski and Chiapello 2003: 134). Viewed thus, projective cities can be compared to a discourse concerning the 'industrial city'. This is a city comprised by centralised managerial control, functional structures, regulations and procedures and stability. It is a world built on efficiency, avoidance of risks and waste, saving resources for the future, long-term planning and progress gained through a scientific outlook, specialised bureaucratic departments and rigid organisational boundaries (Boltanski and Chiapello 2003: 18–24 and 135–36; see also Boltanski and Thévenot 2006).

Projective cities are therefore noticeably different to the industrial city. For example, one special property of a network projective city is that of 'activity', whereby different oppositions, such as stability and instability, work and leisure, waged work and voluntary work, start to dissolve into one another. Through this blurring of opposites, life becomes a series of endless projects where one 'gets involved' in a variety of initiatives across social boundaries, whether these be 'familial, affective educative, artistic, religious, charitable, etc.' (Boltanski and Chiapello 2003: 110). These are networks that are adaptable and flexible, without order or structure, constituted in part through one's talent to access information to gain the requisite skills to 'connect up' to them. They are places 'where everything potentially reflects everything else: a world, often conceived as "fluid, continuous, chaotic", where anything can be connected with anything else, which must be tackled without any reductionist apriorism' (Boltanski and Chiapello 2003: 144).

This chapter explores how a network discourse has come to dominate certain approaches to exploring the informational global world and, more specifically, digital publics. These approaches, which encompass the work of some social theorists and management theorists, as well as some natural scientists, employ the network metaphor to tell us that a complex mixture of global flows, fluids and network formations have now eclipsed the industrial world as we have made a transition to an informational global formation. Life is now said to be less predictable and more contingent than in the industrial past because of these developments (Büscher and Urry 2009: 102).

To analyse these points in more detail the chapter first maps out a prominent strand of thinking in network analysis, which is that of complexity theory. Indeed, complexity theory and network analysis often work in unison, and different theorists see them as being integrally linked together. Moreover, complexity theory is frequently aligned to an analysis of digital technology. As Mansell (2012: 69–71) observes, pioneering work during the 1940s by scientists such as Norbert Weiner and Claude Shannon fuelled an interest by later researchers into how information systems might be self-regulatory. Scientists began to investigate whether communication between the different parts of an information system could be sustained through feedback loops and the 'emergence' of new responses to contingent obstacles encountered. Information systems might therefore 'learn' to adapt to the existing environment and to new environments; and, through learning, information systems gradually become more complex. This chapter therefore examines in a little more detail some ideas in complexity theory. Following this discussion, some different properties of complex networks are briefly sketched out and related to digital technology. This, then, provides a basis for the final substantive section that outlines some common themes in and around complex networked digital publics. These public spheres are said by some to provide new innovative communicative spaces in informational societies for ordinary people to get their voices heard by others.

Complexity theory

Manson (2001) identifies three schools of thought on complexity theory. Algorithmic complexity compresses a multitude of interactions within a system into simple types of measurement. Deterministic complexity, which is also associated with chaos theory, explores the interaction between individual variables that help one to understand the behaviour of a complex system. Aggregate complexity, on the other hand, is more interested in examining the relationships between various entities. As such, this school is less concerned with simple mathematical models than is the case with the previous two groups and instead seeks to understand systems as a whole. It thus focuses on the 'internal structure and surrounding environment; learning and emergent behaviour; and the different means by which complex systems change and grow' (Manson 2001: 409; see also O'Sullivan 2004: 283–84). One useful way, therefore, to comprehend the relationship between chaos theory and complexity theory is to suggest that the former is a specific school of thought within the latter. On this estimation, chaos theory examines the emergence of complex things from simple systems whereas complexity theory more broadly starts from complex systems in order to ascertain how unanticipated patterns of behaviour emerge (Fitzgerald and Eijnatten 2002: 405–6; see also Cilliers 1998: ix; Hatt 2009: 317).

Despite these different schools of thought, it is still possible to isolate some key ideas and points on complexity theory that bring together natural scientists, social scientists and business and management analysts (see Tsekeris 2010). One such idea is that complexity theory is interested in how nonlinear movements operate in systems. Prigogine and Stengers (1984: 139) suggest that linear theories of science explain how a system moves towards a stable and predictable pattern of behaviour. Subsequently, linear theorists are not overly concerned with the initial conditions of a system because they believe a system will eventually evolve into a predictable state of equilibrium. Newtonian mechanics and Euclidean geometry best describe this perspective in science because both seek to explore the world through predictable, invariant and inert properties where small causes lead to small effects (Hayes 1991: 7–8).

In nonlinear systems, however, the emphasis is on how what appears to be a state of equilibrium can suddenly be transformed into a state of non-equilibrium and instability. In management studies, for example, one influential approach adopted a neo-Darwinian position, which 'held that organisations changed through random events that were then selected for survival by competition' (Stacey 2010: 55). From here, organisations were seen to adapt and evolve to a competitive environment. The problem with this perspective was and is that it gives little room for human agency, particularly the agency of management, to influence and change the way that organisations behave. By way of contrast, a complexity approach examines how an organisation forms patterns of interactions and at the same time is being formed by these patterns. Complexity theory thus prompts management theorists to remain open to unpredictable organisational dynamics (Stacey 2010: 61).

Transitions to non-equilibrium can be precipitated by small and unpredictable disturbances in the initial conditions of a system. If this occurs then a system might move to a one of turbulence, bifurcation and crisis. A complex system is thus essentially an open system, which means that it will work in conjunction with its surrounding external environment, or 'noise'. Changes to that environment imply that a system will also most likely undergo change in order to adapt to external alterations, or 'noise' (Cilliers 1998: 99). In the world of business organisations, 'noise' could emanate from inconsistencies between the language used by management and its actions, discrepancies between supply and demand or 'unexpressed needs' in a business. In all of these instances, these fluctuations might go on to produce a crisis point in the organisation at hand (Pascale *et al.* 2000: 146). Eventually a bifurcation point in the system is reached, whereby it undergoes a qualitative transformation (Hatt 2009: 316–17; see also Ball 2004: 131–33). New dynamic states eventually appear, which while ordered in certain ways also exhibit dissipative structures through energy exchanges and transfers with the outside world (Gleick 1997: 24; Prigogine and Stengers 1984: 143).

As Capra (1996: 176) notes, one of the important insights gained from Prigogine's work is the idea that dissipative structures cannot be derived from any one part of a system but instead emerge as a consequence of how the system operates as a whole. Critical for complexity theory in this respect are feedback loops. Organised through a circular motion, feedback loops causally link together different parts of a system. An initial cause will pass through other parts, ensuring that 'the last "feeds back" the effect into the first element of the cycle' (Capra 1996: 56). What transpires from feedback loops is a self-organising system in which the first cause will be modified by proceeding effects in other parts of the system. Negative feedback transpires when, say, one part of the system, A, decreases while B increases. Positive feedback, on the other hand, is predicated on one part of a system, A, producing the same direction of change in B, 'i.e. an increase of B if A increases and a decrease if A decreases' (Capra 1996: 59). Positive feedback thus introduces states of non-equilibrium into a system and can do so through small events; the famous example being a butterfly flapping its wings that go onto to create changes in climate patterns (see Gleick 1997: 20–23).

An important element of complex systems is an attractor, which relates to how a system displays particular patterns of behaviour. Or, according to the business and management analysts, Pascale *et al.* (2000: 69), an attractor is 'analogous to a compass' insofar that it pulls a system in a certain direction and works to 'provide organisms with the impetus to migrate out of their comfort zone'. The simplest example of an attractor is that of a pendulum. Friction causes a pendulum to stop, and this means that the pendulum is attracted towards a specific trajectory, or motion (Capra 1996: 130). In this case, the pendulum displays low rates of energy that become embodied in a stable, linear pattern of equilibrium.

A 'strange attractor', however, is based in nonlinear complex processes. Capra explains that in the case of a pendulum, a strange attractor will result in each swing being unique (Capra 1996: 131–32). High rates of energy thus emerge between equilibrium and random behaviour. 'In other words, strange attractors are paradoxically regular and irregular, stable and unstable, predictable and unpredictable at the same time' (Stacey 2010: 59). Strange attractors therefore epitomise 'unstable spaces' reinforced through positive feedback (Urry 2003: 26–27). They direct systems towards a future not yet realised. In directing them towards this future, though, strange attractors alter the behaviour of a system: 'In that respect, the future is the *means* to alter behaviour' (Pascale *et al.* 2000: 72; original emphasis). Byrne (1998: 28–29) adds that strange attractors represent a phase or condition space because of their high sensitivity to small changes. Once a strange attractor becomes a condition space it creates the potential to move towards a new trajectory. In business and management speak, strange attractors bring about a set of intangible traits in employers and employees: 'desire, excitement, curiosity, power, a quest for knowledge, a competitive wish ... ' (Pascale *et al.* 2000: 72). Managers are able to produce strange attractors by tapping into the resources already found within an organisation, but that perhaps go unnoticed.

For these reasons, Capra (2002) argues that globalisation operates in a manner akin to complex natural systems. Capra (2002: Chapter 5) traces this to the microelectronics revolution in the early 1970s, which allowed information-processing chips to become smaller so that they could then be placed in more machines. This in turn led to a computer revolution across society enhanced by advanced satellite technology. At the same time, this technological revolution encouraged the rise of global capitalism, including the deregulation and liberalisation of financial trading.

> All these measures relied crucially on the new information and communication technologies, which made it possible to transfer funds between various segments of the economy and various countries almost instantly and to manage the enormous complexity brought about by rapid deregulation and new financial ingenuity.
>
> (Capra 2002: 119)

Urry (2003), a social scientist, draws on (among others) the ideas of Capra, a natural scientist, to similarly insist that globalisation is best theorised through the lens of complexity theory. Globalisation, according to Urry, creates 'parallel, irreversible and mutually interdependent processes by which globalization-deepens-localization-deepens-globalization and so on' (Urry 2003: 84). In other words, globalisation is a strange attractor that irreversibly brings together both international and local flows of resources in unstable ways through billions of iterations on a daily basis. Globalisation is therefore also a decentred process in the sense that once-powerful centres of powers such as the nation state are increasingly coming under pressure from global–local processes. 'Nationality gets more constituted through specific *local* places, symbols and landscapes, icons of the nation central to that culture's location within the contours of global business, travel and branding (such as the twin towers of New York's World Trade Centre)' (Urry 2003: 87; original emphasis). In this respect, according to Urry, globalisation is comprised by a number of interacting subunits that through simple interactions with one another create collective behaviour that feedback into the behaviour of each subunit.

Unpredictable dynamics often result from complex systems, but *emergent* patterns might also arise that are not reducible to the micro-dynamics of individual components that comprise a system. For Johnson (2007), these unpredictable phenomena do not rely on a central coordinating apparatus that exists externally to a system. As self-organising entities, emergent properties appear from the internal complex dynamics of the system itself (Johnson 2007: 15). As a result, observes Walby (2009: 74), emergence helps social scientists overcome some of the perennial dualisms in social science such as that between structure and agency, or individual and society. Emergence points towards an explanation of how social systems appear from the actions of people and objects without being reduced to those actions and objects. Different parts of a social system can therefore emerge from another level within the system, while their actual properties can be analysed on their own terms. Emergent objects might very well contain properties from another level, but they also have their own unique properties not reducible to the level from which they emerged. '(I)t is not so much that the whole is greater than the parts as that it is different from the parts' (Walby 2009: 74).

For complexity theorists and those who use complexity theory, networks are a crucial moment in exploring how complex systems evolve. For a natural scientist and complexity theorist, such as Mitchell:

> A network is a collection of *nodes* connected by *links*. Nodes correspond to the individuals in a network (e.g., neurons, Web sites, people) and links to the connections between them (e.g., synapses, Web hyperlinks, social relationships).
>
> (Mitchell 2009: 234; original emphasis)

The leading sociological theorist of networks, Manuel Castells, presents a very similar definition of networks as 'a set of interconnected nodes' (Castells 2010: 19). Castells goes on to suggest that nodes process relevant information in line with the goals and interests of a particular network. In turn, networks organise relevant information between different nodes. What this further suggests is that networks are allocated coded programmes about how to operate. For example, they are instructed to include other networks within their overall remit while excluding others (see also Cilliers 1998: 17). Networks are thus important for complexity theorists because they reveal how systems obtain distinctive patterns (Capra 1996: 82). For these reasons, it is important to spend a little more time describing complex networks. This is the task of the next section.

Complex networks

Watts (2004) suggests that three broad techniques have been developed to investigate networks in sociology. The first is to explore the relationship between network structure, or ties linking members of a population, such as a school or a business, and a social structure, 'according to which individuals can be differentiated by their membership in socially distinct groups or roles' (Watts 2004: 48). The second method is to look at networks as a means to channel information. How this information affects a person depends on his or her individual place in the overall pattern of relations in the network. According to Watts, the third technique of viewing networks in sociology incorporates both of the previous two techniques. This is Mark Granovetter's famous analysis of the strength of weak ties (Granovetter 1973). Granovetter argued that what really matter when it comes to entering and maintaining new social networks are not necessarily strong ties, such as one's close friends, but rather weak ties. For example, by staying within strong ties one is exposed to similar information that everyone within those networks will have access to. By inhabiting a variety of weak ties, such as a network of distant acquaintances for instance, one can be exposed to new information about a variety of different environments. This can prove especially advantageous when embarking on new ventures such as job hunting.

According to Watts, Granovetter's insights were ground-breaking because they demonstrated how the structure of a social network worked in tandem with a person's position in the groups inhabiting it. Granovetter's investigations thus confirmed that the social world was constituted, to a large degree, by small world networks and by densely clustered groups. The famous example of a small world network is the idea that each person will be able to gain access to others through an average of 'six degrees of separation' (see also Buchanan 2002: 64–66 for illustrations from the natural world). Watts (2004: 53–55) adds that a critical moment of social networks is their dynamic capacity and how they evolve over time. Social networks are dynamic because people enter them to do certain things; but when they do things they are also influenced by what others are doing and by the structure of the network itself. In other words, networks evolve through actions and perhaps more importantly through feedback loops associated with distinctive events. As Capra (1996: 82) observes, networks often operate through nonlinear formations in the sense that they move in different directions, and they acquire particular patterns through feedback loops that establish communication between networks. Thus, networks can be thought of as self-organising systems.

Similar views about networks can be found in the business community. For example, Pascale *et al.* (2000) describe networks as being comprised by nodes and connections that emerge through self-organisation without the need for a central administrator. They present the Internet as a classic case of the self-organisation of complex networks: 'Emergence is evident in the growing number of roles the Net performs and the enterprises it fosters'

(Pascale *et al.* 2000: 126). More to the point, continue Pascale *et al.*, the Internet can be thought of as a 'swarm'. An email message, for instance, is comprised of 'bits', or 'packets', that are analogous to bees in the 'hive' of a PC. Once the email has been sent, the hive starts to 'swarm'. Each 'bit' (or 'bee') of the email message is sent down Internet routers, the latter of which functions through its self-organising intelligence to direct the 'bits' through the quickest routes. The 'swarm' of the various 'bits' then reassemble themselves into a message for a receiver. However, routers might 'send some of the bees on what appears to be a roundabout route because the direct route is overcrowded' (Pascale *et al.* 2000: 126). Pascale takes the self-organising and emergence system of the Internet as an illustration of how business organisations as a whole should ideally operate. Business organisations must try to tap into the distributed intelligence of the entire system of nodes (e.g. stakeholders) and connections (e.g. cross-functional contracts) that are relevant to the specific goals of a business (Pascale *et al.* 2000: 127).

One important element of complexity theory, at least in the version taken up by many social theorists, is the belief that it brings into being 'new' materialist politics. DeLanda (2006) provides a way of thinking about this 'new' materialism and its relationship to complexity theory. He claims that many social theorists are interested in how 'structures', such as rules and resources, and 'agency', such as concrete human practices, mutually reinforce one another within a 'seamless whole', which is usually labelled as 'society'. Structures provide the context for meaningful actions to occur, while actions reproduce structures. DeLanda, however, argues that this theoretical position prompts one to explore only those properties of a system internal to the whole. What this approach misses, then, is the ability to understand relations of exteriority. In other words, properties of component parts can never fully explain those relations that constitute the whole.

> In fact, the reason why the properties of a whole cannot be reduced to those of its parts is that they are the result not of an aggregation of the components' own properties but of the actual exercise of their capacities. These capacities do depend on a component's properties but cannot be reduced to them since they involve reference to the properties of other interacting entities.
>
> (DeLanda 2006: 11)

These new strands in social theory, science and business and management theory have become increasingly popular in many quarters, not least because they seem useful theoretical tools with which to explain the rise of the 'new' global (digital) economy. In many respects, this is not merely fortuitous. Globalisation would indeed seem to confirm what many complexity theorists assume – that the world is now inherently complex and that new media digital technologies have added to the energy and information processed through this complexity. The next section starts to begin to explore how this new approach to materialist theory can be applied to develop a version of networked digital publics.

Networked digital publics

Lash (2002: 18–21) argues that new technology sets in motion nonlinearity in three distinct ways. First, technological forms of life lead to a compression of meaning. Units of information and communication bombard individuals from different directions, be they chat forums, consumer ads, emails, social media and so on, and in the process generate noise. Meaning is then attached to this noise at the interface of sense-maker and the environment in order to produce information. As Terranova (2004) observes, this implies that meaning must be reduced to information; that is to say, meaning should be able to be replicated across different communication channels. Background noise must therefore be regulated and kept to a minimum. Think for instance about a political debate between two elected representatives:

> Can we say that politicians are really conveying a persuasive content? Or isn't the main problem of clearing out a channel through a noisy mediascape, of establishing a contact with an audience out there? In this context, the opponent becomes noise and the public becomes a target of communication.
>
> (Terranova 2004: 16)

Second, nonlinearity occurs through the speed-up of time associated with new technology. Online news now reports about events in the world within minutes. As a result, the speed at which information is produced through new media – whether on the Internet, on mobile phones, on email – allows no time for reflection about, or to act on, causes of events. Instead, we act and reflect mainly on consequences and contingences that abound in modern societies. With the rise of new financial mechanisms, for instance, capital accumulation occurs mostly through investments on future, not present, market capitalisation (Lash 2002).

Third, new technology has ensured that social life is now stretched out through nonlinear global networks. Information travels through various 'ports' (e.g. airports, mobile phone ports, modem ports, Internet portals), which increasingly are connected in a nonlinear fashion: 'To move from port to port is to move, not in a straight line but to hop about, to move discontinuously' (Lash 2002: 20). This is to describe the world through the lens of complexity theory insofar that it suggests that no simple, direct-linear relationship exists between the 'micro' (e.g. bits and particles) and the 'macro' (e.g. systematic patterns). Instead, 'it is at the level of the micro ... that mutations and divergences are engendered and it is therefore at the micro that the potential for change and even radical transformation lie' (Terranova 2004: 32). This approach is related to new technological advancements because digital machines and their utilisation of numbers in the form of code have the ability to register precise alterations in matter. 'By extending the principle of counting to fractions and infinitesimal numbers, turning numbers into the infinite combinations of zeros and ones, digitization is able to produce exact and yet mobile snapshots of material processes' (Terranova 2004: 33). Globalisation, for instance, is made up of information and signs that are both 'de-centred' and come to us through global 'flows' based on 'ideas, images, technologies and capital' (Lash and Urry 1994: 321).

Digital technology thus unleashes ways and means to communicate with one another through nonlinear networks. At the vanguard of this process are ICTs that, for Castells, 'separates, in size, speed and complexity, the current process of globalization from previous forms of globalization in earlier historical periods' (Castells 2010: 25). Castells further argues that digital networks are characterised by three main properties. First, they obtain a degree of flexibility, which lies in their ability to reconfigure themselves according to the context in which they operate. They also ensure that information is cheap, accessible and interactive. Second, digital networks exhibit a degree of scalability in so far they have the ability to expand or shrink and thereby become more pervasive throughout society. Finally, they have a degree of survivability to the extent that they operate without a centre and therefore can function in a plethora of configurations (Castells 2010: 23).

A simple illustration of these developments is that of TV. According to Volkmer (2007), TV channels used to report news via a 'sense of place' insofar that news items would be packaged for an audience living in a particular country. With the arrival of satellite technology and the Internet, the way that TV stations reported news and everyday events began to change. There are about 900 satellites in outer space and this means that TV channels can beam images into the homes of *individuals* across the world. That is to say, TV channels can now beam images through a 'sense of space' insofar that specialist news channels target highly specific globally dispersed news communities in their living rooms rather than national populations. Zee-TV, for example, broadcasts to around 25 million Indian expatriates around the world. These channels thereby create transnational communities and micropublic spheres across global localities, and these operate through complex global networks that are flexible, function at different scales and survive through decentred informational flows. This is not to deny that national news outlets are irrelevant or to dismiss the effects of older technological devices such as the radio. However, it is to say that recent technological advancements have made it possible to respond rapidly and continually to news events, to create 'microspheres' based on specialised news channels. Correspondingly, they have established 'self-referential' networks that as well as facilitating normal journalist activities, such as investigative reporting, also provide a public outlet for marginalised political voices that would normally have no other media outlet (Volkmer 2007: 65–69; see also Volkmer 2003).

Another illustration is that of global financial markets. Nonlinear financial networks have become so dominant that they now generate their own feedback loops, and these often give rise to emergent properties. Contemporary financial markets are discernable by the way in which they can be manipulated by computer investment strategies, and this lends itself to complex interactions in financial markets and new levels of turbulence. Indeed, these markets 'produce random patterns of informational turbulence that may destabilize any company, as well as entire countries or regions, regardless of their economic performance' (Capra 2002: 122). As Johnson (2007: 114–15) observes, financial markets are founded on more general market mechanisms, in which information about price movements is fed back to traders who then use this information to make decisions about buying or selling. These decisions then feedback into market prices, which in turn generates information for traders, and so on. Patterns subsequently emerge in financial markets. Financial market can therefore be defined as

> collections of decision-making objects (traders) which are continually feeding off past information about price-movements in order to make their next decisions. Whether it is a group of traders in China, New York or London, makes essentially no difference. Instead, it is the way in which these people make decisions based on past information which is important. It is not the actual decisions themselves, but the *way* in which they make them.
>
> (Johnson 2007: 118; original emphasis)

Communication networks and their ubiquitous nature further implies that social life has become mediated by 'media events'. Most bits of public information are now *media*-ted and the 'social world' is media saturated (Lash 2002). We thus live in a world of immediacy. Castells similarly argues that we live in a time of 'real virtuality':

> It is a system in which reality itself ... is entirely captured, fully immersed in a virtual image setting, in the world of make believe, in which appearances are not just on the screen through which experience is communicated, but they become the experience.
>
> (Castells 2000: 404)

Complex informational societies thus give rise to 'spaces of flows', which are expressions of those network processes which dominate our lives (Castells 2000: 442–43). Time itself becomes more complex in this new communicative realm. Castells names this new time as being 'timeless time', whereby 'time is erased in the new communication system when past, present, and future can be programmed to interact with each other in the same message' (Castells 2000: 406).

Castells uses these observations to claim that we have entered a new global networked public sphere for debate and discussion. Built primarily around new cultural and media objects, this global public sphere is powered not only through television, radio, the print press and the Internet, but also through what Castells terms 'mass self-communication'. Blogs, email lists, YouTube, Facebook and so on have a mass appeal because they are all connected to mass audiences. At the same time, these are forms of self-communication 'because the production of the message is self-generated, the definition of the potential receiver(s) is self-directed, and the retrieval of specific messages or content from the World Wide Web and electronic communication networks is self-selected' (Castells 2009: 55). Naturally, media ownership has become increasingly concentrated in a handful of corporations:

> Time Warner, for example, controls Warner Brothers, which accounts for 10 percent of global film and television production. Time Warner also owns the second largest cable operator in the United States, 47 regional and international cable channels, and the AOL Internet platform over which these productions are distributed.
>
> (Castells 2009: 77)

Yet, argues Castells, it is also true to say that in using mass self-communications individuals strengthen their communicative autonomy.

User-generated content uploaded onto the Internet is one familiar way that individuals gain autonomy through digital media. Moreover, each user who sends a message through new media is at the same time an addressee of a message. Again, this follows on from the view that we live in an age of network complexity in which multidirectional flows of messages move across the globe in often contingent and unpredictable ways and directions and through different spatial scales (Castells 2009: 129–30). In respect to the public sphere, this further indicates that digital technology opens up new possibilities,

> remixing the multiplicity of messages and codes it receives with its own codes and communication projects. Thus, in spite of the growing concentration of power, capital, and production in the global communication system, the actual content and format of communication practices are increasingly diversified.
>
> (Castells 2009: 136)

For some theorists, the very form and content of these communicative networks has brought about a new politicised public sphere. One of the most celebrated theorists of networked publics is that of Hardt and Negri. They employ various ideas from complexity and network theory in order to make sense of new communicative networks. In their remarkable book, *Empire*, Hardt and Negri (2000) extend the insights of Italian autonomist thinking to make sense of the global world today. The autonomist movement in Italy emerged in the late 1960s as a reaction, in part, to both Gramscian-inspired Marxism and the decade-long Christian Democratic Party stay in office. In many respects, these two forces provided a gap for an alternative left-wing intellectual and practical Marxist politics to appear in Italy. Gramscianism claimed that socialism could be achieved by winning the hearts and minds of ordinary people through the existing political and state apparatus (the so-called 'war of position' in Gramsci's use of that term; see also Chapter 6 where some of Gramsci's ideas are discussed in more depth). Experience showed, however, that conventional political parties still had a firm grip on Italian society (Bowring 2004). The frustration felt by some in Italy towards the failure to instigate radical change through everyday politics was manifest in student revolts (1967–68) and workers' strikes (1969). During this period, many involved in Italian militant politics, and discouraged by perceived failures of the Italian Communist Party (PCI) to capitalise upon growing unrest with the status quo in some sections of Italian society, started to rethink Marxist ideas and practice and its relationship to party politics. It was through this background that Antonio Negri emerged in 1973 as an influential exponent of what was known as *operaismo*, or 'workerism', and later became known as *autonomia*.

At its simplest, autonomist writers maintain that it is the power of labour, or 'social labour', which drives the capitalist imperative rather than an objective structural process. Harry Cleaver, who is often associated with autonomist thinking, suggests that Marxism should begin by examining the actual struggles of workers: 'their content, how they have developed, and where they are headed' (Cleaver 1979: 43). To give one illustration, if we think about the most basic and simple appearance of capitalist society, namely the commodity-form, we see that in order for people to exist under capitalism they must of necessity become a commodity themselves. They become commodities by selling their labour power to a capitalist for a monetary wage. It is only through their power to control class relations that a capitalist can employ money to purchase commodities in order to productively use these to make more money. 'The commodity-form is thus a set of power relations. Whether and how it is imposed depend on capital's power, vis-à-vis the working class' (Cleaver 1979: 73).

Capitalism expands by creating new technological means of appropriating relative surplus value; capital slowly becomes dependant on advances in technology, or what Marx terms 'the power of agencies set in motion during labour time' (Marx 1973: 704). These agencies are themselves based on 'the general state of science and on the progress of technology, or the application of this science to production' (Marx 1973: 705). The reproduction of capitalism along these lines, observes Negri (1989; 1991), leads to the creation and reproduction of the 'social individual'. The 'social individual' relates to the increasing diversity of technological tasks undertaken by labour within advanced capitalism, especially as regards capital's increasing reliance on the intellectual capacity of labour. This is the 'total subsumption' of labour to capital by which capital must search out new forms of non-direct labouring value through advances in technology while simultaneously, though unintentionally, creating new networks of reciprocity between the intellectual capacity of labour.

It is within the autonomist tradition that Hardt and Negri begin to move beyond Marxism to explore what they consider to be the main form of globalisation today. New types of socialisation in the world create in their wake new forms by which workers communicate and cooperate with one another through innovative intellectual possibilities. Specifically, Hardt and Negri observe that digital technology and the abstract cooperation it entails is the 'motor of crisis' (Hardt and Negri 2000: 386). Why is this so? Globalisation represents the autonomy of the political because it has unleashed global networks of communication. Communication, along with the linguistic styles that accompanies it, has therefore become a crucial point of struggle: 'The passage to post-modernity ... compartmentalisation of the life world and immediately presents communication, production, and life as one complex whole, an open site of conflict' (Hardt and Negri 2000: 404). Ironically, however, Hardt and Negri also argue that because politics is now inescapably ensnared within communication then the ability to communicate, and what is communicated, becomes immediate to a local event. Think of the Intifada against the Israeli state. This did not, and has not, erupted into a coherent chain of resistance in other countries against state structures. There is therefore an element of 'incommunicability' in social struggles such as these (Hardt and Negri 2000: 54–55). Nonetheless, the very nature of global communication implies that such struggles can leapfrog a chain of nodal points so that their very incommunicability means they are translated into issues of public importance at various points in global civil society that transcend national borders.

According to Hardt and Negri each explicit struggle by the multitude creates 'new public spaces and new forms of community' (Hardt and Negri 2000: 56). What do Hardt and Negri mean by this statement? In one important sense, labour can be thought of today as a 'virtual power'. Labour in global world is simply 'the *power to act*' (Hardt and Negri 2000: 358; emphasis in original). This power is both 'singular', in the sense that labour constitutes the brain and body of the multitude of activists across the world, and it is 'universal', in the sense that a movement from the virtual to the actual and possible is held in common by the multitude through their modes of communication through technology such as the Internet. 'We can thus define the virtual power of labour as a power of self-valorisation that exceeds itself, flows over onto the other, and, through this investment, constitutes an expansive commonality' (Hardt and Negri 2000: 358). Through new media technology, especially the Internet, and through 'post-Fordist' work patterns based on digital modes of work, individuals thus gain access to the 'general intellect' of global communicative interaction. General intellect is another way of saying that there is a 'One' in the world – a digitally augmented mode of communicating across the globe – that comes together through the 'Many' – a multitude of unique identities engaged in communicating about their own experiences with others (Virno 2004: 41–42).

Living through public spaces, and oscillating between different identities, the multitude of activists are connected through intertwining networks of communication. For these reasons, Hardt and Negri bring these new forms of 'immaterial labour' under the umbrella concept of 'abstract cooperation'.

Cooperation is abstract in the sense that communication between different types of labour is immanent to labour itself. While labour is brought together through diverse networks of communication, knowledge and information the actual identities of workers can remain anonymous to one another. Cooperation remains deterritorialised and thus tends 'towards a virtual existence' (Hardt and Negri 2000: 296). What this additionally implies, as Hardt and Negri (2004: 54–55) suggest, is that networks have no centre. Instead, they are distributed unevenly and variably. While patterns can subsequently be observed, their stability is not predetermined but constantly achieved. Networks are thus creative ensembles that operate through communication and cooperation (Hardt and Negri 2004: 83). In this respect, Hardt and Negri find that the 'swarm' metaphor usefully describes the complex and chaotic nature of decentred global networks. This metaphor draws attention to how isolated 'particles' of different dissent groups can 'swarm' together and create intelligent political organisations. As an organisational whole, then, these particles add several layers of complexity to its formation, they are 'attracted' together, which leads to its added collective intelligence (Hardt and Negri 2004: 91–93). Social networks are related to complex formations.

Such struggles by the multitude also create public spaces that collapse traditional distinctions between the economic, political and social domains and, as a consequence, the private and public spheres. Think of scientific knowledge: scientific knowledge is inescapably tied in with economic production; indeed, capital will convert scientific ideas into patents and private property. Nevertheless, this is also a political question because the monopoly upon knowledge obviously is concentrated in the wealthy north hemisphere. These have real effects on the well-being and affective capabilities of people. When pharmaceutical corporations sued the South African government for producing cheap copies of their patented drugs in their fight against AIDS, we can begin to appreciate how knowledge is a fight over the very nature of life itself (Hardt and Negri 2004: 284). This creates a common interest among singular global movements without negating the singularity of specific events of struggle. For Virno (2004: 55), the new 'post-Fordist' society that we all now inhabit operates through digital technology, which at the same time generates 'a publicly organised space' based in part on people cooperating with one another. Communication is thereby made an integral moment of cooperation and lays the basis for a plethora of 'common places' to emerge for a whole host of political actions.

Conclusion

This chapter has been concerned with mapping out some of the characteristics, traits and themes of networked digital publics. Naturally, there are subtle differences between some of the perspectives presented in this chapter. Indeed, Chapter 5 brings out some of these subtle differences in a little more detail. However, it is also worth noting that the view of networked publics outlined previously shares some notable similarities with a number of management gurus. Perhaps this is unsurprising considering that a number of social and management theorists believe we have entered an informational age defined by complex network formations. In their textbook on 'knowledge management' for example, Gamble and Blackwell (2001) claim that work practices have significantly changed in recent years. In particular, there has been a blurring of boundaries between work spaces and leisure spaces, which have been made possible through flat networks. '(N)ow business has to face a new kind of working together, networks of people working in different locations, some even working at home, within a very flat hierarchy' (Gamble and Blackwell 2001: 14). Pivotal for the success of this formation is knowledge mediated through new technologies. Like some social scientists, Gamble and Blackwell argue that we now live in a global network economy characterised by the speed in which information and knowledge can be passed on and received throughout the world by digital means (Gamble and Blackwell 2001: 17).

Populist managerial gurus Ridderstråle and Nordström (2008) also say something similar to Hardt and Negri's observations on the 'singularities' of workers who come together to challenge the existing order through their own specific identities, issues and grievances (Hardt and Negri 2004: 99). For instance, they observe that through their unique knowledge and intelligence that workers *individually* own assets of the organisations they work insofar that knowledge-based organisations are reliant on the individual, or 'singular', emotion, intelligence and knowledge of each worker (Ridderstråle and Nordström 2008: 6). Subsequently, each worker makes a unique and specific contribution to the fortunes of an organisation. Heterogeneity thus needs to be celebrated in organisations if for no other reason than that creative novelty is gained from 'misfits and tension'. Knowing this, employers need not be afraid of encouraging 'standard deviation' from what is average (Ridderstråle and Nordström 2008: 154). For Ridderstråle and Nordström, this should to be pushed as far as to welcome, just as Hardt and Negri do, those 'who are prepared to challenge the status quo, and to break with existing norms and regulations' (Ridderstråle and Nordström 2008: 153).

But to strongly insist, as both some social and management theorists do, that capitalism has made a wholesale transformation to this more fluid, networked and singular formation is to fail to fully understand that capitalism still gains sustenance from a number of historical structural necessities. The most important of these structural imperatives is the constant necessity to accumulate capital for the sake of accumulation and to commodify as much of social life as is possible. This is to ensure that a continuous increase in surplus value transpires, namely as M (money) – C (commodities) – M^1 (an increase in money). At an abstract level, then, capitalists are only interested in quantitative calculations formed by price signals. They are not concerned in the first instance with concrete or contingent 'externalities' such as ensuring that everyone has a public voice in society. The objective pressure to accumulate capital and profits will take priority over these externalities (Albritton 2007: 166–68). For

Marx, it is precisely this historical necessity to valorise capital that helps to explain how and why new ventures and opportunities for capitalist accumulation occur. The blind necessity to accumulate capital likewise generates specific contradictions, such as the overaccumulation of capital, which in turn lead to diminishing profits. Marx (1977: 438–41) argues that when this happens capitalists and their allies are forced to find other profitable ventures. New monopolies, innovative financial mechanisms and state policies are just three different ways that outlets for capitalist accumulation can once again be created.

To draw out the implications of these preliminary remarks about Marx, the next chapter will look in more detail about what Marx actually says about capitalism. This is an important point, if for no other reason than the fact that many informational social theorists start their own respective analyses by claiming we have made a transition from industrial societies to informational societies. Simultaneously, they tell us social theorists of the industrial age need to be transcended to make way for categories more suitable for today's technologically savvy world. Normally, Marx is thrown in as a theorist of industrial capitalism, which of course means that we now need to go beyond many of his critical categories. The next chapter will therefore assess some of these claims and ask whether several contemporary theorists are premature in their appraisal of Marx's worth as a critical thinker for today.

4 Industrial capitalism versus industrial capital

Introduction

According to Mosco, 'myths are stories that animate individuals and societies by providing paths to transcendence that lift people out of the banality of everyday life. They offer an entrance to another reality, a reality once characterized by the promise of the sublime' (Mosco 2004: 3). Myths are not falsehoods as such, but provide a way for people to overcome certain contradictions they face in their daily lives. Myths help us to manage these contradictions by reinterpreting them through cultural objects, jokes, music, narratives, stories and so on. 'In this respect, myths transform the messy complexities of history into the pristine gloss of nature' and present us with solutions that help to make existing social contradictions seems natural (Mosco 2004: 30). And because myths are not mere illusions they provide a window into past meanings of lived experience as well as granting us an understanding of the construction of subjectivity (Samuel and Thompson 1990).

For Bakhtin, one of the more powerful aspects of myths lies in their ability to alter the relationship between 'language and intentions, language and thought, language and expression' (Bakhtin 1981: 369). Myths enter the 'heteroglossic' world of popular discourse and attempt to alter it. Heteroglossia is associated with the contradictions that people face in their daily lives and that give rise to speech diversity in daily encounters.

> (A)t any given moment of its historical existence, language is heteroglot from top to bottom: it represents the co-existence of socio-ideological contradictions between the present and the past, between differing epochs of the past, between different socio-ideological groups in the present ... all given bodily form. These 'languages' of heteroglossia intersect each other in a variety of ways, forming new socially typifying 'languages'.
>
> (Bakhtin 1981: 291)

Heteroglossia is thus attached to centrifugal forces and opens up spaces in society for popular expressions of disquiet against dominant relations. Generating feelings, forms, meanings and stylistic combinations of language, myths seek to erase this heteroglossic living sense of time. In its place, they socially construct a generic narrative associated with an 'automatisation' of time.

Automatisation of time ensures that history and temporal rhythms are seen to move forward through self-enclosed series of events. This is a 'self-sufficient path of the historical development of ... style to style', which excludes real contradictory 'socioeconomic development', struggles between different groups in and around this development and their associated speech diversity (Bakhtin and Medvedev 1991: 159). As a result, myths place time in an 'eternal contemporaneity' without any real sense of renewal. Living always in the eternal present, myths remember the past but only from the present-day (Bakhtin 1984: 105–6). This is a 'monologic' perspective on the world that aims to impart a unified meaning upon the lived experience and history of subordinate groups. Monologic perspectives aim therefore to give 'theoretical expression of the historical processes of linguistic unification and centralisation, an expression of the centripetal forces of language' (Bakhtin 1981: 270).

One of the most powerful myths at the heart of discussions about informational societies is that concerning industrial societies. In order to demonstrate what is original and unique about digital networked societies, many social theorists compare an informational stage of history to a previous industrial stage of history. To recap, some social theorists define industrial societies in relation to the rise of the modern factory system of mass production and the scientific organisation of working practices. Sometimes known as Fordism, this system of production encompassed other social characteristics, most notably a rigidly defined class structure made up of homogeneous groups such as the middle-class and working-class along with the mass consumption of goods. Lash and Urry (1987: 89) characterise this industrial paradigm as being a highly organised one between major industries in a country, its national politicians and its trade unions. Several other social traits include: the concentration of industrial, banking and commercial capital and their regulation by the state; the separation of ownership of business organisations from their managerial control; bureaucratic and scientific management of society through new state-led middle-class occupations; the growth of regional economies based in part on large manufacturing sectors; large industrial cities; and 'a cultural-ideological configuration which can be termed "modernism"' (Lash and Urry 1987: 4).

Lash and Urry are of course but two prominent contemporary social theorists from an array of others who construct similar narratives about a bygone industrial era. Problematically, however, by setting out the industrial stage of history, it is easier for these social theorists to then, quite ironically considering their use of complexity theory, present a linear account of the transition to an informational digital age. In the process, however, the contradictions and heteroglossic diversity within and between each 'stage' is lost to a monologic myth in and around industrial societies.

What is equally interesting about many of these social theorists is that they were once Marxists, but they now claim that Marxism is a theory of the industrial era. Yet, so they tell us, we have now surpassed industrial societies in favour of informational societies, and this means that Marxism is a social theory whose time has also passed, or, more generously, whose main theoretical categories no longer have the same explanatory weight as was once the case. It is therefore important, continues the argument, to reject some of Marx's main theoretical categories in favour of new ones more suited to explaining informational and digital societies.

The aim of this chapter is to interrogate some of these myths about industrial capitalism. It begins by first setting out in more detail Bakhtin's theory of discourse. This is achieved by explaining some its main ideas in relation to examples taken from Anthony Giddens's approach to history. Giddens's insights on modernity and globalisation have been extremely influential in how other social theorists explore contemporary societies. They are also useful in the present context because they demonstrate how a monologic discursive approach plots history through distinctive 'stages' in which social life moves forward within self-enclosed series of events. Giddens's monologic approach thereby proves to be a fitting way in explaining Bakhtin's critical insights.

From here, we will then map out three prominent generic themes about industrial societies that have been made by a number of other contemporary social theorists. The first theme describes industrialism through certain utterances that aim to construct specific images about the abstract and homogeneous nature of industrial societies. For example, words such as 'mass', as in 'mass societies', are employed to describe industrialism and to project an image of the 'homogenous' nature of industrial societies. The second theme sets out to show how Marx employs some of these industrial utterances in how he empirically describes industrial societies. Hardt and Negri, for example, say that Marx's main ideas are founded in a 'factory investigation ... that inquired into the conditions and relations of workers ... ' (Hardt and Negri 2009: 126). For Hardt and Negri, Marx is therefore best seen as an intellectual of the dynamics of industrial capitalism.

The final theme suggests that Marx creates a number of analytical categories that aim to capture the homogenous nature of actual industrial societies. For example, Arvidsson and Colleoni (2012) argue that with the arrival of industrial factories labour could finally be 'subdivided into discrete units that lend themselves to be measured and controlled in terms of the productivity of the time deployed' (Arvidsson and Colleoni 2012: 139). These 'quantitative' conditions provided the context for Marx to develop his labour theory of value. Marx's theory therefore owes its existence to real factory floors and, as such, is a purely empirical phenomenon that develops through the linear flow of history and reaches maturity in the factories of industrial capitalism. For these reasons, Arvidsson and Colleoni, along with many other contemporary social theorists, insist that Marx's labour theory of value is now outdated because the sort of industrial capitalism congruent for measuring labour in abstract units has been surpassed by a new digital form of capitalism.

Certainly, if correct, these three themes prove devastating to Marx's main theoretical contribution to critical social science. If his labour theory of value is no longer applicable then his whole analysis of capitalism is found wanting. So, to what extent are the critics correct to outline these thematic lines of criticism of Marx's work? To assess their claims the chapter moves on to ascertain the extent to which Marx does indeed reduce the abstract contradictory properties of capital to that of actual industrial societies. We will see that for Marx, the separation of labour from the means of production represents the basis for the exploitation of labour power. He is clear, though, that this separation occurs not only in industrial factories, but also in a wide variety of social contexts. It follows that Marx is a more careful and subtle thinker than his critics give him credit for, and he certainly does not reduce the dynamics of capitalism to concrete types of *industrial capitalism*, such as actual industrial factories.

The section that follows argues that Marx first wanted to understand the abstract contradictory dynamics of capital. Only then did he seek to gain an insight into more concrete and empirical types of industrial capitalism. In this respect, his understanding of *industrial capital* is crucial. Industrial capital operates through the two additional circuits of financial capital and commercial capital. Together, all abstract forms of capital go on to create productive labour and productive capital that then goes on to generate surplus value. At the same time, industrial capital reproduces a number of abstract contradictions, which also propels capitalism to produce a certain amount of energy in the system. Through the work of Deleuze and Guattari this can be likened to what they term as a Body without Organs – the conjunction of flows and intensities that spring from the exploitation of labour-power by capital and the constant necessity to generate surplus value. As Deleuze and Guattari say, and contrary to what some informational theorists argue, industrial capital enfolds these flows and intensities in stratified circuits of power. The chapter then makes some concluding observations about the internal contradictions of industrial societies.

Mythic genres

According to Bakhtin, monologic approaches to discourse make a distinction between plot and story. Whereas a story delineates a real event from life, plot is contained purely within a discursive framework itself. Plot in this respect is maintained through a particular discursive device. The role of a device is to make a specific plot perceptible to others, while actual real events and material serve merely to provide 'motivation' for a device. Actual real events and material are therefore secondary to the plotting of a narrative, which in turn justifies the use of a particular discursive device. Material is therefore completely unimportant in the sense that it is replaceable within the contours of a discursive framework and the devices being employed (Bakhtin and Medvedev 1991: 106–8).

By drawing on seemingly neutral material, monological devices are themselves represented in neutral terms (Bakhtin and Medvedev 1991: 111). This can be compared to non-neutral heteroglossic time, which is situated in real historical events wherein crises often erupt. Compared to this form of time, monological time exists not in real historical events but in repeatable 'doings' that are uprooted from a particular locality and simply supplanted to another locality. In other words, monological time 'has no advancing historical movement; it moves rather in narrow circles: the circle of the day, of the week, of the month, of a person's entire life. A day is just a day, a year is just a year – a life is just a life' (Bakhtin 1981: 248). Time, accordingly, becomes abstract, empty and devoid of specific real historical events. Certainly, there is recognition of temporal shifts in human history but these are seen only to operate in stages – feudal, modern, industrial, informational and so on – and each stage comprises self-contained 'static' temporal dimensions to the extent that it only endures in the boundaries of a distinct stage. Stages thus become evolving unities in which all real material can be reduced to the evolving unity of the stage of history in question (Bakhtin 1984: 26).

A common device employed by some informational and 'late-modern' theorists is the manner by which feudal societies are contrasted to modern societies, or when an industrial stage is distinguished from an informational stage. Take Giddens's description of tribal and 'class-divided' agrarian societies. Giddens (1984: 194) says that in tribal societies 'human beings live closely with each other in conditions of co-presence and within the rhythms of nature in their day-to-day conduct, but they also integrate the natural world cognitively with their activities'. These societies are founded on institutions that 'intermingle' directly and immediately with nature. Unlike modern societies, traditional cultures are therefore grounded in the 'immediacy of presence' of face-to-face relationships:

> That is to say, they know only the individual histories, and kin genealogies of each other, as well as many details about physical milieu in which they move, utilising such knowledge as a chronic feature of the continuity of social interaction.
>
> (Giddens 1995: 161)

After traditional societies come class-divided societies, which are characterised by Giddens as agrarian states. Class plays an important factor in how these societies are organised. Ultimately, though, class is not the basic organising structural principle (Giddens 1995: 108). For instance, class-divided societies also rest on authoritative resources supported by the means of violence (Giddens 1995: 112). Authority, however, operates through a division between countryside and city, which, for Giddens, represents one of the main determining characteristics of class-divided societies: 'Without cities, there are no classes and no state' (Giddens 1995: 144). One of the main features of the city is its propensity to generate the authoritative resources from which state power is created and sustained. Cities allow an administrative command structure to develop as 'crucibles of power' based on a division of labour

(Giddens 1995: 145). Class-divided societies need to control vast areas and therefore require the specialisation of an administrative and military command apparatus. Yet, this power-base is often shrouded in religious symbolic markers, such as through temples built for Gods.

Time is also an important feature of these societies, although it is different to that found in tribal societies. There is a 'binding' and embodiment of space–time relations in different material objects and activities. Writing, for example, is invariably accompanied by the invention of calendars and other cosmological investigations. However, these temporal customs are quite different to those found in modernity. Access to writing is the privilege of the few in class-divided societies, so its temporal qualities do not penetrate the lives of ordinary people. In addition, time is embodied in everyday objects and does not exist, as it does under capitalism, as a separate distinct sphere from that of everyday objects. Indeed, time is conjoined to the temporal ordering of a divine power, 'yielding access to the religiosity of things' (Giddens 1995: 132).

The problem with this historical narrative, as depicted by Giddens, is that it describes the evolution of certain historical stages through a number of general descriptive materials. The models Giddens constructs thereby become somewhat static because they encapsulate a wide variety of distinct social relations and social formations under their generic classifications. For example, city-states, empires and feudal societies are all classified as class-divided societies, while capitalist societies and old style soviet societies are classified as industrial societies. Giddens then posits a linear logic that connects these different societies together. 'In *all* these forms of society, following the first emergence of civilisations, the city, in divergent relations with the countryside, has played an influential role' (Giddens 1995: 96; original emphasis). Here, Giddens establishes a generic account of historical development in the sense that he chooses historically invariant factors to explain discrete historical stages, a wide variety of concrete social relations within those stages and transitions between them. Thus, the categories he employs tend to describe the *observable* material of what is being explained. For instance, we saw that Giddens believes that class-divided societies are defined through visible authoritative resources and the means of violence. Similarly, Giddens depicts industrialism through a number of descriptive themes, such as surveillance maintained through the bureaucratic mechanisms of the modern nation-state (Giddens 1991: 16–17; see also Beck 1992: 13–14 for a similar account of modernity).

It is useful to map out Giddens's account of modernity because not only has it been very influential in how some later theorists conceptualise modern and post-modern societies, but also because it gives us a glimpse into how a specific monologic device, in this case the device of 'modernity', incorporates neutral material, for example descriptions about nation-states, in order to illustrate how the device in question plots history through stages. Indeed, we will now see how a number of contemporary social theorists use similar devices to that of Giddens in order to construct their own thematic genres to argue that we have entered an informational age. Far from merely acting as an impartial account of modern societies, these themes help to construct a specific generic explanation of what came before our current informational stage. In fact, they usually make a comparison to a previous industrial paradigm, but do so in a manner that is ideologically loaded. As will also become apparent, this is quite different to a social theory such as Marxism that first maps out a number of historically specific concepts, which seek to capture and makes sense of contradictory and largely invisible systemic processes (Callinicos 1985). We begin first by examining the utterances employed to describe industrial societies.

Utterances of industrial societies

The first theme is an obvious one and is premised on using certain metaphors and utterances to help visualise the industrial paradigm. One of the most prominent utterances in this respect is that of 'mass', as in 'mass societies'. Van Dijk claims that a 'mass' society is

> A modern type of society with an infrastructure of *groups, organisations* and *communities* (called 'masses'), that shape its prime mode of organization at every level (individual. Group/organizational and societal). The basic units of this society are all kinds of relatively large collectivities (masses) organizing individuals.
>
> (van Dijk 2012: 24; original emphasis)

Like many social theorists, van Dijk employs the utterance 'mass' to describe industrial societies as being highly centralised by the state and other command points, as being bureaucratic, as having high levels of density and inclusiveness, as having broadcast mass media and so on (van Dijk 2012: 43). In a comparable way, Bauman (2000: 57) notes that this was a paradigm mediated through 'bulky', 'heavy' and 'solid' machinery that created 'massive labour forces' 'rooted' to particular factories alongside 'immobile' capital. Elsewhere, Urry (2000) similarly observes that many analysts in the past also made frequent uses of the word 'structure' to describe industrial societies because it captured some of the specific traits of those self-enclosed and fairly stable social entities associated with industrialism like nation-states.

Hardt and Negri likewise employ certain utterances to make sense of industrial modernisation. This era is characterised, in part, as being grounded in 'heavy' bureaucracies associated with a centralised state (Hardt and Negri 2000: 277), while industrial factories bred a 'unified' proletariat engaged in 'common struggles' against industrial employers (Hardt and Negri 2000: 262–63). Moreover, there is a 'concentration' of industrial production and 'macroeconomic' management of society (Hardt and Negri 2000: 240–42), which gives rise to 'structures and hierarchies' in a relatively simple division of labour. Subjective social identities are borne in this system that take on 'one-dimensional' character traits, which are also 'functions' of industrial economic development (Hardt and Negri 2000: 243). For his part, Baudrillard says that industrial production fashioned objects of consumption through 'equivalence' and 'indifference' based on the 'serial repetition' of the 'same' commodities (Baudrillard 1993: 55–56). Under this type of employment, workers were managed through a 'scientific organisation of labour' made possible because they all embodied the same 'collective worker' identity in factories (Baudrillard 1993: 15).

This way of portraying industrial societies through certain utterances can also be found in management literature. Peters and Waterman's hugely successful early-1980s management tome, *In Search of Excellence*, expressed a degree of antipathy towards what they labelled as 'the rational model' for managing businesses. In this model, managers are afraid to creatively experiment with working practices and instead prefer a conservative inaction (Peters and Waterman 1982: 47). At the forefront of this conservative attitude is a 'numerative' rationalism that 'seeks detached, analytical justification for all decisions' (Peters and Waterman 1982: 29). Under an industrial, rationalist approach, a business strategist therefore aims to gather precise knowledge about what is in fact unknowable. One might not know yet the end use of a new product but this will not deter rationalist strategists from trying to make detailed market forecasts for its end use. At the same time, 'central staff' will endeavour to show why a particular venture will not succeed if it cannot be quantified (Peters and Waterman 1982: 31). According to Peters and Waterman, it was only by the 1970s that a new mode of thinking challenged this bureaucratic model. This was a move in some management circles towards so-called 'loose-tight' organisational structures whereby a degree of autonomy is 'pushed ... down to the shop floor or product development team' (Peters and Waterman 1982: 15).

Empirical industrial factories and workers

This discussion takes us to the second ideological theme. By constructing an image of industrial mass societies, these theorists can tell us that this stage of history has now been transcended by informational, fluid and networked societies. If this is indeed the case, however, then those theorists who lived during industrial times tended to develop concepts more attuned to an industrial past that, unfortunately, are no longer relevant to most people living today. Karl Marx is the most obvious culprit in this respect. Indeed, numerous modern-day critical theorists reject Marx's delineation of capitalism, believing it to be a remnant of a departed industrial era. Bauman suggests as much when he says that although Marx famously describes modern capitalist societies in *The Communist Manifesto* as being ensnared by the never-ending condition of 'all that is solid melts in air', this should not be taken to mean that Marx's observations can be used to fully understand our present liquid-like informational world. Indeed, Bauman argues, what Marx noted as being the 'melting' of 'profane' relations was in fact the melting of pre-modern fixtures, which had to be cleared away for the dominance of new modern solid structures (Bauman 2000: 3–4). Marx does not therefore speak about our present day fluid condition. What he emphatically addressed with great determination was how capitalism brought the new industrial order into being through the separation of labourers from their livelihood (Bauman 2000: 141). For Bauman, then, the separation of workers from their means of support and subsistence occurs with the actual concrete and everyday formation of industrialisation (see also Castells 2000: 16 for a similar argument).

From this viewpoint, contemporary social theorists tell us that Marx was fascinated by the concrete empirical traits of industrial factories, workplaces and indeed industrial societies. In other words, Marx was mainly writing about a distinctive empirical moment in history, namely industrialism and its various everyday appearances like that of factories. Indeed, one accusation that some theorists make about Marx is that he is besotted with the likes of industrial factories. Hardt and Negri claim for example that Marx mainly focused on uncovering relations of exploitation as these were played out in distinctive places like factories. However:

> In the contemporary world this spatial configuration has changed. On the one hand, the relations of capitalist exploitation are expanding everywhere, not limited to the factory but tending to occupy the entire social terrain. On the other hand, social relations completely invest the relations of production, making impossible any externality between social production and economic production. The dialectic between productive forces and the system of domination no longer has a *determinate place*. The very qualities of labour power (difference, measure, and determination) can no longer be grasped, and similarly, exploitation can no longer be localised and quantified. In effect, the object of exploitation and domination tend not to be specific productive activities but the universal capacity to produce, that is abstract social activity and its comprehensive power. This abstract labour is an activity without place, and yet it is very powerful.
>
> (Hardt and Negri 2000: 209; original emphasis)

Working from within the Italian autonomist tradition, Berardi (2009: 60–61) similarly notes that Marx was primarily interested in the industrial worker and the ability of industrial technology to replace living labour and transform industrial workers into being mere appendages of machines. This being the case, Berardi continues, Marx characterised industrial workers by alienation, atomisation and boredom, whereby their manual labour was separated from their intellectual labour on the factory floor. Even so, workers still discovered pleasure by disrupting and subverting machines through a communist consciousness, communist communities and communist parties (Berardi 2009: 84).

While sympathetic to Marx's analysis, Bernard Stiegler (2010) says much the same. According to Stiegler, Marx was primarily concerned with the emergence of industrial capitalism. During this stage, workers became a commodity, 'and an instrument in the service of a tool-bearing machine' (Stiegler 2010: 39).

Therefore, Marx could not foresee that a new version of capitalism would come into being, which sought to capture a worker's cognitive abilities as well as their physical labour. This is our current dominant stage of capitalism, and it is a stage defined by a hyper-industrial service economy (Stiegler 2010: 33). In fact,

> Marx could not ... have anticipated the role of the exploitation and functionalization of a *new* energy, which is not the energy of the proletarianized producer (labor and pure labor force), nor the motor energy of a new industrial apparatus (such as oil and electricity, which are placed into the service of the steel industry and the culture industries), but rather the energy of the *proletarianized consumer* – that is, the consumer's *libidinal* energy, the exploitation of which changes the libidinal *economy* and, with it, the economy *as a whole*, to the point where the former is destroyed just like the latter, and the former *by* the latter.
>
> (Stiegler 2010: 25; original emphasis)

The original postmodern critic of Marx, Jean Baudrillard, provides an illustration of what Stiegler is driving at here. In *Symbolic Exchange and Death*, Baudrillard notes that the era of producing commodities through labour power was built on capital socialising the means of production and reducing everything to commodities. Solidarity resulted from capital's quest to commodify everything because daily life was reduced to the 'same' equation. Positively, this resulted in the formation of trade unions, which arose to represent the solidarity of workers status as a commodity. For Baudrillard, however, these components of solidarity have disappeared because industrial society has dissolved. Contrary to what Marx argued, we are no longer the 'same' but live instead in an era of media and informational simulations. Organisations of industrial solidarity have become 'separate and indifferent under the sign of television and the automobile, under the sign of behaviour models inscribed everywhere in the media or in the layout of the city' (Baudrillard 1993: 78).

Abstract quantitative units of labour

For this final theme, let us momentarily stay with Baudrillard. He is useful because he was criticising Marx's analysis many years before contemporary leftist critics began their theoretical assault on Marx. Indeed, Baudrillard is clear that once Marx reduced all of social life to industrial factories, it became easier for him to quantify everything in terms of what is produced through magnitudes of surplus value. Industrial production, as Marx portrayed it, therefore equals equivalent amounts of labour in the sense that capitalists can *measure* labour through quantitative techniques to gain equivalent outputs from each worker. This is supposedly Marx's 'law' of value (Baudrillard 1993: 9). By reducing all to sameness, industrial factories thus prepare the way for quantitative measure of one's labour output. It follows that empirical factories provided the social context for Marx to construct his quantitative theory of labour.

Contemporary social theorists have continued Baudrillard's depiction of Marx. Berardi similarly notes that Marx's concept of abstract labour was devised primarily to analyse the plight of the industrial worker, who is seen as the 'bearer of a purely abstract and repetitive knowledge' (Berardi 2009: 60–61). If abstract labour therefore refers to 'the distribution of value-producing time' without taking account of specific concrete qualities, then industrial workers were the epitome of abstract labour because their concrete qualities were unimportant next to their purpose to valorise capital (Berardi 2009: 75). Arvidsson and Colleoni likewise argue that for Marx

> (abstract) labor time is the only source of value, and that capital thus exploits labor by paying it less than the true value of the time in which it is deployed. In other words, the foundations of this approach rest on the supposition that there is a direct linear relation between value and time.
>
> (Arvidsson and Colleoni, 2012: 137)

Industrial factories provide the context for this abstract measurement of labour to reach its maturity and for Marx to develop his labour theory of value. Marx's analysis of the industrial factory thus convinced him that part of the working day in industrial societies is divided between necessary labour-time and surplus labour-time. The former generates enough value to ensure the reproduction of the conditions for labour to exist, while capitalists retain a surplus in the form of profits. In *Capital*, claim Hardt and Negri, Marx argued that the relationship between labour and value is a quantitative one in which a quantity of time of abstract labour equals a quantity of value 'expressed in measurable, homogenous units of labour time' (Hardt and Negri 2004: 145). Under industrial capitalism, therefore, the determinant conflict occurred between workers and capitalists over the wage, 'with workers struggling to raise what was considered socially necessary and capitalists trying to diminish it' (Hardt and Negri 2009: 287). Industrial production for Marx integrated labour with capital through an almost automatic, taken-for-granted process (Hardt and Negri 2009: 291).

Now that these three themes have been outlined, what can we say about them? The first observation to make is to say that without doubt, Marx seems to equate industrial capital with the rise of industrial factories. For example, Chapter 15 of the first volume of *Capital* charts the rise of the modern factory system and its need to use workers more efficiently than previous methods of production. Factories extend the quantity of material for capital to exploit through its complex and extensive division of labour and through its use of sophisticated machines and technology. Technological progress 'serves as a means of systematically getting more done within a given period of time, or, in other words, constantly exploiting labour power more intensively' (Marx 1988: 544). Marx believes that for these reasons factories are better placed to quantify the output of workers into discrete units of time. 'The instrument of labour now becomes an industrial form of perpetual motion' (Marx 1988: 526). Machines in a factory have the necessary technology to make complex calculations about how to quantify the production of industrial workers.

Certainly, then, Marx appears to associate concrete industrial workers with the the the quantitative aspects of abstract, material labour. On closer inspection, however, it soon becomes apparent that Marx in fact discusses the abstract contradictory properties of industrial productive capital and labour at an abstract level *before* he discusses concrete factory conditions. Following this abstract explanation, only then does Marx investigate the progressively more complex and concrete forms that industrial capital assumes. Indeed, before the factory mode of accumulation Marx investigates what he terms as manufacture. He clearly states that manufacture is not the same as factory production: 'Modern manufacture – I am not referring to here to large-scale industry which is based on machinery … ' (Marx 1988: 485). But if this is the case, what might constitute some of the social traits of manufacture? It is to this question we now turn.

Capital beyond industrialisation

To answer this question we first need to define some of Marx's key concepts. Labour-power is defined by Marx as the capacity of labour – 'the aggregate of those mental and physical capabilities existing in the physical form' – to create use-values for sale (Marx 1988: 270). A capitalist therefore purchases labour as a commodity in order to utilise its capacity, or labour-power, to produce use-values to sell in the marketplace and make profits. 'As a commodity, labour-power has a unique characteristic in that the "consumption" of labour-power is itself the expenditure of labour and so the production of value' (Clarke 1991: 115; see also Marx 1988: 302). By purchasing labour-power through wages, a capitalist can then generate surplus value. This arises from the difference between what capitalists pay for wage-labour and means of production and the labour actually spent in production. 'Thus labour-power is paid for as a commodity at its value, like any other commodity, but having been purchased the labour-power can be set to work to produce value in excess of its own value' (Clarke 1991: 115). The next question is to ask is, which social formation does Marx think furthers the interests of capital in early capitalism?

According to Marx, it is 'manufacture', not industrial factories, that develops the production techniques and division of labour that proves so revolutionary for capital's expansion. In this first instance, a capitalist brings together different workers in a workshop who have independent trade skills. They devote their energies to producing unique objects that draw on their skills and training. While workers might initially continue to labour like artisans, the external pressure of competition soon forces a capitalist to make them perform labour in a disconnected and isolated manner carried out side-by-side and next to one another. In this second main division of labour, a capitalist is less interested in the apprenticeship and training a worker has, than with the ability of a worker to sustain a regular output. In the manufacture workshop, these workers thus lose their independence. 'The commodity, from being the individual product of an individual craftsman, becomes the social product of a union of craftsmen, each of whom performs one, and only one, of the constituent partial operations' (Marx 1988: 457).

Marx's point in spending a considerable amount of time to describe and analyse manufacture is because he believes that it represents a more concrete and complex form of socio-economic co-operation that capital requires in order to procure relative surplus value from workers. There are two steps to his argument on this issue. In the first instance, Marx sets out why co-operation between workers is so important for the extension of the capitalist mode of production.

> Capitalist production only really begins ... when each individual capital simultaneously employs a comparatively large number of workers, and when, as a result, the labour-process is carried on on an extensive scale, and yields relatively large quantities of products. A large number of workers working together, at the same time, in one place ... in order to produce the same sort of commodity under the command of the same capitalist, constitutes the starting-point of capitalist production.
>
> (Marx 1988: 439)

In the second instance, Marx says that this form of co-operation 'assumes its classical shape in manufacture' (Marx 1988: 455). Why does he believe this about manufacture? Specialisation of labour and then combining this into a single unit and mechanism means that manufacture bestows 'the social process of production with a qualitative articulation and a quantitative proportionality' (Marx 1988: 486).

Both points lead Marx to argue that manufacture creates the conditions for the transformation of the capitalist mode of production through the fundamental commodity of labour-power. This is noticeably different to factories, which focus more on developing the instruments of labour from the tools of handicraft to the machines found on the factory floor (Marx 1988: 492). Manufacture therefore develops the co-operative nature of the division of labour that becomes so integral for the hegemony of capital to take root in society. Clearly, then, Marx does not reduce labour-power or the main abstract characteristics of capitalist production to industrial factories or even to the rise of modern industrialisation. As we know, he even suggests that manufacture is a plausible candidate for the advancement of capitalism before the arrival of industrial factories. This is because manufacture pushes forward the onward march of capital by furthering the conditions for the valorisation of capital. The latter occurs by a capitalist pursuing at least two interconnected goals.

In the first place, he wants to produce a use-value which has exchange-value, i.e. an article destined to be sold, a commodity; and secondly he wants to produce a commodity greater in value than the sum of the values of the commodities used to produce it, namely the means of production and the labour-power he purchased with his good money on the open market. His aim is to produce not only a use-value, but a commodity; not only a use-value, but value; and not just value, but also surplus value.

(Marx 1988: 293)

Manufacture thus renders all of these abstract processes more complex and concrete.

These are all important observations in the move to criticise the myth of industrial capitalism constructed and perpetuated by contemporary social theorists. As we have seen, these theorists reduce Marx's major abstract categories to the empirical industrial factory floor. Yet we can now appreciate that this conceptual move is simply wrong. Certainly, Marx discusses industrial capital but he does so initially at a relatively high level of abstraction. In other words, Marx is concerned initially to outline the essential traits of capitalist reproduction irrespective of their concrete manifestation in factory conditions. For these abstract conditions to exist, Marx argues that a set of class relations must be in place. A capitalist owns any surplus produced because he or she owns the means of production and labour power exactly in his or her capacity as a capitalist. The labourer owns only his or her labour power and can thus only be connected to the conditions of labour under the dominance of capital. Each meets not in the workplace but in the market, in the sphere of circulation. The capitalist holds money capital, the labourer owns nothing but labour power because he or she is separated from the means of production and thus the means of their subsistence. This relationship is not therefore an interpersonal relationship between workers and capitalists, but is instead an objective class relationship between free wage labour and capital (Clarke 1991; Larrain 1983).

Hence, although ... the possessor of money and the possessor of labour-power relate to each other only as buyer and seller ... and are thus from this point of view simply in a money relationship with each other, the buyer appears right from the start as the possessor of the means of production which form the objective conditions for the productive expenditure of labour-power by its possessor. In other words, these means of production confront the possessor of labour-power as somebody else's property. The buyer, conversely, is confronted by the seller of labour as another's labour-power which pass into his control, and has to be incorporated into his capital in order for this really to function as productive capital. The class relation between capitalist and wage-labourer is thus already present, already presupposed, the moment that the two confront each other ...

(Marx 1992: 114–15)

Still, while it is now patently clear that Marx does not reduce some of his core theoretical categories to that of industrial capitalism, we need to unpack these points further in order to get a grip on the way in which capital operates through a number of circuits that in turn provide capitalism with a contradictory momentum. This is the job of the next section.

Industrial capital as a body without organs

To be clear, the class relationship between capital and labour is grounded in alienated labour because it is mediated through the continual separation of labour from its means of subsistence. Labour can only gain access to its means of subsistence through a wage by transforming itself into a commodity to be bought and exploited by capital. This alienated relationship is both the presupposition of capitalism and its continual result.

> (The worker) emerges from the (exchange) process as he entered it, namely as a merely subjective labour-power which must submit itself to the same process once more if it is to survive.
> In contrast to this, capital does not emerge from the process as it entered it. It only becomes real capital, value valorising itself, *in the course* of the process. It now exists as capital realised in the form of aggregate profit, and as such, as the property of the capitalist, it now confronts labour once more as an autonomous power even though it was created by that very labour.
>
> (Marx 1988: 1061; original emphasis)

Immediately, therefore, we are alerted to this basic objective class relationship in Marx's work that he thinks endures in capitalist societies irrespective of which particular modes of accumulation also occur. Following this, Marx then starts to consider other abstract preconditions of the reproduction and valorisation of capital. We have of course already flagged some of these up in respect to labour-power and surplus value. Indeed, Marx argues that the real drive of capital is to increase surplus value, and surplus value is generated through the class relation between capital and labour (Harvey 2013: 85).

However, there are a number of other abstract processes, or circuits, that need to be in place for capital to reproduce itself, and it is here that we finally come to Marx's definition of industrial capital. Accordingly, Marx shows that 'industrial capital' should not simply be conflated with industrial factories and similar industrial empirical forms. Rather, it is vital to isolate the determinations of the class relationship of capital at a fairly high level of abstraction. After all, observes Marx, everyday objects of capital, such as money capital, already assume that more abstract processes are in place for specific circuits of capital to gain momentum. Money capital, for example, 'presupposes the availability of the class of wage-labourers in sufficient numbers across society' (Marx 1992: 118). Marx, however, further insists it is productive capital that ensures surplus value is generated. Productive capital purchases labour-power and the means of production in order to consume these and convert them into commodities that will generate more value. Ideally, therefore, the products produced should be a commodity 'impregnated with surplus-value' (Marx 1992: 131).

But, how is surplus value produced? The answer lies in the circuit of productive capital, which Marx writes as follows:

$$P \ldots C^1 - M^1 - C \ (LP + MP) \ \ldots P.$$

(Marx 1992: 144)

In this circuit, a capitalist has already obtained labour-power (LP) and the means of production (MP). These are then set to work to produce (P) new commodities (C^1), which are sold for money to make a profit (M^1). By making a profit, the capitalist can then purchase more commodities (C), including labour-power and the means of production, so that the production process (P) starts again. The dotted lines represent the moment when the circuit is interrupted. In this case, it is the moment when the capitalist produces yet more commodities (C^1) and money (M^1) to start the production process over again.

However, productive capital is also connected to two other circuits: money capital and commodity capital. In the circuit of money capital, a capitalist goes into the commodity and labour markets as a buyer so that his money is transformed into commodities, represented as M – C. Then, the capitalist engages in productive consumption of these commodities and produces more commodities through production. Commodities emerge with a greater value than their elements of production. The capitalist then returns to the market as a seller and the commodities are transformed into money, and they thus pass through C – M circulation as $C^1 - M^1$. The money capital circuit can therefore be represented as:

$$M - C \ldots P \ldots C^1 - M^1.$$

(Marx 1992: 109)

In the circuit of commodity capital, we have yet another metamorphosis of capital. This is represented as:

$$C^1 - M^1 - C \ldots P \ldots C^1.$$

(Marx 1992: 167)

In this circuit, C^1 is both the result and premise of the other two circuits. This because 'what is M – C for one capital already involves $C^1 - M^1$ for another' (Marx 1992: 167). The difference in this circuit, however, is that it begins with circulation in its entirety as two opposing phases. One commodity (C^1), which is impregnated with surplus value, has already been transformed into capital

(M^1). This is then used to create another commodity (C) in the production process (P) in order to generate more commodity capital (C^1). This circuit therefore creates both surplus value and surplus products in the form of surplus commodities.

The reason why these three circuits have been sketched out is that, for Marx, they represent an interconnected unity; they all work together, albeit in contradictory ways. More importantly, however, Marx uses the term 'industrial capital' to describe the unity of these three circuits.

> The two forms that the capital value assumes within its circulation stages are those of *money capital* and *commodity capital*; the form pertaining to the production stage is that of *productive capital*. The capital that assumes these forms in the course of its total circuit, discards them again and fulfils in each of them its appropriate function, is *industrial capital* – that is pursued on a capitalist basis.
>
> (Marx 1992: 131–33; original emphasis)

The following circuit can thus represent industrial capital:

$$M - C \; (LP + MP) \; ... \; P \; ... \; C^1 - M^1.$$

> (Marx 1992: 137)

In this relatively simple formula, we know that M represents money capital that is exchanged for the commodities of labour power (LP) and means of production (MP). Both LP and MP are put to use in the process of production (P) to create commodities (C^1) of more value than was initially laid out in the production process. Transforming an object into commodity capital (C^1) enables a capitalist to sell the commodity for more money than was spent in production. Profit (M^1) can then be accumulated.

Importantly, as Harvey (2013: 51) notes, industrial capital does not operate smoothly across these different circuits. Far from it. In each circuit, contradictions occur that halt the smooth flow of circuit of industrial capital and demonstrate the need for state action to suspend these contradictions. Indeed, Burnham (2006) shows that at a systematic level the state must engage in a permanent offensive of resolving and offsetting the inevitability of crises in the various stages of the circuit of capital. For example, at the initial stage of money capital, $M - C$ (MP + LP), there is the real possibility of inflation in the procurement of means of production and labour-power through factors such as acquiring the necessary means of production and workforce in a way that does not negatively affect balance of payments. In addition, state policies have to be created that regulate the flow of money within and between countries so that money capital can be converted into productive capital and then back to money capital. A state also has to ensure that its workforce remains in a competitive and healthy position vis-à-vis the population of other nation states, hence the requirement of welfare policies. The circuit of productive capital brings to the fore the importance for state officials to tackle industrial relations and unrest and the importance of investing in policies such as labour skills. The final circuit of money capital (M^1) reveals the importance of factors such as tax revenues and the perennial problem of the reasonable amount of tax the state can collect (Burnham 2006: 77–79; see also Burnham 2002).

The contradictory nature of these circuits and its need to valorise surplus value gives capital a certain energy. Marx talks endlessly about how capital transforms itself as it moves through these different circuits. This metamorphosis is premised on the ceaseless requirement for capital to accumulate surplus value for the sake of accumulation, and to reconvert surplus value into capital for the sake of production (Marx 1988: 742). This blind necessity leads to an external constraint for capitalists to invest in new machines, or constant capital, so that they become more competitive at the expense of investing in labour-power, or variable capital. At the same time, this energetic force is conspicuous in how capitals are over time centralised in the hands of a few capitalists. Monopolies soon emerge, and in the process create world markets that ensnare more people within its nets to be prepared to be exploited. Yet, this also demonstrates the source of capital's vitality. Capital 'flourishes, unleashes the whole of its energy ... only where the worker is the free proprietor of the conditions of his labour, and sets them in motion himself' (Marx 1988: 927).

The energy that capital exhibits through its circuits can be likened to what Deleuze and Guattari term as the Body without Organs (BwO). By this strange name Deleuze and Guattari hope to capture the processes by which the energies associated with desires is transferred through flows and connect up with one another through circuits. Desire therefore acts as a 'machine' by behaving as a 'desiring-machine'. At its simplest, this refers to a desire to produce reality. We desire something and so we find ways to produce it in reality to satisfy our desired need for it. Therefore, 'if desire produces, its product is real. If desire is productive, it can be productive only in the real world and can produce only reality' (Deleuze and Guattari 1984: 28).

But how does desire produce reality? Desire first imparts a 'passion' that has to be fulfilled. In other words, desire must attach itself to its object of desire (Deleuze and Guattari 1984: 28). A desiring-machine, which is one element of more general desiring-production, is therefore any organ that makes a connection with another object. More precisely, specific machines cut into the flow of another machine to gain energy. A baby's mouth is a machine that connects to its mother's breast to gain energy from the flow of milk. The one machine – the baby's mouth – is an organ-machine connected to the breast and flow of milk that acts as an energy-machine. This being the case:

> (T)here is always a flow-producing machine, and another machine connected to it that interrupts or draws off part of this flow (the breast – the mouth). And because the first machine is in turn connected to another whose flow it interrupts or partially drains off, the binary series is linear

in every direction. Desire constantly couples continuous flows and partial objects that are by nature fragmentary and fragmented. Desire causes the current to flow, itself flows in turn, and breaks the flows.

(Deleuze and Guattari 1988: 6)

Flows interrupt other flows and in the process bring together, break apart and fragment different partial machines and thus produce new machines.

Every machine, in the first place, is related to a continual material flow (*hylè*) that it cuts into. It functions like a ham-slicing machine, removing portions from the associative flow … (E)very machine is a machine of a machine. The machine produces an interruption of the flow only insofar as it is connected to another machine that supposedly produces this flow.

(Deleuze and Guattari 1984: 38–39)

Desiring-machines therefore maintain flows between partial objects and as a result produce new connections. As Bogue (2003: 60–61) observes, desiring-machines are comprised by many machines that then make connections to other machines. A baby's mouth is a machine that is also a breathing-machine, a crying-machine and so on. At the same time, the baby is comprised by numerous machines associated with the alimentary canal (stomach-machine, urethra-machine and so on), that are then converted through energy routes such as different circulatory-machines, hormonal-machines, etc. These are all interconnected circuits of energy connected with, and drift and move through, the flow of milk. Bogue also notes that other circuits are present here.

The infant's alimentary circuit, for example, being connected to ocular circuits (the infant's eye-machine focused on a living room lamp, say), olfactory circuits (the nose-machine coupled to flows of kitchen odours), tactile circuits (epidermal machines in touch with heat, fabrics, flesh, mists, air currents).

(Bogue 2003: 61).

The BwO therefore represents a number of circuits of energy that cut and connect into one another in often contingent and unpredictable ways (Deleuze 2005: 32; Deleuze and Guattari 1988: 300; Deleuze and Guattari 1984: 315–16).

As a constant evolving process, production is as a result a product itself because it creates states of being. Under capitalist production, the various circuits of industrial capital aim to cut into these circuits and flows of energy in order to direct them into its own circuits. In fact, Deleuze and Guattari say that industrial capital is the form that captures other commercial and financial 'flows' and transforms these into capitalist circuits based on the production of surplus value. Industrial capital performs 'a tighter and tighter control over production' and brings other flows under its abstract and decoded control and regulation (Deleuze and Guattari 1984: 246–47). After all, industrial capital is productive capital because it is only interested in quantitative calculations of surplus value irrespective of the qualitatively different forms of labour that produces surplus value. Money dominates these processes because it ensures that the connections between different circuits of capital remain in a creative synthetic flow with one another (Deleuze and Guattari 1984: 12). In this respect, industrial capital represents an attempt to control the energy and desire of labour in order to procure surplus value. That is to say, the organs of labour-power and its productive energy must be captured by capital and transformed into an organism of exploitation through the acquisition of surplus value. Through the circuits of industrial capital, capital proclaims to labour: 'You will be organised, you will be an organism, you will articulate your body' (Deleuze and Guattari 1988: 176–77).

Unlike informational theorists who see capitalism today as being immersed in concrete flows and networks, Deleuze and Guattari are fittingly more nuanced and subtle in their explanation. They recognise that capitalism is stratified through specific 'forms, functions, bonds, dominant and hierarchical organisations, organised transcendences' (Deleuze and Guattari 1988: 176). Flows and networks always operate through historically specific capitalist forms.

Conclusion

As should be by now patently obvious, Marx does not equate industrial capital with industrial capitalism. Those theorists who suggest otherwise are therefore wrong to do so. More to the point, the analysis presented in this chapter gives us a basis to argue that the contradictions of industrial capital are still present in contemporary capitalism, albeit they exist in a new form. Furthermore, they provide a way to analyse the socio-economic models put forward by some contemporary theorists. As we know, these models are constructed through rather static accounts in which material serves merely to illustrate certain devices that plot history through a linear progression of 'stages'. This point can be developed further through the category of contradiction. According to Bakhtin, who works from a Marxist perspective, contradictions are inextricably united in one another. This monistic viewpoint suggests that, 'dialectical negation is born and ripens in the bosom of the negation itself. Thus, socialism ripens in the bosom of capitalism. The phenomenon itself inevitably prepares its own negation, gives birth to it out of itself' (Bakhtin and Medvedev 1991: 165).

Some contemporary theorists also suggest that 'contradiction' inhabits the stages of history, although not in the sense of Bakhtin's or a Marxist viewpoint suggests. Interestingly, Beck claims that modern industrial societies contain a contradiction between 'the *universal* principles of modernity – civil rights, equality, functional differentiation, methods of argumentation and scepticism – and the exclusive structure of its institutions, in which these principles can only be realized on a *partial, sectoral*, and *selective* basis' (Beck 1992: 14; original emphasis). Yet, this contradiction is premised on an *external relationship* between a number of universal principles and their empirical mooring in empirical institutions. This is not, then, a necessary and essential contradiction within the very abstract structure of an object, but is a description of 'a temporal succession of two phenomena that are unconnected or only connected extraneously and accidentally … ' (Bakhtin and Medvedev 1991: 165).

This is an important point because it suggests that we need to move away from the sort of non-dialectical and non-contradictory socio-economic models constructed by some social theorists in and around the supposed transition from industrial societies to informational and networked societies. This chapter has argued, for example, that there are a number of problems with the non-dialectical models constructed by contemporary social theorists on industrial capitalism. They push a non-dialectical description of industrial capitalism onto the abstract and contradictory properties of industrial capital. Not only has this meant that they misinterpret Marx's original analysis of industrial capital, they also tend to overlook the internal contradictions and tensions of the more empirically based descriptions of actual industrial Fordist societies.

In what ways, though, did Fordist industrialism embody certain internal contradictions? Clarke argues that what has become known as Fordism represented a specific form of the contradictory tendencies of capitalism. As will be argued in more depth in the next chapter, capitalism develops unevenly because it wants to expand its productive powers but must do so within the limits of the market. Capital sees these limits as barriers that must be overcome in order to realise surplus value. Fordist industrialism was one way that capital sought to do this by revolutionising the means of production (Clarke 1988). At the same time, its contradictions meant that it developed in an uneven manner. Williams *et al.* (1987) point out, for instance, that Henry Ford's innovations in mass production were originally limited to manufacturing cars and some electrical products primarily because no added advantages were gained by mass-producing other consumer goods such as furniture. In the UK, moreover, only a limited number of companies ever employed assembly-line production, while many of those mass production companies in existence had inter-related car models structured around a variety of models rather than one standard model. Indeed, by the 1960s the Toyota car manufacturer in Japan was already experimenting with 'mixed lines' production based on assembling two or more models of cars on one line.

Furthermore, as Clarke (1988) further notes, after the Second World War people expected better living standards for the sacrifices they had endured in recent years. The institutionalisation of wage bargaining and better wages certainly ensued, but this was at the expense of linking higher wages to actual rises in productivity. This became particularly troublesome for major employers and the government because productivity in manufacturing was not especially higher than in previous years. Productivity in other areas such as agriculture, transport, buildings and distribution did, however, increase, but profits nevertheless came under pressure from increased wages that people enjoyed in the 1950s and 1960s (see also Foster and Magdoff 2009).

Overaccumulation of goods thereby transpired in some sectors of the economy. Income policies became one of the main ways in which governments sought to control these processes, but this merely politicised struggles over wage policies. This in turn led to higher inflation. To compensate for a squeeze on wages, credit was made increasingly available to people to continue their consumption patterns, but this simply separated production from consumption to greater degrees (Clarke 1988).

The next chapter continues to highlight specific contradictory tendencies of capitalism, although this time the emphasis is shifted to the present-day financial form of capitalism. The reason for doing so is not only to continue the critical analysis of informational theorists started in this chapter, but also to begin to understand how they apply their theoretical armoury to make sense of our financialised times. Indeed, as we will see, they construct an integral link between new modes of financialisation and digital publics. Yet, we will also see that the internal contradictions at play in industrial capital are at play in today's financialised capitalism. This then opens the way in Chapter 6 to begin to present an alternative Marxist account of finance and digital publics.

5 Financialisation and digital publics
Beyond discourse and performativity

Introduction

Some years before the 2008 crash, many critical social theorists had been studying the impact that global finance was exerting on everyday life. They had noted the rise and dominance of new financial devices in economic markets, the likes of which had not previously been seen on the world stage. Complex mathematical formulas and models sought to explain to a select few who had the necessary theoretical training that new opportunities for massive profits were open to those who were prepared to take risks in how they invested on the money markets. Soon, terms such as 'collateralised debt obligations' were appearing in trading rooms around the world in order to describe this new and exclusive financial utopia. A growing number of social theorists also started to notice that finance was becoming sexy and seductive; indeed, finance was looking like it could actually take on a 'performative' guise. More reality TV shows began to appear during the 1990s, for example, extolling the virtues of financial investments in forms such as property, while other shows praised the techniques used by contestants to become a hotshot apprentice in business. Financial lifestyle magazines were suddenly popular, with their glossy pictures showing how happiness equalled the amount of financial investments made in everyday life.

Given this, it is perhaps unsurprising that many social scientists have become interested in how financial networks and financial models assemble and order economic markets. This approach is particularly keen to analyse how financial markets are integrally related to digital media, and how micro interactions between both result in calculative mechanisms that socially construct and market risks in society (Sum 2013: 545). Today, many who follow this latter analytical approach to finance recognise that digital media is a central actor in how economic and financial markets operate across the world. 'Just think, for instance, of what is involved nowadays in trading equities or derivatives', Pryke and du Gay note. 'A superabundance of data. From price movements to secondary market feeds, cascades into dealing rooms to confront traders and heads of desk. The sheer volume of data requires not just quantitative but qualitative techniques to help interpret the numbers' (Pryke and du Gay 2007: 345).

To understand this point in more depth this chapter starts to tackle some of the claims put forward by informational theorists about global finance. This is an important area to investigate, not only because we are still suffering the negative consequences of the 2008 global financial crisis, but also because an array of informational theorists suggest that the way in which global finance operates today is intimately tied with digital information and the public sphere. Critically exploring their respective views on global finance thereby provides a basis to deconstruct certain prominent arguments in and around digital publics. For example, it presents a way to show how particular views about global finance often parallel some beliefs found in business and management literature on financial markets, and, following this, to open the way to build an alternative Marxist perspective on the relationship between digital information, finance and the public sphere in Chapters 6 and 7.

The chapter starts by outlining three overlapping schools of thought on global finance and digital publics advanced by informational theorists. First, we explore the claim that global finance is now inherently part of the network society. Second, the idea that global finance exhibits degrees of performativity is outlined. Finally, we will set out the argument that insists that global finance is embroiled in autonomist networks of the multitude and communicative labour.

While it is true to say that these schools of thought reveal many important traits about the global economy and the public sphere, they also reproduce a number of problems in their respective analyses. Broadly speaking, they tend to operate at a concrete and contingent level of analysis. This means that they do not take enough notice of how capitalism is mediated through a number of necessary contradictions and inversions, which are reproduced in distinctive forms at more concrete levels. This point is extended into four main lines of criticism. First, that by bracketing certain contradictory dynamics of economic markets, some social theorists unintentionally reproduce an account of global finance that is remarkably similar to that found in mainstream and populist business and management literature. Second, these theorists too readily over-identify with the concrete and contingent nature of global economic markets and their associated publics. Third, they sometimes indulge in degrees of technological determinism in making certain arguments. Finally, they sometimes seem to reduce finance and the public sphere to being instances of discourse rather than viewing both as refracted moments of the same contradictory 'real' essence of capitalism.

Finance and the network society

For some time now, those who argue that we have been witnessing a move towards a flatter, more networked world have also noted the growing importance of what is termed as financialisation. There are several different and over-lapping meanings of the meaning of financialisation in relation to networks and digital media. Lash and Urry (1987: 204) note that during the 1960s a private market for extensive loans had significantly increased across Europe and in the US. Spearheaded by European banks that fell outside of stricter monetary regulations by national states, a market in Eurodollars grew quickly during this period. The way in which these banks got around normal monetary rules and regulations was to lend money to other investors, particularly American companies, in dollars. By doing so, the banks escaped normal regulatory constraints and in the process helped to establish an offshore money market for the sales of Eurodollars. An indicator of a growing deregulated international flow of finance across borders, Lash and Urry further argue that this market for private finance was and is different to finance under 'industrial capitalism'. In the latter, financial activity 'occurred within a nation-state and was based upon the dominance of banking groups stemming from a given *national* currency' (Lash and Urry 1987: 207; original emphasis). Nevertheless, this 'organised' form of finance has now become 'disorganised' primarily because industry and finance have grown into two separate international circuits. While both overlap with each other, it is global financial networks that presently dominate many profit margins in capitalist countries:

> In Britain ... the profits of financial corporations rose as a proportion of net corporate income from about 10 percent in 1968 to nearly 60 percent in 1980; in France the increase was from 10 percent to about 25 percent, and in Germany from 20 percent to 50 percent.
>
> (Lash and Urry 1987: 208)

Castells argues that such changes are an indicator that we have entered a globally complex network society. 'Thus, global financial flows have increased dramatically in their volume, in their velocity, in their complexity, and in their connectedness' (Castells 2000: 102). Castells notes the importance of new media as being a key influence on this expansion in financial networks. After all, communication networks have enabled billions of dollars in transactions to occur across the globe every few seconds. Technology moreover helps investors to number crunch financial transactions and put into practice complex financial models, all of which helps to make financial calculations. Apart from the enlargement of international banking, along with the likes of global investors making acquisitions in overseas stocks and money markets, there has also been a vast increase in the degree and size of currency trading with daily turnover rates in trillions of dollars. Since the 1980s, successive governments have supported these practices by passing lax financial regulation. Speculation by hedge funds in particular has been empowered. Overall, Castells observes, capital flows have become increasingly autonomous of 'the actual performance of economies' (Castells 2000: 106). A world of communicative networked financial transactions is also non-linear and thus highly unpredictable.

Indeed, according to Lash (2011: 116), the so-called financialisation of everyday life is an indication of how social life has become more intensive and heterogeneous. Unlike industrial capitalism founded on identity and sameness (e.g. the codification and commodification of life through

homogeneous abstract labour), 'cognitive capitalism' is predicated on difference and 'uncodifiability'. Borrowing from a host of theorists that include
Castells, Lash claims that capitalism has entered an intensive phase consisting
of 'bits' of information. These bits of information communicate with one
another. This is seen most readily in the difference between industrial capitalism and networked financialised capitalism. For Lash, capitalists can only
exploit knowledge under industrial capitalism during the commoditised labour
process in the form of units of time. Under informational capitalism this is no
longer the case. These days, capitalism is reliant on ordinary people inputting
their own everyday knowledge into co-creating the product in question. This
is a type of knowledge that exists as an externality and cannot be codified. 'It
is a knowledge of attention, care, intelligence (capacity to understand context),
learning and, above all, innovation' (Lash 2011: 116). Networked digital capitalism encourages this type of knowledge to circulate; we need only to think
about how social media operates to understand the logic of this argument. At the
same time, this networked digital capitalism provides new routes for knowledge
about brands to circulate globally. Indeed, according to Lash, brands are built
through their distinctiveness to other brands, by their ability to harness and build
intellectual property, and by their aptitude to mobilise ordinary knowledge to
speak about the distinctive image of the brand to other ordinary people. 'The
brand is effective through its "difference-value"' (Lash 2011: 127; see also
below on the discussion of autonomist Marxism).

In making these claims, Lash also draws on a specific poststructuralist
approach to finance that has become very influential in that last few years.
This stresses how financial networks are created through financial categories
and models themselves, which not only 'describe economies … but are
intrinsic to the constitution of that which they purport to describe' (Langley
2008: 25). In this respect, finance can be analysed as being 'performative'
insofar that financial models and other financial devices and objects create a
certain calculative logic amongst agents and objects and this in turn helps to
shape the economy. We know explore this approach in more depth.

Performativity, information and economic networks

According to MacKenzie, there are different ways to understand how theories
'perform' certain functions in the world of economics. For instance, 'effective
performativity' refers to those moments when the use of economics 'makes a
difference' to those instances in which it is applied. 'Barnesian performativity',
named after the social constructionist theorist Barry Barnes (see Barnes 1995),
argues that performativity designates the point at which an object is brought
into being at the moment it is performed in concrete events. In relation to
economics, this would mean that 'the use in practice of an aspect of economics
is to make economic processes more like their depiction by economics'
(MacKenzie 2007a: 56). Options provide an illustration of this meaning of
performativity. Options are a type of financial derivative. They are based on

the idea that one trader has the right to either buy an option at a stated time for a fixed price, for example to give $5 to another trader for the option to buy crude oil at $75 in six months, or sell an option at a stated time for a fixed price (Scott 2013: 68). When best to buy an option in the first place was of course a perennial problem in dealing in options. This problem was 'solved' by the Black-Scholes model in 1973, which stipulated that 'it was possible to construct a portfolio of an option and a continuously adjusted position in the underlying asset and lending/borrowing of cash that was riskless' (MacKenzie 2007a: 58). MacKenzie shows that the Black-Scholes model started to change the behaviour of option traders. The model was highly regarded in academic circles, simplistic enough for traders to understand its basic principles and was publicly available through newly established personal computers. As a result, the model helped to construct economic reality in accordance with its own principles. The Black-Scholes model thereby opened up a space for economic agents, for example derivative traders, to make 'rational' calculations about the decisions they make in line with the model.

MacKenzie is influenced by actor-network theory (ANT), and through ANT it becomes clearer how the public sphere is implicated in assembling financial and socio-economic models. A key term in ANT is that of 'actants' and this refers primarily to the coming together of human and non-human actors through networks of heterogeneous materials. For ANT, the important question is how various actants are mobilised, contrasted and then held together – or ordered – through and within organisational entities (Law 1991: 6). Organisations are thus translating devices insofar that organisations order actants into a recognisable network. Actants are subsequently effects of performative organisational translation; that is to say, actants are not fixed things but, rather, gain an identity through ongoing negotiation and translation. Each actant's identity is thus contingent, mobile and uncertain. The aim for ANT, then, is to analyse how what might appear to be relatively enduring objects are in fact 'produced, assembled, collected, or kept up' through actor-networks (Latour 2005: 184). ANT theorists therefore seek to go beyond seeing organisations as being 'fixed structures'. Organisations are not stable and do not exhibit routine behaviour. 'Stability' is an effect of negotiation among a wide range of actants (Munro 1999: 431).

ANT scholars thereby see objects and organisations as coming together through a 'semiotics of materiality' insofar that both social and natural entities gain their identities by being produced and ordered through an assemblage of concrete objects, networks and relations (Law 1999: 4). Importantly, this perspective emphasises by what means different publics are mobilised into a specific assemblage of actants. This is to explain how an object '*has been allowed to be deployed as multiple* and thus allowed to be grasped through different viewpoints, before being possibly unified in some later stage depending on the abilities of the collective to unify them' (Latour 2005: 116; original emphasis). Economic calculations, for example, are made about objects through algorithmic statements that ascribe a particular identity to an object and, at the same time, make the object 'different' to other objects. New attachments are therefore assembled between itself and other objects, which include designers, marketers, advertisers, packagers, shopping centres, specific groups of consumers and so on.

Arguably, however, a performative approach to economics is better suited in analysing the construction and ordering of economic reality through micro interactions than it is in mapping how these interactions might constitute moments for opposition and resistance in and against financial global capitalism. However, this theme preoccupies autonomist thinkers.

Autonomism and global finance

As Chapter 3 outlined, autonomist theory stresses that in recent years a cadre of 'immaterial' and 'intellectual' labour has gained increasing importance in how the global economy operates. These individuals include scientists, state functionaries and people working in information technology. What autonomists are at pains to point out, however, is that changes in technology, and movements towards more sophisticated technological achievements, are made by capital *in response* to working class struggle against the imposition of alienating conditions (see Witheford 1994; Dyer-Witheford 1999). Thus, the exploitation of labour-power by dead and constant capital, such as increasingly sophisticated machines, is transposed to more and more areas of capitalist society in order to control variable and living labour. But the mobility and extension of exploitation also helps to unintentionally create new 'figures of struggle and new subjectivities' against capital exactly because intellectual labour, and social networks connecting them, expand (Hardt and Negri 2000: 61). It is for this reason Negri claims that the 'growing complexity of society is the growing precariousness of domination ... In effect, the more the laws of the transformation of the value form are realized, the more they demonstrate their efficacy as forces of deconstruction, deconstruction of Power' (Negri 1996: 159).

Within this general framework, autonomist writers have started to explore global finance. After the 2008 crisis erupted, Marazzi for example sought to apply some autonomist ideas to make sense of the global financial architecture that had built up over time. According to Marazzi, financialisation arose within the demise of Fordism in the 1970s, which anyhow had reached its limits in gaining an adequate amount of surplus value. During the 1980s, profits were increasingly made through financial markets and financial devices, such as through interest on loans or through shareholder value (Marazzi 2010). More ominously, financialisation has also signalled the willingness of capital to encourage ordinary people to take on more debt. This was an important stage for capital in overcoming the problems of Fordist accumulation. By fostering everyday debt in the form of credit cards and the like, the citizens of the postwar welfare state were slowly converted into individual risk-takers prepared to become an individual economic subject. 'In the debt economy, to become human capital or an entrepreneur of the self means assuming the costs as well as the risks of a flexible and financialized economy … ' (Lazzarato 2012: 51). Debt forces one to shoulder more of the costs and risks that were once the prerogative of the welfare state.

In the 1990s, financialisation also became associated with the growing prominence of digital technologies in everyday life. As Terranova (2010) observes, the dot.com crash of 2001, which brought down wildly over-hyped new media companies, did not signal the end of the so-called new economy. Instead, a new vocabulary soon appeared that sought, among other things, to get investors excited once again in potentially making huge amounts of money from digital enterprises. 'Web 2.0' in particular conveyed an image that masses of people could be lured to the Internet with the promise that they could personalise and co-create webpages. New platforms and applications such as MySpace, Facebook and Google quickly surfaced that encouraged users to upload personal details about their immaterial desires, passions and tastes, and establish networks with other like-minded souls. These Web 2.0 sites were also innovative in harnessing the data from users to sell to third parties for profits (Terranova 2010: 155).

For autonomists, these developments have meant that surplus value is now extracted from the bio-economy of a global body of individuals and their immaterial labour. What Marazzi has in mind here is the value creating capacity of prosumers – those who both consume a product and help to produce it at the same time. For example:

> (S)oftware companies, beginning with Microsoft or Google, usually beta test on the consumers the new versions of their programs, but also the programs belonging to so-called software open source are improved by a multitude of people, by 'productive consumers'.
>
> (Marazzi 2010: 38)

Web 2.0 companies are therefore successful, in part, because they draw in ordinary people who are willing to co-create platforms such as Facebook. These companies can subsequently harness the consumer data of the technological 'free' labour of these individuals and use this to extract surplus value. There is then an enormous potential reservoir of surplus value to be had. Indeed, profits are based on capturing value outside the immediate sphere of production in the world of prosumers. Money is thereby made by reducing costs inside the production process and by drawing on knowledge outside of its confines (Marazzi 2010: 60). Certainly, there has been an increase in the quantity of surplus value extracted, explains Marazzi, but it is accumulation external to the immediate factory floor. Accumulation rests on value being produced by society as a whole and not necessarily just inside factories.

As these accounts testify, financialisation is integrally related to the rise of Web 2.0 companies. After all, the stock valuation of many Web 2.0 companies is partly reliant on the way in which those companies are valued through public communities of users. Financial actors, for instance, draw on 'the affective investments of a multitude composed of market actors, as well as, increasingly, members of the public at large' in order to gain information about the reputation of companies to ascertain whether they are worth investing. Facebook of course provides the perfect illustration of these affectual financial calculations (Arvidsson and Colleoni 2012: 142).

Elsewhere Arvidsson (2013: 374–76) says that these online affectual and immaterial actions of users also constitute publics made possible by their devotion to a 'thing' in common. This 'thing', Arvidsson claims, can therefore be a common devotion of attention, for example, watching a play or a common cause such as a political cause. This is a communality without necessarily being a close-knit community, and it is a communality that expresses the manner in which consumer publics operate in digital media. Most obviously, those who go on social media sites often comment on particular consumer good and thereby become part of a common 'buzz' around the good in question. In this way, Web 2.0 companies can try to capitalise on the publics generated by users, especially the dispersed desires of users. These companies will try to capture what Terranova calls 'lateral' surplus value; 'selling advertising, the property and sale of data produced by user activity, the capacity to attract financial investments on the base of the visibility and the prestige of new global brands like Google and Facebook' (Terranova 2010: 156). More positively, this implies that people are becoming more skilled at communicating with one another about their immaterial desires and of doing so through specific associations, projects and publics. After all, 'the most recent information technologies allow us to think human communication in freer terms' (Marazzi 2011: 147). New spaces for different experiences to comingle and express grievances and conflicts open up in this new communication environment.

Now that we have outlined the three schools of thought on financialisation and digital publics, we need to unpack some of their assertions in a little more depth. One obvious point to make in this respect is that some inadvertently paint a picture of the world that is remarkably similar to the ideology of new management discourse. We now explore this point in more detail.

Network models of finance and management gurus

While some differences are apparent, many social theorists nevertheless often describe the causes of the financial crisis in terms analogous to mainstream economists, management consultants and mainstream financial analysts. Take for example Castells's explanation for the causes of the 2008 financial crisis. He argues that six factors combined to produce the crisis. First, deregulation of financial capital enabled finance to travel across the globe unimpeded. Second, new media technology helped to develop highly sophisticated mathematical financial models, which then badly managed financial transactions. Third, the securitisation of every economic activity ensured that finance gained hegemony in the global economy and encouraged a virtual and non-transparent capitalism to take root. Fourth, the US mortgage crisis of 2007 had a huge effect throughout the world because it could travel across the new and various financial networks. Fifth, brokers and dealers were allowed to engage in highly risky financial activities. Finally, an imbalance between new economic powers such as China and capital-borrowing countries fed into a credit-led expansion in the USA and Europe (Castells 2011: 187–91).

But, the causes that Castells identifies here are also ones given by business and management gurus in order to explain why the 2008 crisis erupted. In terms similar to Castells, for instance, the ex-financial trader and now financial consultant Satyajit Das (2010) argues that the financial crisis was the outcome of deregulated markets and highly complex although ultimately meaningless financial models that failed to take account of the reality of economic markets. One illustration given by Das is that of financial ratings, which have been a crucial mechanism in selling highly complex securities to investors. Since the 2008 crash, it is now even more evident that these ratings were highly dubious, based as they often were on theoretical market values rather than real values. Bolstered by a lack of regulation, investors nevertheless 'ascribed magical properties to the alphabet soup of letters assigned to a security' (Das 2010: 339). They were soon drawn into the murky world of virtual banking and trading schemes that were supposed to 'off-set' risk but in reality made finance more risky and more speculative. In a comparable vein, the financial analyst and journalist Anatole Kaletsky (2010) argues that while there have been many benefits to the deregulation of global economic markets it also allowed debt to grow and fester because 'it was genuinely impossible to tell in advance what would be sustainable levels of debt' (Kaletsky 2010: 99). Moreover, this blind spot in the global financial economy was made worse by an obsession with free market ideology doggedly pursued by financiers, economists and politicians (Kaletsky 2010: 100).

All of these public intellectuals therefore describe the causes of the financial crash in very similar terms, such as through a lack of monetary regulation, increasing risk-taking by traders, hegemony of finance and free markets, dominance of irrational and complex financial models in setting prices, increased flows and fluidity of global finance, and so on. But there are other noticeable similarities too. We know that in order to make their claims, many social theorists have consciously adopted new metaphors such as 'fluidity', 'mobility' and 'networks' to describe informational societies and global finance. Interestingly, these discursive terms are also prevalent in much business and management literature. Some begin from the viewpoint that nation states can no longer control financial transactions across the globe. Drucker (1993b) is typical in this respect when he says that in the past each nation state could control money through mechanisms of sovereignty. In our 'transnational' times, however, this is no longer possible because the amount of money traded on a daily basis greatly exceeds the power of any one nation state. He announces:

> No central bank any longer controls money flows ... (T)he amount of money traded every day on the transnational markets ... so greatly exceeds

anything needed to finance national and international transactions that the flows escape any attempt to control or limit them, let alone manage them.

(Drucker 1993b: 143)

For Papows (1999), this new financial formation is fundamentally related to new media. Banks across the world have adopted new technology in their day-to-day operations and this drastically reduces costs in the financial sector and brings about a whole host of other benefits. 'Radically lower operating costs, new delivery channels, new and converging products, outsourcing opportunities, emerging new payment infrastructures, new retail intermediaries, and a largely green field of international expansion all combine for an exciting and tumultuous future ... ' (Papows 1999: 143–44).

While some social theorists therefore present critical accounts of global finance, these accounts can nevertheless be accommodated within conventional business wisdom about the global crisis. To elaborate on this critical point in a little more depth, let us briefly return to Castells's description of the 2008 financial crisis. As we know, he thinks that the crisis can be explained through several factors, not least the fact that the rise of new digital networks enabled finance to 'flow' around the globe, which were accompanied by complex financial devices, securitisation, the mortgage crisis and so forth. Without doubt, all of these factors are important ones in helping to understand the crisis. Still, they do not go far enough in providing a critique of mainstream economic and management insights on its causes. Take the claim that the crisis is said to have originated, in part, from the housing bubble brought about by securities on subprime loans. While this was certainly a factor in the crisis, it does not necessarily imply that it was a cause of the crisis. As Sotiropoulos *et al.* (2013: 120–21) observe, the rise of a new housing programme in America in 2002 was based on a neoliberal ideological crusade that claimed home ownership was a way for American 'minorities' and those on relatively low incomes to enter the credit system. At a time when neoliberalism was placing a downward pressure on wages and on a number of social services, encouraging these groups to enter the housing market became a technique for policy makers to secure neoliberal hegemony *and* give ordinary Americans a route to overcome the social constraints on living standards imposed prior to 2002. Thus, the housing crisis is in fact a *consequence* of a deeper restructuring of class relations in America (see also below and Chapter 6). This restructuring can itself be seen as the result of deeper underlying contradictory crisis tendencies in the capitalist mode of production. This vital point, though, is missing in accounts given by the likes of Castells. However, this in turn leads to a further set of problems, which we now explore.

Over-identification of concrete and contingent networks

Anthony Giddens's argument that globalisation is formed through concrete processes has been an influential one in the social sciences and humanities.

This account stems from Giddens's earlier work in which he conceptualises social structures as emerging from concrete processes. For example, he says that 'structure, as recursively organised sets of rules and resources, is out of time and space, save in its instantiations and coordination as memory traces, and is marked by an "absence of a subject"' (Giddens 1984: 25). Yet, Giddens also says that structures are both the medium and outcome of social agents who exist in time and space in distinctive social systems. As such, '(s)tructure is not "external" to individuals' (Giddens 1984: 25) but enables and constrains human action.

Giddens's ideas on social structures being both the outcome as well as the medium of concrete human agency are captured in his theory of globalisation. He says that globalisation is an inevitable development of modernity and involves the 'stretching' out of relations between the local and the global. 'Globalisation can thus be defined as the intensification of worldwide social relations which link distant localities in such a way that local happenings are shaped by events occurring many miles away and vice versa' (Giddens 1990: 64). Local empirical contexts occupied by agents and their actions thus have affects many miles away and vice versa. But keeping in line with his idea that structures are the *effects of human action*, Giddens also argues that globalisation is primarily constituted through 'networks' comprised by concrete actors and concrete events (see Giddens 1990: 64–65). Perhaps for this reason, some of his ideas play an important role in the arguments of other contemporary theorists. One such idea is the belief that concrete 'things' – people, money, technology, knowledge and so forth – are lifted out or disembedded from their local social contexts and reconstituted and restructured elsewhere in the world across open-ended distances of time-space (see Giddens 1990: 21–29).

Lash and Urry (1994: 243–44), for example, draw on Giddens's argument that electronic communication media has opened up a space for news stories, once separated from one another in time and place, to be reported back to diverse audiences.

> Stories from many different places occur alongside each other in a chaotic and arbitrary fashion, such stories serving to abstract events from context and narrative … There is thus a literal time-space *compression* as this collage of disconnected stories intrude and shape everyday life.
>
> (Lash and Urry 1994: 244; original emphasis)

Like Giddens, Lash and Urry therefore move from the concrete everyday world, to global networks, and then back to the concrete and everyday networked world. As we can see, the concrete everyday world of communication networks is thus turned into a defining feature of globalisation. This is also readily apparent in Lash's argument that

> The network society … puts order into the previous disorder of dis-organised capitalism. It imparts a new systematicity to the previously

fragmented world system ... The network society creates a new order and hierarchical chain of linked global cities, of urban space and cyberspace.

(Lash 2002: 127)

Some autonomist writers also hold comparable views about globalisation. In their theory of resistance to global power relations, Hardt and Negri highlight the potency of concrete and contingent struggles of resistance in specific local events that are connected up globally. As they say:

> The global cycle of struggle develops in the form of a distributed network. Each *local* struggle functions as a node that communicates with all the other nodes without any hub or centre of intelligence. Each struggle remains *singular* and tied to its *local* conditions but at the same time is immersed in the common web.
>
> (Hardt and Negri 2004: 217; emphasis added).

Here, Hardt and Negri suggest that different singular concrete struggles come together to constitute interlocking networks of the multitude in singular contingent events of concrete struggle.

An equivalent viewpoint can be found in the work of some ANT scholars. They reject well known social dichotomies such as agency-structure, macro-micro, individuals-groups and so on. Understanding societies requires an altogether different way of thinking. Does capitalism, for example, require one CEO to direct its operations, or is it held together through a multiple concrete networks that criss-cross one another in complex ways? Latour (2005: 167–72) prefers the second option, which is why he rejects theoretical and methodological binary oppositions and instead advocates a 'flat ontology' for investigating social relations. Latour advises social researchers to recognise and take seriously the idea of the *impossibility* of staying in either a structural context or local interactions for too long. Globalisation provides us with an illustration of these instructions. Globalisation is constructed through diverse *places*, and each place is only 'larger' than other places through degrees of connectedness.

> This move has the beneficial effect to keep the landscape flat, since what earlier, in the pre-relativist sociology, was situated "above" or "below" remains side by side and firmly on the same plane as the other loci which they were trying to overlook or include.
>
> (Latour 2005: 176)

Keeping the landscape 'flat' implies seeing globalisation as being comprised by a variety of everyday *concrete* actants. 'What is now highlighted much more vividly than before are all the connections, the cables, the means of transportation, the vehicles linking places together' (Latour 2005: 176).

These claims all seem to be reasonable enough, yet on closer inspection there is also something lacking with them. In their eagerness to reject untenable dichotomies they all seem to want to approach the 'social' from the world of concrete and contingent relations that when brought together make up the global world. Ontologically speaking, they therefore exhibit what Jessop (1990) terms 'empty realism'. A world is said to exist beyond the processes of thought, but the different causal properties of the entities residing in the world are thought to be inaccessible abstractions; or, rather, the abstract and internal causal properties of entities, and how these properties relate to other entities, are thought to be inaccessible. The only solution therefore open to the social scientist is to focus on the observable concrete and contingent relations between entities and objects (Jessop 1990: 294). Probabilistically, of course, this viewpoint therefore makes it extremely difficult to investigate how a concrete object is internally related to, mediated by, and is a refraction of a wider historical system that operates in part through abstract processes beyond a concrete level. Everyday objects are not merely connected and associated with a whole host of other concrete objects in different places, but are also contradictory historical forms of distinctive historical systems at different levels of abstraction.

Severing the link between the abstract form and content of capitalism, these contemporary approaches to the global thereby lose 'sight of the social connections which penetrate' a concrete object of enquiry (Bakhtin and Medvedev 1991: 77). We are told, for example, that struggles to combat the worst excesses of global capitalism must be fought at the level of the concrete and contingent. Yet, as Žižek (in Butler *et al.* 2000) perceptively notes, this position leads one to *over-identify* with contingent concrete sites of struggle against historically specific power relations. Thus, it also loses sight of the ideological relations that intersect an object and thereby over-identifies with the concrete and contingent level of everyday activity (see also Fine 2005; Kirsch and Mitchell 2004).

A simple illustration of this practice can once again be taken from Latour. Supermarkets, he says, preformat people to become general consumers. To translate a person into an active and understanding consumer, however, requires a further set of devices to be constructed. In particular, a person has to be equipped with the ability to *calculate* and *choose* what objects to consume in an actual local supermarket. What devices, though, does Latour mean here? According to him, supermarkets must provide potential shoppers with devices that will enable them to carry out calculations in a competent manner. These devices thereby include:

> (L)abels, trademarks, barcodes, weight and measurement chains, indexes, prices, consumer journals, conversations with fellow shoppers, advertisements, and so on. The crucial point is that you are sustaining this mental and cognitive competence as long as you *subscribe* to this equipment.
>
> (Latour 2005: 210; original emphasis)

Latour's command is therefore to empirically trace the history of each one of these devices in order to try to ascertain how 'they circulate through their own conduits' (Latour 2005: 211). One must therefore investigate how concrete devices are mobilised in concrete network configurations in order to understand real people and their worries.

I doubt very much that most social researchers will initially find much that is wrong in what Latour says here. Difficulties nevertheless inevitably arise when Latour insists that this concrete and contingent level is the main one to stay within when conducting research. Problematically, however, by only residing at this level makes it extremely challenging to try and understand other 'layers' of conflict, power and reality that will unavoidably contribute towards defining a particularly locality. In the case of Latour, he sees battles over hegemony between different groups with different resources of power as being battles for control over concrete and contingent devices and objects. In other words, he implores us to bracket out of the analytical picture any idea that power resides in some central ghostly spectral figure, or that it is 'descended from some mysterious context' (Latour 2005: 211). The social is comprised not by this mysterious figure, he insists, but through real people, real objects and real networks. Clearly, though, Latour and those who paint a similar picture of socio-economic markets and globalisation are fixated with the concrete and contingent at the expense of any other level of analysis or forms of social mediation. A critical standpoint is thereby reduced to making analytical judgements about concrete and contingent struggles between groups over concrete devices, objects and networks. At its most extreme, this position reproduces a relativistic attitude that deliberately rejects any idea that one social construction of the world is superior to another one. It argues that one must simply investigate how some types of technology, actor-networks or performative objects manage to attain a consensual place in a particular social context. While this viewpoint makes many interesting observations about technology, its relativism, unfortunately, does not give due weight to how technology is always mediated through social and political conflicts and struggles. One need only think about how new technology is implemented in the workplace to understand this point. This will invariably lead to 'winners' and 'losers' in a workplace, which in turn is related to the politics of the workplace around issues such as power differentials between workers and managers (Boreham *et al.* 2008: 36).

One important reason why over-identification with these devices thereby occurs is because such struggles have been *abstracted away* from the wider antagonistic structuring principle that defines the terrain for contingent struggles in the first place (Žižek 2002: 190). For example, many informational theorists expound a network approach to transformational changes in media corporations. As we know, this viewpoint explores how concrete micro processes of power operate through different institutional network configurations. Castells, for example, 'speaks of concentrated ownership and the structural capacity of groups and individuals to control access to networks and to shape their form and function' (Fitzgerald 2012: 387). However, major media corporations such as Bertelsmann, News Corp and Time Warner not only operate through concrete institutional network configurations, the position of Castells and, more radically, Latour, but also through underlying class forces and class powers. As we know, financialisation and neoliberalism empower the global operations of capital. They have enabled a few media corporations to assemble different media companies and sectors into single concentrated conglomerates and thus to dominate the global media landscape. One need only think of how News Corp dominates newspaper markets in Australia and the UK to understand this point. At the same time, these companies engage in intra-corporate competition, which is fuelled by their need to expand their corporate assets. Time Warner, for instance, is attuned to the need to take on debt in order to finance growth and restructure its corporate assets in order to make its 'investment portfolio' attractive to investors (Fitzgerald 2012: 393). Again, though, these are representative of abstract class processes that mediate and are refracted into everyday life (see also Chapter 6 for more examples of this point).

Žižek goes further in his critical observations by arguing that a concrete and contingent viewpoint is in fact congruent with the ideology of financialisation. After all, finance enables individuals to disconnect themselves from the underlying realities of capitalism and, in the process, bolster the idea that we are indeed living in creatively 'new' technologically sophisticated times. Žižek is therefore surely correct to observe that one of the main ideological fetishes today is that related to finance.

> Do phenomena usually designated as those of virtual capitalism (the futures trade and similar abstract financial speculations) not point towards the reign of the 'real abstraction' at its purest, far more radical than in Marx's time? In short, the highest form of ideology does not reside in getting caught in ideological spectrality, forgetting about its foundation in real people and their relations, but precisely in overlooking this Real of spectrality and in pretending directly to address 'real people and their worries'. Visitors to the London Stock Exchange get a free leaflet which explains that the stock market is not about mysterious fluctuations, but about real people and their products. This really is ideology at its purest.
>
> (Žižek 2008: 11–12)

The festishism that Žižek alludes to is centred on a knowledge-based form of capitalism that positively encourages us to contribute to everyday concrete form, Internet chat forums for example, about our 'real worries'. As we do so, we believe we are being active in society by contributing to social and political debate whereas in reality the content of our contribution becomes one of many other contents swirling around in cyberspace; contents that never really make active connection with other contents nor address the underlying reality of financial capital.

It is useful to return to Deleuze and Guattari on these matters. Naturally, some of their theoretical observations lend themselves to a certain interpretation of global processes in which concrete 'assemblages', 'flows' and 'networks' of global processes are given analytical importance over and above more 'structural' accounts. However, it must not be forgotten that Deleuze and Guattari are very much taken with Marx's ideas about how capitalism operates. This is why they clearly state that any talk about capitalist 'flows' must also be conjoined with an investigation of how technical advancement is always mediated through distinctive social relations based on the exploitation of labour and accumulation of surplus value. Why is it crucial for them to emphasise this point? Without recognising the significance that social relations hold for understanding how capital develops, they suggest, it is easy to get carried away into thinking that the way to increase capitalist profits, and hence the power of capitalism, lies solely in technological improvements. Not so, say Deleuze and Guattari, because capital can in fact increase profit by holding onto existing 'obsolescent equipment'. This leads them to observe:

> An innovation is adopted only from the perspective of the rate of profit if its investment will offer the lowering of production costs; without this prospect, the capitalist will keep the existing equipment, and stand ready to make a parallel investment in equipment in another area.
>
> (Deleuze and Guattari 1984: 254)

'Flows' of technological innovation cannot themselves adequately explain capitalist progress. Instead, one must look to how these 'flows' are brought into the overall profitability of a firm as this is related to the reproduction of the moments of capital as a global whole (e.g. various global market processes, commercial capital, financial capital and so on) (Deleuze and Guattari 1984: 254–55). To think otherwise, Doogan notes, is to stray dangerously close to ideological celebrations of computer-assisted 'theoretical knowledge' for its own sake (Doogan 2009: 49). Such celebrations can soon lead to an excessive level of praise being heaped on the potential of new media, especially social media, to unlock innovative channels of communication among ordinary people. In some instances, it is said that these also facilitate new opportunities for ordinary people to construct radical public spheres in and against government agendas. Castells argues that digital technology establishes global networks of mass self-communication, buoyed in part through self-generated and self-communicated messages by ordinary users (Castells 2009: 54–55). Anyone can use these communication platforms to post blogs, information, images, videos, comments and so on, and they can also watch and read what others users have posted, and this makes these types of communication devices inherently open to popular expressions of democracy (Castells 2009: 67). While this might seem to elicit more spaces of popular communication across society, in practice not all types of discussion through these media are listened to with equal force. Obviously, social media reflects elite culture that is prevalent in capitalist societies, which means that a few prominent and well known sites will get lots of people reading them, while only a minority of people ever read websites of politicians, or non-mainstream media sites (Fenton 2012: 134). In other words, there is not a huge number of ordinary people engaged in mass self-communication about matters of public importance. What one often finds, however, is that these new technological devices are celebrated in an almost deterministic manner. It is to this point that we now turn.

Technological determinism

Webster says that technological determinism is a belief that technologies determine the path of social change irrespective of other social factors such as classes, exploitation, politics, social identities and so on (Webster 2006: 44). Naturally, contemporary social theorists discuss the impact that social factors such as inequality have on the use of technology in society. To give one illustration, Castells is aware that digital technology brings with it new social divisions and inequalities. Knowing this, observes Fitzgerald, it is therefore strange that he spends so much of his time focusing on technological innovation as the main factor in economic growth rather than looking at the ownership and control of capital along with how this affects the politics in and around the expropriation of surplus value in the workplace and inter-capital competition. Without this emphasis one often gets the impression from reading Castells that technological innovation occurs as an end in and of itself within the context of 'a perpetual innovation economy' (Fitzgerald 2012: 71). He says, for example, that the invention of the steam engine in the last third of the eighteenth century, and then the invention, application and use of electricity in the nineteenth century, transformed the manner in which energy was generated and distributed. When both eventually came together, the result was to revolutionise production: 'It was the electrical engine that made possible and induced large-scale organization of work in the industrial factory' (Castells 2000: 37–38). Similarly, Castells claims that technological advancements during the 1970s provided the basis for a new mode of socio-economic development to be built associated with our present informational economy. Microprocessors, telecommunications and microcomputers all helped to create new flexible networks. Indeed, he goes as far as to say that they were part of a wider set of 'autonomous dynamics of technological discovery and diffusion' during the 1970s (Castells 2000: 61–62). In both of these historical cases, then, Castells describes technological modes of development mainly through a single-toned vision insofar that technology is simply taken to be a factor of production. Technological progress is a neutral 'fact' associated with efficiency gains acquired through the historical expansion of certain technologies. Technological innovation almost becomes embroiled in a historical destiny (for example, see Castells 2000: 255).

A type of technological determinism is also noticeable in ANT. Consider how Callon examines economic markets as 'socio-technical arrangements or *agencements*' (STAs) (Callon 2007: 140). Broadly speaking, STAs refer to specific combinations of heterogeneous human, material, technical and textual devices. Depending on how these combinations are arranged, STAs have different capacities to act in various ways (Çalişkan and Callon 2010: 9). STAs are especially prominent in the new economy where a wide variety of different services are objectified into packages, or 'things', in order to be valued (Çalişkan and Callon 2010: 7). Of importance to the competitive nature of contemporary economic institutions and organisations, then, is their ability to mobilise intellectual capabilities of consumers (Callon *et al.* 2005: 40). This much is clear when Callon *et al.* observe that it is with new information and communication technologies that the 'logic of singularization reaches its peak':

> With information renewed on the screen, with links and cross-references, and with scroll menus that multiply options from which users can and must choose, the Internet is a machinery that is *entirely* oriented towards the singularization of products.
>
> (Callon *et al.* 2005: 42; emphasis added)

In this quote, Callon *et al.* look to be claiming that the informational economy is 'new' because it is steered by (global) technological knowledge and machines. Yet, this idea confuses cause with effect (see Žižek 2009: 140–41). Deleuze and Guattari are once again instructive here. In *Anti-Oedipus*, they argue that in capitalism technical machines (e.g. information communication technologies) certainly appear to obtain a degree of independence from industrial capital. These technical machines also seem to obtain coded qualities of the sort identified by ANT. However, continue Deleuze and Guattari, this is only partially true. The novelty of capitalism is that industrial capital actually decodes social flows through the incessant drive to procure surplus value irrespective of meaningful coded beliefs or qualities. In other words, industrial capital pushes an axiomatic desire on to the whole of society to produce quantitative amounts of surplus value. Capital's energy is maintained by this continuous search for profits and, ultimately, this will always take priority over and above the need to determine the qualities of economic transactions through specific beliefs and meanings (Deleuze and Guattari 1984: 268). On this understanding, Callon's insights on the qualification of products do not take full account of the logic of abstract equivalences, the latter of which is a necessary precondition for capitalist production. It is only the axiomatic decoded nature of capital, namely M-C-M[1] (money buying commodities to make more money), which imposes a universal abstract and decoded quantity of measurement on all of society (Deleuze and Guattari 1984: 270). As a result, technical machines, such as STAs, do not bring about capitalism, but rather become themselves elements of the drive to accumulate surplus value. 'Knowledge, information, and specialised education are just as much parts of capital ("knowledge capital") as is the most elementary labour of the worker' (Deleuze and Guattari 1984: 255). This point leads naturally on to the final substantive area of critical analysis, which is an exploration of a discursive and performative account of global crises.

Beyond purely discursive and performative accounts of global crises

Without doubt, the social theorists explored so far provide far-reaching insights into the state of global finance. Moreover, they offer detailed, precise and rich accounts of the complexities involved in the concrete micro interactions between key actors, objects and players. These interactions are traced across an array of social and cultural encounters through and across different spatial contexts, from the local to the global. Their research has given us new understandings of not only how global finance operates, but also why crises occur in how finance operates. To take one illustration, MacKenzie (2011) explores the 'toxic assets' that helped to bring about the 2008 global financial crisis. Important to his analysis are 'collateralised debt obligations' (CDOs), which are the pooled together by banks of various debt cash flows from assets (e.g. mortgages or car loans) into asset-backed securities (ABS). Generally speaking, ABS are like pools of loans that are packaged and sold to other investors. According to MacKenzie, the crisis in these assets can be traced back to the different competing evaluation cultures within financial markets and financial organisations, particularly between the different evaluation cultures of ABS key players and CDO specialists. For example, MacKenzie observes that

> By the end of the 1990s, CDOs had largely split off organizationally from the world of securitization and ABSs from which they had sprung: they were the province of different teams or even different departments of banks. There were therefore often fierce battles over which team or department should have responsibility for the new and highly profitable ABS CDOs.
> (MacKenzie 2011: 1810)

This being the case, new divisions of labour emerged in major financial ratings institutions over CDOs and ABSs and relationships between ABS specialists and CDO specialists were sometimes fractured and difficult for various reasons.

Elsewhere, MacKenzie (2007b) remarks that financial traders often have conflicting interests and so they have to pay careful attention to the specification of what is considered a standardised derivative. Hedgers can be at odds to speculators, while similar conflicting interests are noticeable between traders who have bought a derivative and those who have sold it. Conflicting interests are not inherently fixed, but they mean that the contract design of derivatives becomes a political issue 'that requires balance and compromise' across different evaluation and trading cultures (MacKenzie 2007b: 361). However, by failing to work within and across these evaluation cultures, both groups of financial specialists inadvertently 'helped permit mortgage-backed securities to become riskier, and those securities in turn facilitated ever riskier mortgage lending' (MacKenzie 2011). When crises, dilemmas or problems in economic and financial markets therefore emerge these are thought to occur primarily at the level of discourse, narratives and representations associated with different cultures or communities of actors.

MacKenzie's analysis thus points towards the necessity to talk to key players involved in financial markets and organisations, to explore qualitatively how they think, their habits, their tacit assumptions and so forth. Yet, as we can also acknowledge, MacKenzie condenses his albeit fascinating account of 2008 crisis to that of *dominant* discursive performative economic models in the sense that the focus of attention is on key financial players who employ mainstream economic models to make real-life decisions about investments. Thus, in this instance, the performativity literature leans towards favouring the impact that mainstream economic theory has had on society, particularly how it has successfully 'constructed' economic markets through their economic models. That is to say, the performativity approach leans towards an analysis of how particular mainstream economic models have successfully constructed reality in its own image. As Bryan *et al.* (2012: 308) note, this further implies that performativity theorists have spent less time in their accounts looking at rival economic explanations of markets, particularly those associated with heterodox economic approaches such as Keynesian or Marxist theories, and how these rival accounts have tried to articulate opposition to mainstream economics in the public sphere.

This critical point leads to another, related observation. Montgomerie (2009) usefully argues that one characteristic of relatively new financial devices is that they transform credit-based streams into bonds that can then be sold on markets to raise more money. The same capital stock thus creates a new pool of credit. For financial traders these practices disperse risk among investors. For those interested in the performativity of markets, these risks are ways that financial markets construct a set of calculative tools that construct risk narratives. These then go on to encourage individuals to take on more debt. Montgomerie (2009) nevertheless quite rightly points out that the discourse and performativity approach takes these risk narratives constructed by financial traders at face value. 'If the financial crisis has taught us anything, it is that credit derivatives were not dispersing risk as they claim' (Montgomerie 2009: 6). While representations of knowledge, alongside the social construction of economic subjectivities and evaluation cultures, are obviously important, they cannot account for the way in which financial companies generate asset-based securitisation and new streams of loans to everyday consumers by carefully targeting debtors and drawing on socio-political mechanisms to further this cause. For example, those employed in financial industries rely on state hegemony to support their practices. Once the state is brought into analytical play, however, there is a need to establish a theory of the state and how it operates through hegemonic projects that selectively favour some groups, interests and practices in society over and above others. As the next chapter shows, the contemporary neoliberal state has pursued a neoliberal project in society that favours the interests of financial practices over and above other interests. At the same time, it has done so to stem the demand of rival demands and theories about the global economy, to paper over its contradictions and to dampen dissent against the neoliberal project.

Of course, MacKenzie is well aware that financial models break down during a crisis. Such cracks and fissures in a particular financial model also open up public spaces for alternatives to be put forward by others. At the same time, however, he tends to explore financial crises at the level of discourse, narratives and socially constructed representations associated with different cultures and communities. For example, MacKenzie (2007a) also suggests that performativity in economic markets, namely the way in which an economic model leads to practices that in turn confirm the original economic model, can come up against its opposite. This transpires through 'the use of an aspect of economics altering economic processes so that they conform less well to their depiction by economics' (MacKenzie 2007a: 76). Empirical economic practices therefore no longer conform or follow a specific economic model. One decisive factor in exacerbating the 1987 stock market crash, for instance, was the gradual failure of some economic financial models to match how global market financial traders had started to work. In addition, 'new' economic models were developed during this period that helped to establish a certain pattern of actions by investors that then fed into the crisis.

In both the 1987 and 2008 crises, MacKenzie therefore focuses on how models and communities of agents socially construct crisis through 'counterperformativity' (see also Thrift 2005). Macartney notes, though, that one key problem with this type of explanation is that the material causal factors of a crisis are separated from their discursive assemblage. The difficulty here is that economic and financial performativity are reduced once again to concrete and contingent actors, cultures and objects. What this account subsequently neglects is the fact that while these actors, cultures and objects are obviously vital in how markets operate, they are themselves subject to competitive pressures that operate 'behind the backs' of concrete and contingent processes. In other words, much in the social constructionist and performativity literature abstracts away from how capitalist social relations actually function. Capitalists do not undertake their activities based purely on belonging to 'evaluation cultures' or by being part of an assemblage of actants. Instead, capitalist social relations mediate them all. They are, as Clarke shrewdly observes,

> capitalists seeking to realize their commodity capital in money form; capitalists seeking to transform their money capital into the form of means of production and labour-power; workers seeking to sell their labour-power, or to purchase their requisite means of subsistence; petty commodity producers seeking to dispose of their own products.
>
> (Clarke 1990–91: 452)

In his quote, Clarke alludes to the constraints placed on each capitalist to conform to the external and internal necessities and needs to engage in capitalist exploitation.

The *real* drive of capital at an abstract level even in capitalism today is not in fact a drive to ensure that finance is 'performative', nor to ensure that each person's needs are met, or to ensure that consumption prevails. The real drive of capital is still to increase surplus value by embarking upon a quasi-autonomous competitive path to exploit labour more efficiently so that it can accumulate money to an ever-greater extent. There is a barrier, however, to the degree to which capital can expand its productive powers. In order to enhance its productive capacity, capital will develop its technological capability.

Indeed, technological innovation is always the main way for capitalists to remain competitive because this creates the conditions for relative surplus value to occur. 'As fixed capital in the production process, technology is both the vehicle for the expansion of capital and also the impetus for such development' (Smith 2010: 155). Investing in technology is also contradictory because the more that technology expands, the more chance there is that living labour will be displaced from the production process. As a result, capital cuts away its main source for the realisation of surplus value in the form of money. This is because labour is devalued through its displacement from the relations of production. Devaluation occurs, for example, through a steady decline in the value of wages and by a number of workers losing their jobs. Labour's capacity to consume is thereby restricted. Technological development results in the overproduction of commodities that cannot be sold in the marketplace. This tendency to crisis is not an epochal event but is 'permanently inherent in the process of capital accumulation, as an ever present aspect of the class struggle ... ' (Clarke 1990–91: 448).

None of this is to deny the causal efficacy that economic models and theories can play in the economic behaviour and practice of financial traders. However, this approach tends to overstate the performativity of discourse, ideas and knowledge without reciprocal emphasis on the material basis of these performative actions and devices. This leads once again to an over-identification of concrete practices in order to account for the causes of economic crises. This critical point can be illustrated if we turn once more to Castells. He says that

> the current crisis stems from the destructive trends induced by the dynamics of a deregulated global capitalism, anchored in an unfettered financial market made up of global computer networks and fed by relentless production of synthetic securities as the source of capital accumulation and capital lending.
>
> (Castells *et al.* 2012: 2)

Castells further notes that a 'me first' culture, in which an individualist ethos now dominates socio-economic decision-making, has encouraged a new breed of corporate managers to narrowly focus of short-term profit-maximising strategies at the expense of long-term sustainable growth. Unpredictable consequences resulted that eventually erupted in 2008. Thus, for Castells, such unpredictability was one of the reasons why the 2008 financial crisis erupted. Clearly, however, Castells focuses his attention at a concrete level of analysis without the necessary appreciation of underlying external pressures placed on each capitalist to accumulate profits for the sake of accumulation.

Unlike a purely discursive or performativity approach, therefore, it is important to explore how underlying contradictory causal powers operate and are reproduced within contingent and concrete circumstances. Not only can an external world therefore be rationally confirmed and its causal and contradictory properties noted, but this materialist viewpoint also welcomes the unintended consequences of social relations. After all, unintended consequences always contain the possibility of attaining causal powers outside the reaches of the discourse that initially gave them life (Jessop 1990: 298). A purely discursive or performative approach, while providing astute observations about global economic markets, has a tendency to render external constraints on discourse as being secondary to what is seen as being the more important question of how discourse and narratives are assembled and mobilised. In this respect, discourse is in danger of being transformed into 'isolated, finished, monologic' dialogue precisely because it comes close to being 'divorced from its verbal and actual context' (Voloshinov 1973: 73). 'Discourse' is no longer seen to have a qualitatively distinct identity to the non-discursive but instead both become blurred and merged together.

Conclusion

Discursive and performative approaches to finance, economic markets and the public sphere 'generally default to representing knowledges as initiators or prime movers of social processes' (Bryan *et al.* 2012: 306). Capitalism, however, is comprised not only by specific types of knowledge, but also by historically specific contradictions that are part of its very identity. This is to embrace a dialectical viewpoint about the world. When one talks about dialectics, however, one is not simply saying that they want to view the world through some sort of dualistic prism. In order to criticise what they consider dialectical thinking to be, some social theorists certainly characterise dialectics along these dualist lines so that they can then easily dismiss it for their preferred concrete-contingent viewpoint. Latour is good at playing this game. He claims that dialectics sees interactions as being 'overflowed by some structures that give shape to them'. In turn, 'those structures themselves remain much too abstract as long as they have not instantiated, mobilised, realised, or incarnated into some sort of local and lived interaction' (Latour 2005: 169).

It might come as a surprise to Latour and others of a similar theoretical persuasion, but those who embrace dialectics would undoubtedly have no problem in rejecting his characterisation. Indeed, many Marxists already discard such a theory, seeing it as being more associated with theorists such as Giddens than with Marx (Bhaskar 1993). Marxists thereby abandon such dualistic perspectives ('abstract' *and* 'concrete') in favour of a truly dialectical

94 Financialisation and digital publics

one that seeks to highlight how 'abstract' contradictory tendencies must assume a 'concrete' contradictory form. More precisely, dialectical thought develops concepts that arise from within social relations themselves with the aim of discovering that which socially constitutes concrete objects beyond their immediate appearance. If the *appearance* of capitalism is based on society being comprised by dualistic relationships – the state *and* economy, for instance – then a dialectical analysis seeks to move beyond this fetishistic exterior in order to ascertain its inner contradictory mode of being – for instance, the state and economy as each being *moments* and qualitative *forms* of the same deeper social relation. Dialectical thinking critiques those social forms that appear inevitable and natural by probing their social constitution beyond how they immediately appear. 'Concepts are thus moments of a reality that requires their formations, and it is the business of conceptual thinking to subvert the critical subject by denouncing its deceitful publicity according to which its thing-hood is either self-constituted or a natural phenomenon' (Bonefeld 2009: 126–27).

One way, therefore, to understand the relationship between discourse and 'reality' is indeed to theorise them in relation to struggles in and around social and political projects that aim to win hegemony in society. We need to be aware of how political and state projects such as Thatcherism have gained hegemony in society through a number of ways of winning consent and by coercing other groups in society. Such political hegemonic projects are mediated by the capitalist state, the latter of which is derived from 'the silent compulsion of economic relations'. Under capitalism, politics and economics share an internal relationship (Holloway and Picciotto 1978). In contemporary times, the socio-economic project of financialisation is coupled with a neoliberal state project. The next chapter develops all of these points by outlining an alternative framework for understanding the relationship between financialisation and digital publics.

6 Financialisation, neoliberal state projects and the public sphere

Introduction

Since the 2008 crash, governments, global institutions, policy makers and public intellectuals have argued that knowledge-based and service economies provide the means for capitalism to recover. Engelbrecht (2009), for instance, cites from a 2009 OECD policy document, which aims to revitalise post-2008 economies. The document states:

> Many of the existing stimulus packages put some emphasis on deploying ICT infrastructure and a 'networked recovery' – i.e. the notion that ICT infrastructure and its use are a tool to revive the economy through new innovative services and offer solutions to pressing social problems.
>
> (cited in Engelbrecht 2009: 407)

Similarly, creative economy guru Richard Florida argues that one way to recover from the crisis is to invest in the creative sector. He says that the Bureau of Labor Statistics predicted that 15.3 million new jobs will be created in the USA between 2008 and 2018. Most of these, roughly 13.8 million, will be in creative, professional and service occupations. For working-class jobs, construction and transportation will be growth sectors, but overall working-class jobs will increase by only 1.5 million jobs. Another 1.2 million jobs will be lost in manufacturing (Florida 2010: 118). This and other data lead Florida to suggest that the US and other major economies need to invest more in knowledge-based and service sector occupations in order to help rebuild the economy. 'The service economy offers a tremendous potential for tapping the creative contributions of frontline workers and turning them into improved productivity' (Florida 2010: 122). Companies in the service sector have the capacity to tap into the creative potential of their workforce, encourage employees to present ideas to improve the company in question and then open up routes for employees to be promoted for their innovations within the company itself.

As we know, of course, one strand in the cultural political economy argues there is a close relationship between finance, information and knowledge. As Pryke and du Gay observe, finance has significantly altered the way in which it operates through new technologies, knowledge and practices that enable finance to perform its ventures in new ways. Digital constructions and representations of financial transactions on trading floors is just one illustration of how financial trading is dependent on cultural practices of information (Pryke and du Gay 2007: 343). Yet, as Clarke (2010: 390) perceptively observes, while countless people might now have less or little faith in neoliberal free markets to fix problems and provide avenues for profitable ventures, it is still nevertheless the case that many others still believe in the virtues of an entrepreneurial society based on 'choice' and 'freedom'. They want to ensure that the continual contracting out and privatisation of public services and the wider public sphere should proceed unabashed.

What this last observation alerts us to is how neoliberals and financial practitioners have pushed forward the financialization agenda through the state. Indeed, neoliberalism operates closely with the state in implementing 'free markets' across society. In fact, they both promote an audit and target culture in the public sector that establishes internal markets and competition between services. By using the state to open up the public sector and by privatising major industries, the way is therefore open for private companies to take over the running of some service providers in the public sector and public sphere (Mirowski 2013: 57). In theory at least, neoliberals therefore consciously seek to use the state to push forward free markets into society. This implies developing state policies such as deregulation, protection of intellectual property, opening up society to global flows of entrepreneurial activity, using digital technology to further neoliberalism in society and providing fertile ground for elites and experts to govern policy making rather than formal democratic apparatuses (Harvey 2005: 64–67).

When one reads certain strands in cultural political economy, it is often difficult to see how the state operates in constructing this management ethos in the public sphere, except at the level of the concrete. As we know from previous chapters, many of these theorists argue that the powers the nation-state once enjoyed have now been dissolved to variety of public–private bodies and networks at local, regional and global levels. The aim of this chapter is to demonstrate, on the contrary, that the *neoliberal state* is a vital mechanism for financialisation to gain hegemony in civil society. The neoliberal state has sought to do this through the public sphere by persuading ordinary people that it is in their best interests to become individual subjects of finance. The first section of the chapter therefore briefly sketches out some characteristics of hegemonic state projects through recourse mainly to the ideas of Gramsci and Poulantzas. Following this, the chapter outlines the meaning of neoliberalism and financialisation and then shows how both are related to digital technology. Next, the chapter maps out the nature of neoliberal state projects and financialised hegemonic strategies. This lays the ground to then see how these hegemonic strategies have sought to articulate a financialised 'common sense' through (digital) public spheres in society, which insist that financial debt is an assured route to prosperity. Some conclusions are then presented.

Hegemonic state projects

As we have seen, there has been some debate among academics about how we should think theoretically about credit and debt. For his part, Langley (2013) pursues a poststructuralist account in order to make sense of the explosion of debt. According to Langley, a Marxist approach cannot account for the way in which finance actively constructs reality, populations of people and individual subjectivities the moment that finance is being deployed in society. Financial devices are not external or outside of society, a position that Marxists apparently espouse; that is to say, unlike the viewpoint perpetuated by Marxists, finance 'is not a pre-existing material reality that is legitimated through ideological representation' (Langley 2008: 31).

One example that Langley presents to illustrate his argument is that of credit scores. These days, Langley observes, credit scores occur through databases run by large financial companies. In the UK, one of the largest credit scoring companies is Experian. Through the Internet, individuals living in the UK can pay a fee to Experian and regularly monitor their own credit score. While a person's credit history is still monitored by the bank they have accounts with, since the 1980s people in the UK have also been increasingly monitored through databases maintained by large companies. In practice, this means that these companies create risk-scores and risk profiles of distinctive populations through data received from a variety of financial sources. These coded populations are assigned risk categories based on factors such as payment history, amounts of credit owed, length of credit history, new credit and types of credit (Langley 2013: 14).

Individuals are subsequently placed into population risk categories and are targeted and sold financial products according to their risk category. 'Probabilities for default for different categories of consumer are determined on the basis of inference from statistics on the past credit records and behaviour of the population' (Langley 2013: 8). Credit scoring companies thus see a person's own credit history as an ongoing activity; a person is assigned various risk codes and then placed into distinctive populations. At the same time, however, these companies also have resources on their websites that give advice and guidance about how individuals can use information around their credit scores to transform themselves into good 'entrepreneurial selves'. For example, individuals are encouraged to raise their credit score if it is low, and given advice about how to achieve this goal. In addition, they tell individuals how they might manage uncertainties in their lives and gain access to future routes of credit.

Without doubt, Langley presents an engaging and convincing account of one important feature of credit and everyday life. Even so, Langley himself admits that his account is focused exclusively on a concrete everyday level of analysis. For him, power relations must be studied through their everyday manifestations and not at a higher level of theoretical abstraction, such as that of the global institutional or state regulatory level (Langley 2008: 37). While containing many interesting insights, Langley's account subsequently fails to fully reflect upon, and understand, the nature of *hegemonic state projects*. In other words, Langley provides no theoretical grounds to analyse how the capitalist state inevitably affects, shapes and structures a strategic terrain for concrete actors to act within and for some to be co-opted into a political hegemonic project. As Montgomerie notes, the 'concrete' approach to finance has a habit of overlooking how 'various political and institutional complexes allow global finance to proliferate through unequal relations between new emerging markets and well-established global financial centres' (Montgomerie 2008: 245). Since 1948, for example, major capitalist powers have assembled their resources together into a global public credit system mediated through global institutions such as the World Bank and the IMF. These institutions then operate, manage and support a complex financial system that connects other governance bodies, poorer countries and multilaterals. Those who manage this system can also then reassure private firms that the risk attached to investing in certain areas of the world can be managed exactly because the country, project, company or bank in question also has international financial institutional capital invested in it (Bracking 2009: 53–54). One does not have to subscribe to global conspiracies to agree with the simple point that such systems and agreements between powerful economic players represent centres of institutional power in the world.

Developing a theory of the state is crucial in this respect. Indeed, reading the arguments made by some contemporary theorists one would think that the state is no longer important in regulating societies, or that its power has considerably diminished. Langley tells us, for instance, that disciplinary power in the form of self-enclosed modes of surveillance operating in distinctive social contexts has been on the wane for some time. In its place one now discovers that the control of dispersed populations throughout society is made possible through computer databases (Langley 2013: 5). This, though, is a fanciful claim, if by a decline of 'disciplinary power' Langley also means a decline of state power. If anything, state power has increased in the last few decades, as witnessed by the increasing draconian empowerment of police power and anti-terror laws that regulate and monitor spaces of dissent in cities (see Roberts 2014).

Arguably, then, Langley has mistaken the *appearance* of how capitalism is now mediated by decentred flows and networks of information, for the *reality* of how capitalism actually operates. As Deleuze and Guattari (1988) observe, capitalism is shaped through two basic forms, that of free labour and independent capital.

> Capitalism forms when the flow of unqualified wealth encounters the flow of unqualified labour and conjugates with it … This amounts to saying that capitalism forms with *a general axiomatic of decoded flows.*
> (Deleuze and Guattari 1988: 500; original emphasis)

The very nature of capitalism, grounded as it is in axiomatic decoded flows of abstract commodity relations, makes it appear as if capital no longer requires a political force to regulate society. After all, it looks to be the case that capital can move anywhere it wants in the world in the search for profits. Labour, too, is no longer beholden to a particular employer, but can 'choose' whom it wishes to work for. Accordingly, 'it seems that there is no longer a need for a State, for distinct juridical and political domination, in order to ensure appropriation, which has become directly economic' (Deleuze and Guattari 1988: 500). Deleuze and Guattari, though, say it is wrong to make this claim. While capitalism operates through decoded flows, it must also exploit specific sectors and employ particular models to realise surplus value; hence, capital requires ways to code these sectors and models. States therefore help to 'moderate' the axiomatic decoded flows of global capital by reterritorialising them within borders and recoding them for purposes of surplus value extraction. 'So States are not at all transcendent paradigms of an overcoding but immanent models of realisation for an axiomatic of decoded flows' (Deleuze and Guattari 1988: 502). We require, then, a way to theoretically explore how abstract and simple, and concrete and complex, social processes are brought together in hegemonic state projects that serve to articulate the political, economic, ideological aspirations of certain dominant groups over the rest of society. Such hegemonic projects should be seen as an unstable set of alliances that selectively co-opt other groups to join its hegemonic goals while coercing other groups who are thought to be outside of its group.

Antonio Gramsci's theory of state hegemony is instructive in this respect. For Gramsci, any group aiming to win support and thereby gain hegemony for a political strategy or project has to recognise that it needs to capture state power and gain support in society. As a result, it had to recognise the two-fold nature of winning support, or gaining hegemony, insofar that support is gained through 'civil society' and 'political society'.

> What we can do, for the moment, is to fix two major superstructural 'levels': the one that can be called 'civil society', that is, the ensemble of organisms commonly called 'private' and that of 'political society' or 'the State.' These two levels correspond on the one hand to the function of 'hegemony' which the dominant group exercises throughout society and on the other hand to that of 'direct domination' or command that is exercised through State and juridical government.
>
> (Gramsci 1986: 12)

Gramsci believed therefore that neither political force nor economic relations could explain the dominance of a certain group. Rather, such dominance can only be successful if it wins both state power and 'intellectual and moral leadership' with allies in civil society. It achieves this by claiming to represent the interests of these other groups. At the same time, the dominant group uses its hegemony to maintain that its interests represent the general interest.

Under Gramsci's definition, then, the state encompasses civil society as well as its own particular claims to legitimacy. This leads Gramsci to adopt his celebrated formula: state = political society + civil society (Gramsci 1986: 239; 261–63). Jessop notes that Gramsci's interpretation here implies that he is less concerned with the form of the state under capitalism than with its modalities under specific historical moments in class struggle. 'Thus it is much more important to examine how Gramsci analyses the modalities of state power and the periodisation of forms of the state than to consider his various definitions of the state' (Jessop 1982: 147). This being the case, Gramsci believed that the state was constituted in and through class struggle as well as through popular struggles with other social forces and groups. As such, the state was an apparatus for both coercion and consent: consent because the state could only secure hegemony through civil society; and coercion because state power was embodied in its 'legitimate' enforcement of law and order through the army and police. Thus, for Gramsci, the capitalist state is an 'integral state', or the state in its 'inclusive sense' of being inclusive of civil society.

Gramsci insisted that hegemony is achieved when the state organises an 'historical bloc'. Of immense importance in this respect is the role played by what Gramsci terms as 'organic intellectuals'. These are individuals or organisations within the state and civil society that help to win support for a hegemonic project. To articulate the ideals of a hegemonic project to different groups in society, they engage in a 'war of position'. This refers to a long drawn-out battle to embed hegemonic ideals and practices in specific areas of civil society through compromise and restructuring, with one main aim being the containment or destroying of rival popular hegemonic projects. Organic intellectuals thereby help to create a 'power bloc'. This is defined as 'a fairly stable alliance of dominant classes or class fractions whose unity depends on mutual self-sacrifice of immediate self-interests and their commitment to a common world outlook' (Jessop 1990: 42). By successfully enrolling a selective number of other groups and organisations into this power bloc, a historical bloc is the result, which cements together a contingent relationship between an accumulation strategy and hegemonic project formed through state strategies. In our present-day time, this would be the accumulation strategy of financialisation and a neoliberal hegemonic bloc formed through neoliberal state strategies.

The capitalist state thus attempts to steer and negotiate policy agendas between different groups and institutions in civil society within the parameters of a hegemonic project while at the same time endeavouring to reproduce the structural conditions of capitalism. Poulantzas (2000: 32) is therefore surely correct to observe that the capitalist state creates a number of fragmented and dispersed 'discourses' that not only address different classes, but also organise intersecting strategies of power in society. In this respect, Deleuze and Guattari usefully remark that the state transforms the public sphere in civil society. The state has to ensure that its laws are *consistent* and applied in a non-arbitrary manner throughout civil society, and thereby ensure that each person has equal access to certain 'rights'. The state must therefore work from a perspective that sees people as being 'individuals' who share a number of 'rights', while the state must also instigate 'personal relations' in society based on a free flow of discussion in society, rather than each person being forced to be a member of a community as occurred under feudalism. Law subsequently becomes 'subjective, conjunctive, "topical"' (Deleuze and Guattari 1988: 498). Each person, as an autonomous individual with rights, gains a sense of subjective freedom that can reach 'the point of delirium', while, at the same time, working within more sober 'qualified acts that are sources of rights and obligations' (Deleuze and Guattari 1988: 499). While this new sensibility appears to treat all as affectual individuals with their own subjective desires, in reality the capitalist state will endeavour to uphold the general interests of a dominant class and the various groups associated with the dominant class, for example, the financial bourgeois class in our neoliberal times.

These tasks obviously place a great strain upon how the capitalist state organises hegemony within civil society and it ensures that hegemony is constituted through different relational struggles between forces around power. These struggles move both through and beyond the state and often seem to have very little to do with class relations. If we think of struggles around gender, for example, or around race and ethnicity, these frequently occur outside the immediate boundaries of the state and in many cases never find refuge in an explicitly class-based politics. Nonetheless, the state intervenes in all relationships of power and as a result assigns 'class pertinency' to social relations by enmeshing 'them in a web of class powers' (Poulantzas 2000: 43). We must remember that the capitalist state by its very definition obtains its social form from a distinctive class relationship and acts as both a concentration of that relationship and as a set of mechanisms that spreads to and infiltrates other power relations.

None of this is to imply that the state administers civil society in a carefree fashion by getting its own way. Nothing, in fact, could be further from the truth. As a condensation of power, the state internalises struggles and contradictions that occur around and between various power relations as it seeks to establish the dominance of a particular class force. Contradictory state tactics are often the upshot from these dynamics. Different power relations in civil society try to discover a space through these processes in order to affect state policies in various ways. But we must be clear what we mean here. The capitalist state is traversed by contradictions at both the level of its own bureaucratic structure and through different relations competing for power (e.g. dominant class interests, social movements and labour interests). If we think momentarily of the bureaucratic structure of the state itself in relation to its apparatuses composed of departments and functionaries such as, for example, the army, education, judiciary, welfare and culture it is possible to note certain dilemmas and problems. For instance, each apparatus has its own history and given interests and will seek to gain advantages in a network of power relations often against other apparatuses. Each apparatus will therefore pursue its own priorities, sometimes against the priorities of other apparatuses (Poulantzas 2000: 134).

The attempt to achieve hegemony is therefore an active and ongoing process and *evolves over time*. A political project must take special note of the historical conjuncture within which hegemony is sought and must be prepared to engage in 'war of position' in developing hegemonic capacity with a number of strategic alliances over time, as well as prepared to change its aims and goals to sustain hegemony. The aim of a dominant group, moreover, must be to infiltrate civil society and maintain an organic unity of conflicting interests. It can do this by creating a 'national-popular' outlook through invoking the prevailing beliefs and common-sense perceptions of a selective number of groups adequate to the needs of social and economic reproduction. At the same time, the state will engage in coercive tactics against groups deemed to be outside of its hegemonic project. It is in this respect that the state requires a way of administering and organising civil society through seemingly coherent state projects. These points will now be illustrated further in respect to neoliberal state projects and financialised hegemonic strategies.

Neoliberalism, financialisation and digital media

According to David Harvey, neoliberalism 'proposes that human well-being can best be advanced by liberating individual entrepreneurial freedoms and skills within an institutional framework characterized by strong private property rights, free markets and free trade' (Harvey 2005: 2). More practically, according to Jessop, neoliberalism argues for the deregulation of markets and the breaking down of economic and financial transactions within and between countries. It calls for the privatisation of the public sector and nationalised industries in the belief that the welfare state is a cost of production rather than a source of demand. Flexible labour market and wage policies are pursued, in part, by weakening of trade union power. Regressive taxation policies are put in place that favour 'entrepreneurial activities, and the conviction that developing countries in the world would benefit in respect to wealth creation and the alleviation of poverty if they followed neoliberal policies' (Jessop 2002: 259–60).

Neoliberalism has always embodied distinctive strategic goals. Indeed, it has changed its basic form throughout the twentieth century up until today. Emerging in Germany during the late 1920s, and comprising thinkers such as Walter Eucken, Franz Böhm, Alexander Rüstow, Wilhelm Röpke and Alfred Müller-Armack, the Freiburg School explicitly thought that 'entrepreneurship is not something that is "naturally given", akin to (Adam) Smith's idea of the natural human propensity to truck and barter. Instead it has be fought for and actively constructed' (Bonefeld 2012: 636). These 'ordoliberals' strongly held on to the belief that the pursuit of private property, self-interests, entrepreneurial determination and so forth, had to be socially ordered through the state. After 1945, other leading economic figures developed these liberal ideals. Most notable was the economist Milton Friedman, whose work at the University of Chicago with liked-minded colleagues critiqued Keynesian demand management of the economy in favour of deregulation and monetarism. Unlike ordoliberalism, Friedman's and his followers' neoliberalism was more anti-state and advocated a larger degree of pro-market strategies in policy-making (Peck 2010: Chapters 1 and 3). These later 'new liberals', like their ordo-liberal cousins, were not, however averse to using the strong arm of the state to apply neoliberal principles. For instance, one of the first experiments in implementing neoliberal policies in fact arrived in an authoritarian state system in Chile when in 1973 Augusto Pinochet staged a *coup d'état* against the democratically elected government of Salvador Allende. As well as rounding up, imprisoning and killing many in the opposition, Pinochet also called on the help of neoliberal economists to apply their brand of free market economics (Crouch 2011: 15).

Arguably, it was Margaret Thatcher who gave neoliberalism a public global face during the 1970s even though neoliberal economic policies had already been tried and tested in 1970s Chile, and Ronald Reagan would give neoliberalism a public lease of life in the 1980s. Thatcher, however, won an election in 1979 in part through neoliberal rhetoric and this was her importance. As she consolidated power it soon became clear that her government wanted to promote free markets, lessen the grip of state control on particular parts of the economy, privatise as much of the welfare state and nationalised industries as possible and boost consumer choice and investments (Jessop *et al.* 1988). To make these sorts of drastic changes the Thatcher government had to use state mechanisms to enact strong law and order programmes against some sections of society as well as populist privatisation programmes that appealed to other sections of the population (Hall 1988). Peck and Tickell (2002) thus refer to this as the 'roll back' stage of neoliberalism in the sense that the aim of neoliberalism was to attack and roll back the frontiers of the Keynesian welfare state.

By the 1990s, neoliberalism entered a second stage based on 'softer' policy agendas such as the Third Way and public–private partnerships (Kiely 2005). Tickell and Peck (2003) suggest that this encompassed a 'roll out' period of neoliberalism in which governments endeavoured to consolidate and embed neoliberalism into new areas of civil society. A third broad change occurred through the US neoconservative agenda under George W. Bush in which neoliberalism became attached to military intervention in so-called 'insecure' regions around the world (Kiely 2005: 32–33), while today we have arrived at a phase of austerity neoliberalism (Bruff 2014). It must also be borne in mind that along all of these routes neoliberalism has remained a contested project, with opposition being mounted at various points. For example, in Britain during the early 1980s different political opposition groups mounted fierce challenges to Thatcherism. The Greater London Council under the leadership of the left-wing politician Ken Livingstone is one notable illustration. Thatcherism also constantly altered its social composition from the late 1970s throughout the 1980s and early 1990s, moving through passive, aggressive and consolidated phases (Jessop *et al.* 1988).

Unlike some contemporary social theorists who see neoliberalism as being articulated by institutions and individuals with broadly similar agendas of creating calculative and enterprising subjects (Langley 2008), a hegemonic approach recognises that a range of organic intellectuals with often different and conflicting viewpoints can articulate that neoliberalism. For example, some in leading global institutions such as the World Bank insist that while it is true that global free markets contain negative effects it nevertheless reduces poverty around the world especially if it operates in a 'humanitarian' context. Others, on the other hand, argue that neoliberal globalisation requires proper management. These people work from a more liberal and soft agenda and include a variety of public intellectuals such as Paul Krugman and Jeffrey Sachs. They often chastise global economic institutions such as the International Monetary Fund (IMF) for their market orthodoxy. As such, they reject an orthodox approach to neoliberalism pursued by the likes of the World Bank. They believe instead that only a multilevel analysis, comprising economic institutions, economic integration, state mechanisms, values and social divisions, can really get to grips with, and therefore manage, global problems around the world brought about by neoliberalism. They have faith in the ability of economic global competition to rectify problematic issues around the world but only if this is done in an administered way that is also seen to be fair. 'At the end of the day, the agenda is to stabilise globalising capitalism. It is to modify neoliberal globalisation without tugging at the roots of underlying structures' (Mittelman 2004: 22).

We should expect such divisions in debates around neoliberalism once we realise that neoliberal ideals adopt different forms in different contexts. Jessop (2010: 172–74) usefully notes four. First, there is the most radical form, which is neoliberal system transformation. Here, a radical and quick overhaul of a system is attempted in favour of neoliberalism. Soviet-bloc countries tried to do this after the fall of Eastern Europe communism in 1989–91. The result can vary from marginal success to failure. Neoliberal regime shift is the second form, and this is most readily associated with the Thatcher and Reagan governments of the 1980s. In this case, Atlantic Fordist regimes of accumulation and regulation associated with Keynesian demand management and welfare states are transformed to ones favouring the free flow of capital over welfare and labour rights. Neoliberal structural adjustment programmes are the third type, and here the focus is on developing countries. Those countries deemed 'security risks' because of high levels of poverty and often unstable governments are given 'support' through the likes of aid and loans by external organisations such as the World Bank; however, this aid only emerges as long as the designated 'troubled' countries are willing to follow neoliberal economic ideals. Finally, Jessop identifies neoliberal policy adjustments, which are modest changes in countries deemed necessary to stay globally competitive. Nordic capitalism and Rhenish capitalism are typical examples.

Since the 1960s, capital has also discovered new ways to accumulate money-capital within the financial sector. 'Real accumulation', as Lapavitsas (2013: 201–4) observes, tends to be generated by industrial capital. It develops the means of production and its related labour process by producing physical outputs, building transport networks to distribute physical outputs, maintaining and enhancing communication networks to this end too, realising outputs in the form of money that will be reinvested in production, building up stocks of capital, and so forth. Financial accumulation, on the other hand, denotes the mobilisation of loanable capital in the sphere of circulation that is also undertaken by financial institutions. Financial investors thereby gain profits by expanding the flows of loanable capital. Profit is subsequently made through claims on others. These claims can also take the form of financial assets such as by purchasing bonds or derivatives in a financial market. As this market develops, loanable capital starts to cultivate its own trading irrespective of its relationship to real accumulation.

Such has been the impact of financialisation on the economy in terms of profits that nonfinancial firms have increasingly relied on the financial sector to increase their own profits. For example, a substantial number of nonfinancial firms in the US depend on portfolio income (total earnings gained from interest, dividends and realised capital gains on investments) as a means to gain profits. When compared to corporate cash flows (profits plus depreciation allowances), portfolio income shows a marked increase among nonfinancial firms from the 1970s onwards. 'In the late 1980s, the ratio peaks at a level that is approximately *five times* the levels typical of the immediate postwar decades' (Krippner 2011: 35; original emphasis).

Financialisation and neoliberalism are also inherently knowledge-based forms. At a relatively high level of abstraction, capitalism is heavily reliant on knowledge. Producing objects requires one to apply what Carchedi (2011: 221) terms as mental use-value, that is, our perception, theorisation and comprehension of objective reality that can then be transformed in order to create objects. Mental use-values are integrated into capitalist labour processes to help procure surplus value, 'if the labourers work for a longer time than that necessary to reconstitute their labour-power *and* if they transform existing use-values into new ones' (Carchedi 2011: 221; original emphasis). Knowledge is therefore always employed in the capitalist labour process to create commodities for exchange. But, as Jessop further notes, in order to render different types of knowledge as commodities a number of procedures are required. Knowledge, for example, is not a scarce resource and is collectively produced. To transform it into a commodity, then, certain conditions must be put in place. Indeed, 'it only gains a commodity form insofar as it is made artificially scarce and access thereto is made to depend on payment (in the form of royalties, license fees, etc.)' (Jessop 2002: 14).

This is an important point because it suggests that the use of knowledge by capital is partly based on the ability of capitalists to employ their power to enclose it for their own profitable uses. For De Angelis (2004), enclosing common resources in fact represents one of the most powerful mechanisms available for neoliberal capital to increase profitable revenues. We see this, for example, in the enclosure of 'social commons' such as the welfare state. These particular 'commons' is where people normally gain access to social goods, but in the last few decades it has been under attack from neoliberal policies. 'Knowledge-commons', including the freedom to share knowledge, are similarly being enclosed through intellectual property rights, while 'land-commons' such as public space in cities and towns have also been increasingly privatised (De Angelis 2004). Financialisation, neoliberalism and knowledge-based work practices can therefore work hand-in-hand to enforce the power of capital in civil society. In fact, those academics, policy makers and business gurus who employed the knowledge-based discourse overlooked the importance of these financialised practices until it was far too late (Thompson and Harley 2012: 1376).

At a more concrete level, financialisation, neoliberalism and knowledge operate together in diverse ways. Breaking down global trade barriers and imposing neoliberal markets on countries has enabled transnational digital companies to relocate parts of their production to those countries that provide cheap labour for the manufacture of parts of products. In 2007, for example, Apple introduced the iPhone to the world. Now selling into their millions, the iPhone has been a huge commercial success for Apple. By 2009, however, Apple had off-loaded the manufacturing of its components to nine different companies located in Germany, Japan, South Korea and the US. These components are then shipped across to China where they are assembled and then sent around the world to consumers (Hart-Landsberg 2013: 21).

Financialisation, neoliberalism and knowledge also worked closely together in helping to prepare the way for the 2008 crisis. After all, digital technology played its part in building up the financial bubble in the first place, not least by allowing speculative activity to reach new levels of intensity by trading through communicative channels (Engelbrecht 2009: 408). A further consequence of this has been to encourage venture capital to invest in struggling companies and take high risks in returning companies to being profitable organisations. By the 1980s, venture capital began to invest in the growing market in initial public offerings (IPO), which funneled money into high-tech industries. During the 1990s, the Clinton administration encouraged the growing significance of financial capital, along with its more concrete form in the guise of venture capital, in order to promote the US economy through a variety of measures. Imposing margin requirements on stock market speculation was rejected by the government, allowing a debt-financed boom to get underway because many rich households spent more in the belief that the value of stocks and shares had risen (Pollin 2003).

By the late 1990s, the US stock market had grown by more than 60 percent. Yet, this can be accounted for by the huge increase in in technology stocks that soared upwards by 300 percent between 1997 and 2000. 'At the peak of the bubble, total market capitalization approached US$15 trillion, while the technology stocks soared above US$45 trillion, or 35% of the total, up from 12% in 1997' (Perez 2009: 784). Financial speculation also fed into new technology. Henwood (2003) reminds us of the Internet boom in the 1990s. Launched unofficially through the 1995 IPO of Netscape, which led to a speculative mania of investments in Internet companies, the hype surrounding these investments soon fizzled out when it was realised that the value of many of these companies was desperately overinflated. In 1998, for instance, a small Internet company with big losses, TheGlobe.com, was offered on the stock markets at $9 a share. By 2000 it was trading at $97, only to see this plummet to 0.075 by 2003 due to its continual losses (Henwood 2003: 189).

In saying this, there is truth to the statement that finance enables individuals to disconnect themselves from the underlying realities of capitalism and, in the process, bolster the idea and ideology that we are indeed living in 'new' creative and technologically sophisticated times. Technology also often serves to mask the irrationalities of global finance. Think momentarily about the following claim made by Ohmae (1994: 152). In a 'borderless world', he says, it will always be the case that 'money finds the best and most comfortable place to live'. Investors will put their money where they can expect the highest returns. 'Borderless financial markets' (Ohmae 1994: 152) are made all the more porous by new technology, and this means that 'money slips across borders in the blink of an electronic eye' (Ohmae 1994: 167; see also Papows 1999: 143–44). In this instance, then, an ideology surrounding informationalism becomes entwined with an ideology associated with financialisation. Both come together in the belief that open global borders are good for the world in and of themselves, that 'modernist' and 'industrial' societies now belong in a bygone era, that the welfare state needs to be radically overhauled and made to get people back to work, that societies make progress through new technologies, and that individuals freed from the shackles of institutions can prosper in the world (Neubauer 2011: 211). The next section starts to look in more depth at how this ideology becomes part of a wider state hegemonic project.

Neoliberal state projects and financialised hegemonic strategies

Neoliberalism has always strategically used the state to further its aims and goals. In the words of Philip Mirowski, 'a primary ambition of the neoliberal project is to redefine the shape and function of the state, *not to destroy it*' (Mirowski 2013: 56; original emphasis). Indeed, a more than plausible argument can be made that suggests that under globalisation the nation state has increased its various capacities 'for defining and enforcing property rights, extracting revenue for privileged capitalists, and fostering the centralization and administrative and political resources' (Tabb 2005: 53). This is an extremely important point if for no other reason than the fact that neoliberalism is often thought to only promote free markets in society. This is not true. While supporting free markets neoliberals have also been keen supporters of a strong interventionist state in selective areas of society.

Within state apparatuses itself, new neoliberal organic intellectuals have been created. In the UK, for example, Margaret Thatcher managed to take hold of the state to impose neoliberal practices in the public sector and nationalised industries. For instance:

> Between 1979 and 1994, the number of jobs in the public sector in Britain was reduced from over seven million to five million, a drop of 29 percent. Virtually all the jobs eliminated were unionized jobs ... The government (also) used taxpayer money to wipe out debts and recapitalize firms before putting them on the market (for example, the water authority got five billion pounds of debt relief plus 1.6 billion pounds called the 'green dowry' to make the bride more attractive to prospective buyers).
>
> (George 2000: 32)

Through these policies, new intellectual labour has proliferated in the guise of 'expert' consultants in the UK public sector that steer policy provision and provide guidance in this neoliberal policy environment. One study, for example, found that during its period in office in the mid-2000s, New Labour spent more than £2.2 billion a year on consultants for its different government departments (*The Guardian* 2006). A mechanism through which new experts have gained power in the public sphere has been through the increasing dominance of public–private partnerships (PPPs) that operate between the public sector, private business, quangos and the voluntary sector. For advocates, PPPs enjoy the potential to create new opportunities for collaboration and socialisation in communities. As Lindsay *et al.* (2008: 716–19) observe, partnerships assume a variety of forms, not least principal-gent relations based for example around the contracting out of public services, inter-organisational negotiation by for example the coordination of resources, or systemic coordination by multi-agency governance. Lindsay *et al.* also note many mutual benefits for those involved in partnership networks, such as sharing knowledge between different partners to solve common problems, flexible and responsive solutions to issues as they arise, the constant testing of innovation, mobilising local knowledge and expertise and finally building capacity in organisations.

The neoliberal state also forces local authorities, voluntary organisations and 'third sector' groups into compulsory and formal partnership networks with business. These different 'partners' often come together with different ambitions and assumptions concerning the remit of specific partnerships. Community members for example might enter a partnership with a set of beliefs about a local development that is contrary to the interests of a particular business involved in the partnership network (Newman and Clarke 2009: 61). In addition, those 'partners' who are forced to follow the non-negotiable audit culture and target-setting agenda of particular contracts often resent the 'partner' who has implemented the contract in the first place, distrusting their competence to work in a true partnership network. Communication between 'partners' can then start to break down. This is often the case when service delivery becomes increasingly centralised in the hands of big corporations who take over the running of particular services. Rather than sharing the risks and benefits, costs soon instead take precedent over the actual effectiveness of the service (Milbourne and Cushman 2012: 19). Forcing 'partners' to work together certainly generates cooperation, but it can also create antagonism and conflict in a 'network'.

The neoliberal state, moreover, has taken the lead in encouraging and forcing managers in the public sector to cut costs without affecting service provision. This has been imposed on public sector managers in various ways. For instance, public sector managers in the UK have been urged by successive governments to redefine the boundaries between different types of public sector work within the same occupation. Creating more job boundaries around specific sets of skills and grades within the same service strengthens the hand of management to then closely monitor the performance of each grade. 'Within this more pressure is being applied by managers as they seek to claw back terms of conditions and reduce union power at the level of the employer' (Seifert and Mather 2013: 459). There is good reason of course why the state wishes to push through these changes in the public sector. Knowledge-based services, which include insurance and pension funds, real estate, hardware and software consultancy, advertising, architectural design and research and development, have all been given a new lease of life through the privatisation of the public sector. Public sector outsourcing alone is worth billions in the UK (Wood 2006). By enacting these polices the neoliberal state has managed to alter the bureaucratic apparatuses of the capitalist state in a direction favourable to neoliberalism.

These changes have in turn transformed the class composition of advanced capitalist societies. While commercial-clerical workers have seen an increase in their numbers, and while industrial workers still exist in manufacturing sector, Duménil and Lévy claim that neoliberalism provides fertile grounds for a resurgence of higher incomes for the upper echelons of the capitalist class. Financial institutions in particular have gained hegemony through neoliberal policies. Central banks now ensure that strategies are adapted that maintain stable prices over and above social and welfare policies such as full employment. Such policies have in turn furthered the financial interests of this capitalist class (Duménil and Lévy 2011: 56). A middle-class group of managers has been significantly altered during the neoliberal phase too. Gradually in the 1980s, the tasks of managers became those that ensured shareholder value and the like benefited owners. 'At the top of managerial hierarchies, managers are involved in the dynamics of neoliberal corporate governance to such degrees that the financial facet of management tends to overwhelmingly dominate' (Duménil and Lévy 2011: 84). It has thus become the norm to give managers 'incentives' in the guise of stock options to ensure high performance. These can be transferred into shares later when prices in the company are high. Shareholder value – managers who would share in the value of a company after it had been subject to restructuring – have therefore become a vital form of restructuring businesses (Glyn 2006: 58).

This activity was part of the deregulation of the banking sector that was once again supported by the state. During the 1970s, a number of important changes occurred in the banking sector, especially in the US banking sector, which effectively deregulated banking markets. For example, Lazonick and O'Sullivan (2000) note that in this period a number of money-market funds appeared that presented higher rates of returns for savers than those offered by regulated banks. To open up the market for loans, the American government in 1978 deregulated the interest rates, which meant that banks could now compete on the interest rates they offered to savers. A few years later in 1982 the Garn-St. Germain Act opened up opportunities for different savings banks to trade in junk bonds and participate in risky financial ventures in order to increase their own money supply and then compete with other banks for a share of household deposits (Lazonick and O'Sullivan 2000: 17). Once the socio-economic ground started to be transformed in the direction of financialisation the way was then paved for major financial institutions to capitalise on this and push forward the agenda even further. In the UK, Rothschilds, Barclays, Merrill Lynch, Goldman Sachs and Citibank were just a few such institutions who in the early 2000s were building on changes that had already been established over the last two decades, ensuring in the process that the changes became 'commonsense' and the 'norm' in government policy agendas (Macartney 2011: 62).

As we know, to gain hegemony and create a hegemonic project, financialisation requires a number of organic intellectuals in civil society who help to articulate the 'common sense' traits of financialisation in civil society. One important group of organic intellectuals in this respect are a new breed of capital market intermediaries who have grown in force under the patronage of neoliberal capitalism. In their study of the UK Folkman *et al.* (2007) bracket these intermediaries into two main groups. First, responsive functionaries deal with juridical requirements of market capitalism along with their stream funds into secondary markets of shares and bonds and they include audit partners, consultants, corporate lawyers and stock market analysts. Second, 'proactive initiators of deals, corporate restructuring and investment arbitrage opportunities' are associated with hyper-innovation in capital markets and include hedge fund managers, traders and dealers (Folkman *et al.* 2007: 557). Folkman *et al.* go on to to say that while these intermediaries do not represent a coherent calculating group they are nevertheless connected through a penchant for a capitalism constantly restructuring itself 'because deals (be it acquisition or demerger, new issues or buybacks, securitization or rebuilding risks) are the source of fees' (Folkman *et al.* 2007: 561). These financial intermediaries also mobilise various resources and they construct and choreograph new networks in order to reproduce their identities and social positions. For example, securitisation requires specialist investors, financial institutions, financial models, specialist financial language and so forth (Hall 2009: 181).

Other organic intellectuals have also been enrolled to articulate the 'common sense' nature of financialisation to the rest of the population. One major organic intellectual is that of media publics. Studies in the UK suggest that major media sources routinely report the opinions about the 2008-ongoing financial crisis from financial elites rather than those that emanate from critical non-mainstream economists. In his study of the first six weeks of coverage of the 2008 financial crisis on the BBC's leading current affairs and news Radio 4 *Today* programme, Berry (2013) discovered a clear bias towards interviewing elites from major financial institutions located in the City of London. For example, during the six weeks the *Today* programme featured 233 source appearances. From this figure, Berry found that:

> (R)epresentatives from the financial services community are the largest group of sources accessed (35.1% of all source appearances) followed by politicians (32%). Since the main three British political parties during this period were all committed to free markets and 'light touch' regulation, there is a narrowness in the range of opinion available to listeners.
>
> (Berry 2013: 257)

Other sources given a large amount of airtime included business lobbyists, neoclassical economists and financial journalists who all favoured neoliberal solutions to the crisis. Few if any of these sources sought to warn the public before the financial crisis erupted, while those commentators that warned of a looming impending crisis before 2008, such as trade unions and radical economists, were given significantly less airtime.

Kay and Salter (2013) discovered similar results in their analysis of the BBC Online coverage of the Coalition Government's Comprehensive Spending Review 2010. Presented on 20 October 2010, the Comprehensive Spending Review outlined the Coalition Government's wish to cut public spending and announce an era of public austerity in British society. By analysing three different BBC websites that went online just before and after the announcement of these austerity measures, Kay and Salter explored the extent to which the BBC opened up spaces for critical public dialogue on the Comprehensive Spending Review. What the authors discovered was that critical dialogue was noticeable by its absence on these websites.

For instance, one of the BBC websites entitled 'What is the Spending Review' set out to be a 'guide' in the form of slides to the Spending Review and to explain 'why it matters'. On this particular webpage, no coverage was given to any real alternatives to the budget cuts. Instead, the slides suggested that the cuts were an inevitable result of the crisis rather than a political choice. Moreover, banks and welfare recipients were framed as being equal participants in public spending decisions, whereas, as Kay and Salter note, they were anything but. 'In March 2010, the total outstanding support explicitly pledged to the banks by the Treasury was £612.58 billion ... Welfare spending at that time stood at around £87 billion over a year' (Kay and Salter 2013: 8). The only real alternative to the cuts that was highlighted on the slides was that associated with the Labour Party's response, which as Kay and Salter observe, was very similar to the Coalition Government's policies, and so did not represent a real alternative at all. These organic intellectuals thereby reinforce the dominant viewpoint that financialisation is the only game in town.

However, Froud *et al.* also air a note of caution about the financialisation of national economies, which in many respects ties in with one of the main contradictions of capitalist reproduction. Capital will seek to develop its productive powers without limits by accumulating money-capital and yet at the same time it will always be compelled to operate within the limits of the market. This contradiction is reproduced into finance in its own unique way. For instance, while fund managers and financial markets expect and require huge returns on their investments, managers of corporations are constrained in what they can generate in terms of earnings due to limits in product markets. This problem is compounded by the fact that financial investors and companies are not a homogeneous set of actors in the financial market but represent divergent interests. Venture capitalists who expect a fast return have different expectations to pension funds that operate with more predictable and medium-term outcomes (Froud *et al.* 2002: 106–7). To overcome this contradiction, financial capital has moved into other spheres of society in order to generate profits. Of special importance in this respect is the financialisation of households.

Household debt and the pursuit of financial hegemony in the public sphere

In the 1980s, Leys (2001: 53) notes, Margaret Thatcher's government set out on a journey to commercialise everyday life. Its aim was to build an enterprise culture in Britain by unleashing market mechanisms in the public sphere. Nationalised industries were soon privatised and shares in them offered up for sale, schools had to train children for business, the tax burden was shifted from rich to poor and welfare benefits were further means-tested. While opinion polls have consistently showed that many express a degree of hostility to Thatcherite policies, Leys is probably correct to observe: 'The reality was that while Thatcher's reforms were seldom popular, they had become an accepted part of daily life' (Leys 2001: 53).

Over the last few decades, households have increasingly felt an external pressure to invest in this Thatcherite project through a type of 'coupon pool capitalism'. Most noticeably, in the US and UK there has been substantial pressure brought to bear on households to invest in their own future through securities so they might provide funds for old age and retirement. The coupons acquired are then managed by a pension fund or insurance company or directly held by a household (Froud *et al.* 2002: 127). Clearly, dangers lurk in these practices. The most obvious one is that it encourages non-financial corporations to redirect their investments from the productive sectors of the economy to financial sectors. Take for example the explosion of the credit card industry. Securitisation of credit means that, like a number of financialised devices, banks can bundle credit card receivables together into a pool of loans. A trust known as a special purchase vehicle administers a pool of loans. Investors can then purchase certificates in this trust. The advantage for banks is that they can take receivables off their balance sheets and earn a profit on the loans further to what they pay for on the securities. Recycling pools of funds is thus made easier for banks because when these are off their balance sheets the loan pool is simply re-capitalised through new asset-backed securities rather than deposits. For third parties, low-risk securities imply that the funds are lowered in the interest charged to cardholders. Profits magically increase (Montgomerie 2006: 313). In reality, funds for real investments decline (Orhangazi 2008).

Credit cards are also important because they represent an instance of how banks and other financial institutions have sought to make money. For some theorists, credit and debt are not so much associated with class strategies as they are about controlling diverse populations across society (see Langley 2008; 2013). Yet, in moving the theoretical boundaries away from class-based accounts, one loses sight of how debt is indeed linked to social class. Neoliberalism, after all, operates by intensifying labour to procure a higher average output per worker, while at the same time keeping wages stagnant. High levels of profit are thereby made at the expense of relatively low wage levels. In the UK, report Elliot and Atkinson (2012: 237), just 54 percent of the national economy is accounted for by wages, a drop of four percent from the 1970s. In more practical terms, this means that the UK workforce now misses out on an extra £60bn a year in their wages. This trend has been accompanied by pay cuts since the onset of the 2008 crisis.

> Once adjusted for inflation, real incomes fell by more than 7 percent between 2009 and 2012, the biggest three year drop on record. Even in the brief periods when the economy was actually showing some signs of life, living standards were hit by a rising cost of living, and in 2011 household incomes dropped by 3 percent. Such a fall was on a scale not seen since the slump of the early 1980s, which was followed by a period of strong growth in living standards as inflation dropped to a low of 2.5 percent by mid-decade, while earnings growth fell below 7.5 percent.
>
> (Elliot and Atkinson 2012: 238)

Under these conditions the key for business to ensure that individuals keep consuming, and thereby maintain high profits, is to make credit available and encourage people to take on higher levels of debt. In the US, household debt as a percentage of disposable income has increased to 130 percent, while in Europe this figure stands at about 90 percent. The ratio between total debt and GDP in the US rose to 358 percent by 2008 (Dienst 2011: 60–61). Debt is therefore such an important issue during these times because it allows accumulation to proceed (Nesvetailova 2005: 405–6).

Montgomerie (2009) shows that one way in which financial companies encourage people across different social classes to take out more loans is to transform debt into a virtue in order to maintain certain lifestyle consumer patterns. There are various moments to this new restructuring of lifestyles. Financial providers, such as large commercial banks and consumer credit issuers, have been allowed to bundle up existing loan pools and then issue bonds on the streams of income coming from debtors. More money is then generated and more loans are issued to consumers. As a result, 'these practices have made lenders dependent on borrowers staying in repayment for longer periods' (Montgomerie 2009: 10). Lenders thus target those already in debt to take on more debt. It is in this sense that debt is no longer thought to be something that one avoids if possible. It has instead become a way to maintain certain standards of living.

> For example, there has been a 74 percent increase in health premiums for the average US family with health care coverage, which has led to 29 million American adults incurring unsecured consumer loans to make up for the gap between medical coverage and actual costs.
>
> (Montgomerie 2009: 17)

In 2011, it was estimated that £200 million was owed on credit cards in the UK (Elliot and Atkinson 2012: 71).

Credit card issuers have created, moreover, class-based and racialised strategies in how they pursue certain groups already in debt. This is because those who take on a lot of debt are often those who underuse normal banking facilities, such as regularly using a bank account. Evidence suggests that these groups of people are located in relatively deprived, low-income households and in ethnic minority households (Soederberg 2013). Soederberg goes on to show how the strategies employed by credit card issuers rely on the state to ensure that their tactics are successful. In the US, this has occurred through various pieces of legislation. The Obama Administration passed the Credit Card Accountability, Responsibility and Disclosure Act (CARD Act) in May 2009. While the CARD Act seems to provide stronger regulations on credit card issuers by, for example, ensuring that interest rate increases cannot occur in the first year, some of the major problems of the credit card industry remain untouched by the Act. Credit card companies still have the power to charge their own rate of interest at the beginning of a contract and then to increase this after one year. As a result, 'although interest rates stabilized in 2010, the spread between the prime rate set by the Federal Reserve (3.25%) and the average APR on unsecured cards (14.06%) was the widest in the past two decades' (Soederberg 2013: 508).

Digital publics have mediated these debt strategies in different ways. Banks trade in interest-bearing capital, or $M - M^1$. Credit represents sources of interest-bearing capital for banks and through new technology they have been able to generate innovative mechanisms to accumulate large amounts of interest-bearing capital. Information technology has thereby transformed how banks manage financial risks. They can treat their customers as large and distinct uniform populations. Naturally, and as we noted earlier in the chapter, many contemporary social theorists make similar arguments about credit. What is important to add, though, is that these strategies have furthered and strengthened the concentration and, by default, structural power, of global banking operations. Think of credit-scoring techniques employed by banks. Data of up to 30,000 loans is required to start to calculate the performance of loans. 'This favours large banking organisations possessing data from their own pool of previously extended loans' (Lapavitsas and Dos Santos 2008: 46).

These practices, in turn, require a huge number of ordinary people able to go online and gain information about what credit is available to them from banks and other financial institutions. As well as websites set up by banks for these purposes, numerous other websites appeared extolling the virtues of, and relaying information about, financial and credit products available to ordinary people. Online financial analysts, experts and journalists, along with personalised social media pages, have all given rise to new financial digital publics for people to gain information about credit. 'Most importantly, interactive technologies generated a financial blogosphere. Major blogs contained a mix of information, news, commentary, company analyses, and trading recommendations' (Hope 2010: 660). Moreover, financial digital television has low production costs but high commercial value. This is one reason for their increase in recent years, which also corresponds with proliferation of everyday financial devices in society (Lee 2012).

Governments have also sought to widen the basis of these digital publics. Martin describes one scheme that was introduced by the Securities and Exchange Commission (SEC), which is an agency of the US government. Among other things, SEC regulates the securities industry in the US, and passes laws to this effect. In 1994, it created a website that made government-mandated documents that corporations must file about their activities freely available to everyone. Before this time people had to pay a fee to a private company to obtain this information. The rationale for setting up the site, therefore, was that it would assist in democratising financial information and help people learn basic skills of financial literacy. Nearly 50,000 people a day were going on the site soon after its launch (Martin 2002: 127–28).

Overall, according to Comor (2008: 105), digital technology shrinks the timeframes required to make careful decisions about what one purchases. Speed and efficiency become the norm when accessing information online, and this negates the space required to make careful and considered evaluations about what to consume. Certainly, a sense of panic often sets in when one is bombarded with information about fluctuating prices in and around basic goods. Nowhere is this clearer than in the case of housing. One obvious form of debt in many countries today is indeed that produced through the mortgage market. In fact, mortgages represent an ideal case study of the relationship between the neoliberal state and winning hegemony for financialisation, if for no other reason than the fact that mortgages represent the highest form of household debt in most major capitalist countries (Lapavitsas 2013: 238).

Mortgages are also a good indicator of how debt and finance create new social divisions in society. In February 2013, the UK-based housing charity Shelter claimed that if the cost of food over the last 40 years had increased in line with the escalation in UK house prices then the weekly shopping basket would by today's prices cost about £453.

> In 1971, a typical weekly shop for a family of four cost £10.40, and the average home £5,632. By 2011 the price of the average home had shot up to £245,319 – over 43 times more expensive. This puts the average weekly shop at £453.23.
>
> (Shelter 2013)

Shelter goes on to show that if this remarkable rise in house prices was applied to individual grocery goods in an average weekly shopping basket then some very ordinary food items would soon become unaffordable for many. A four-pint carton of milk would cost £10.45, a loaf of sliced white bread would be £4.36, while shoppers could expect to pay £53.18 for a leg of lamb.

These dramatic rises run in parallel with some other notable changes in the UK housing market. In 2013, government figures revealed that home ownership in England had fallen to its lowest level since 1987. In 2011–12, 65.3 percent of households were homeowners, while in 1987 we discover a comparable figure of 64.6 percent. From 1980 until 2003, the number of homeowners had showed a steady increase, with 56.6 percent of households being homeowners in 1980 to a peak figure of 70.9 percent in 2003. Nevertheless, after 2003 the gradual decline in home ownership started to take effect. Meanwhile, the number of people privately renting homes in England has increased. In 1980, the number of households privately renting was 11.9 percent. This figure then fluctuated between 9.1 percent and 11.7 percent up until 2005. After 2005, however, the figure gradually increased above 1980's figure of 11.9 percent so that by 2011–12 the number of households privately renting stood at 17.4 percent (English Housing Survey 2013: 47).

Today, then, we know that the Thatcherite dream of a home-owning democracy in the UK has at least for the time being bitten the dust. Nevertheless, Thatcherism has been successful in helping to create neoliberal subjects across the UK by consolidating a neoliberal and financialised hegemonic project. How is this so? During the 1980s one of Margaret Thatcher's flagship policies was to promote home ownership for all or, as she liked to put it, creating a 'property owning democracy'. This was part of the Conservative Party's hegemonic project in the 1980s to privatise the public sector and set loose free markets across society more widely in the (neoliberal) belief that such policies represent a rational calculative approach towards economic decision-making and policy intervention.

To be sure, the Conservatives were perceptive enough to realise that one way in which they could gain hegemony for the Thatcherite project was to articulate the supposed benefits of free markets in the private domain of people's lived experience in their homes. As Hay (1992) observes, the Thatcher government *selectively* focused on a number of problems that had occurred in some sectors of council housing. The post-war welfare settlement certainly empowered local authorities to engage in a number of slum clearances in major UK cities, to be replaced by new housing developments. New council homes varied in quality, however, and were subject to successive government cuts and the promotion of the private sector in meeting housing needs. By the 1960s, preferential treatment was being given to building high-rise flats in inner cities, but this had the unintentional consequence of exacerbating a number of social inequalities and social divisions between different social groups in cities. Some families were placed in well-built modern council homes, while others were housed in poorly-built and alienating high-rise blocks.

After their election in 1979, the Thatcher government took advantage of these contradictions in post-war housing. It introduced the 1980 Housing Act, which gave council tenants up to a 50 percent reduction in the market value of their homes while removing rent subsidies for those that remained council tenants. Another Housing Act in 1984 increased the selling of council homes so that by 1987 about a million council houses had been sold off. By 1996, this figure had reached 2.2 million homes. Four years later the Housing Act in 1988 removed rent controls and this meant that landlords could now negotiate yearly contracts with tenants. Buying homes to then rent them out, the so-called buy-to-let phenomenon, soon became an attractive option for existing and pro-spective landlords (Cumbers 2012: 48; Hay 1992: 56; Leys 1989: 119). Of course, the government knew very well that by selling off council homes so cheaply it was cultivating a sizable support base among 'aspirational' working-class families. In the words of Hay:

> The sale of council houses constitutes a thinly disguised restructuring of the political agenda and of civil society itself, for, in offering individual families a route out their proletarian impasse into the free market, Thatcherism has succeeded in the recommodification of housing, replacing the interests of the family in the public sector and state welfare with those of the free market and the private sector.
>
> (Hay 1992: 56)

In the 1990s, more regressive taxation systems were introduced through policies such as the Mortgage Interest Relief that allowed richer households to transfer housing wealth to other areas of consumption. Second mortgages meant that equity could be used to further welfare spending for households, such as using equity for residential care for elderly relatives. New mortgage products flooded the market during this period that further encouraged the use of homes as sources of income for welfare use (Lowe *et al.* 2011: 109). Evidence thus indicates that an expanding amount of fixed assets contained in housing have leaked out through mortgage equity withdrawal (Smith and Searle 2008). By 2011, it was estimated that UK mortgage debt stood at a massive £1.2 trillion (Elliot and Atkinson 2012: 71). We must remember, though, that Thatcherite housing policy also had to operate through coercion as well as consent. For example, those working-class families who refused to buy their homes saw a withdrawal of their rent subsidies leading to average rent increases of 66 percent between 1980 to 1981 (Hay 1992: 56). Housing policy has therefore been strategically selective in its effects.

Yet, it hardly bodes well for those devotees of free markets that despite all of the huge changes to the UK housing market over the last three decades the actual number of homeowners languishes at the level found in 1987. In fact, the biggest rise in UK home ownership of nearly 25 percent occurred from the 1950s to the early 1970s, but this was a period when the welfare state was still relatively unscathed by the neoliberal onslaught (Office for National Statistics 2013). In other words, *it was the welfare state, not Thatcher's privatisation programme, which created a steady increase in homeowners.* The subprime mortgage crash likewise revealed an underlying problem with global finance more generally. Financial risks involved in investing in forms such as CDOs are underestimated, while credit is made too cheap for these investments (Blackburn 2008: 91; Kregel 2008: 24).

Nevertheless, these problems are of secondary importance to how the state can co-opt housing into its neoliberal and financial hegemonic project and then disseminate this project to selective British public spheres.

In these circumstances, housing has played a vital role in schooling people in the details of everyday finance and in taking financial risks in their daily lives. Moreover, housing has become caught up in media publics inundated with dreams, images and visions of lifestyles, personalisation and self-management through finance. By entering the housing market, one immediately becomes part of the media landscape that plays on the idea that money and finance should be democratised, especially by letting ordinary people participate in the opening up of the free flow of finance across and between societies. Financial literacy should not therefore be the prerogative of a small elite but should be open to all so that everyone has the opportunity to learn the basic rudiments of financial management and the skills to make money (Martin 2002: 121–28).

Conclusion

Privatisation of public services leads to lower wages for many employees working in those sectors, not least because trade unions lose their bargaining power with employers. Lower wages, though, implies that people have less money to save for mortgages. As the Office for National Statistics (2013) notes, declining wage growth and rising inflation in the UK has meant that people actually have less savings. Indeed, huge increases in UK house prices have served to push home ownership even further from the reaches of many British citizens. Average house prices England and Wales were for example six times the average gross wage in 2001. Fast forward ten years and average house prices were nine times higher than average wages, with new buyers being hit especially hard by the need to find larger deposits for mortgages.

But shareholder value empowered managers of corporations in another way. 'Downsize and distribute' became the mantra to satisfy financial investors rather than 'retain and reinvest'. In other words, 'top managers downsize the corporations they control, with a particular emphasis on cutting the size of the labour forces they employ, in an attempt to increase the return on equity' (Lazonick and O'Sullivan 2000: 18). Financial restructuring has therefore been as much about restructuring employment relations in the workplace as it has been about generating profits.

This, of course, signifies a qualitative transition in how corporations operate, which, in some respects, can indeed be captured by informational metaphors of 'flows' and 'fluids'. After all, as Froud *et al.* (2002) note, financialisation of corporate practices leads to a speeding up of management practices as they enter daily rapidly-changing financial markets and they negotiate with fund managers who are prepared to undertake mobile transactions. Nevertheless, contradictions are always apparent, lurking behind the rhetoric that proclaims the world is now more mobile and fluid. Neoliberals, for example, start from a position that the marketplace is a sphere in which equal individuals exchange goods so that they can consume them. Individuals are said to interact in the marketplace through perfect information on factors such as the price of goods on offer. However, 'the sole purpose of capitalist production is not the production of things to meet human need, but the constant thirst for profits to maintain the accumulation of capital' (Clarke 2005: 54).

This external pressure on each capital makes it extremely challenging to gain perfect information. In a highly competitive environment where, of necessity, one must accumulate profits for the sake of accumulation, then, as Crouch (2011: 43) notes, information will have a price and this then becomes a major transaction cost. Fully informed opinions about market transactions thus come with a price tag attached to them, ensuring that the wealthier one is the more informed one can be in making economic decisions. Capitalist markets are inevitably structured by inequalities at different levels of abstraction. In this respect, neoliberalism actually increases inequalities in gaining access to information.

It must also be borne in mind that such contradictions and dilemmas also provide fissures and gaps for alternative publics to flourish and develop their own strategies to combat these social problems. In respect to the UK housing market, for example, voluntary groups and housing associations campaigning for an egalitarian ethos in the UK housing market and sector have still managed to retain a voice in the public sphere. Groups from black and ethnic associations in the UK, for example, have been successful in setting up management committees with the aim of identifying and meeting the housing needs for families from ethnic backgrounds. The 'Black and Minority Ethnic Voluntary Housing Movement' (BVHM) has experienced some success in campaigning for greater awareness on the relationship between housing and community identifications. Part of the reason for such success has been its ability to be seen as holders of specialised knowledge on all related issues. As such, many housing governance bodies, such as the Housing Corporation, have included the BVHM in various housing partnership networks (Harrison and Reeve 2002). Moreover, New Labour emphasised the need to foster 'joined-up government' and PPPs in the late 1990s that, in part, helped to establish community-based approaches to housing regeneration along with the principle that egalitarian ideals should be encouraged through community empowerment and activism (Manzi 2007: 262). The next chapter further elaborates on some of these contradictions in public spheres in and around contemporary workplace organisations. In particular, it assesses the extent to which they open up new possibilities for politicised digital publics to grow and flourish in and against neoliberalism.

7 Creative organisational publics

Introduction

As part of the broad-based argument that we have entered an informational, networked era, some also contend that numerous organisations now operate along the lines of decentralised network formations. The archetypal illustration often presented is that of the Japanese 'lean' decentralised motor industry. Castells (2000: 178–79) says that the Japanese model of manufacturing, which emerged during the 1960s, rejected vertical, rational bureaucracies associated with large corporate mass production companies. 'Toyotism', named after Japan's Toyota car manufacturer, replaced these bureaucratic organisational forms. In this decentralised system of working, a company will subcontract out parts of its business to other firms when the need arises in order to respond flexibly to changing consumer tastes and install more efficient chains of production between suppliers and subcontractors. Moreover, the devolved structure of the organisation enables management to diffuse some decision-making powers down to workers and employees. Lash and Urry tell us that this type of organisation engages in 'reflexive accumulation'. What this alludes to is the predominance of information-intensive research and development in production over and above labour-intensive work practices. Like Castells, Lash and Urry say that Japanese firms typically display this pattern. These firms represent 'the totality of Japanese production systems, including teamworking, multifunctionality and collective responsibility' (Lash and Urry 1994: 75), all of which reinforce collective reflexivity in Japanese production.

A number of influential management gurus see this move towards decentralised organisations as representing the most appropriate way for businesses to make large profits in today's high-tech world. In their celebrated business manifesto, *Wikinomics*, Tapscott and Williams, like Castells and Lash and Urry, similarly view knowledge capitalism as opening up new possibilities for decentralised and horizontal firms to prosper. However, they argue that the liberalisation of markets in China have enabled some Chinese companies to take the decentralised Japanese model further. They focus on the Chinese motorcycle industry, which, in recent years, has engaged in a system of 'micro-manufacturing'. This is the idea that a 'truly global firm' is one that 'breaks down national silos, deploys resources and capabilities globally, and harnesses the power of human capital across borders and organizational boundaries' (Tapscott and Williams 2008: 306). Local factors are critical in this respect. Small to medium Chinese motorcycle firms are increasingly realising the possibilities for profit within the complex global world they inhabit. For example, ICTs make it possible for these companies to manufacture a specific product for somebody located in another part of the world as long as the particular design has been uploaded. 'Micromanufacturing' of goods will thus increase along with personalised manufacturing based on local individual consumer tastes.

Tapscott and Williams are also clear that the best way to harness these new global economic forces is to reject organisational centres of power that revolve around hierarchies and instead generate self-organising collaborative processes that might involve 'hundreds of different companies' involved in designing and producing a product. This economic form is based on a modular system of self-sufficient and self-organising local units that come together to pro- duce an emergent product. 'The process relies on the ability of suppliers to quickly test, develop, and retest how well their parts integrate with those of other local suppliers' (Tapscott and Williams 2008: 222). Tapscott and Williams are alluding to the ability of communication networks to link individuals together across time and space in order to make a product. The contemporary work- place is thereby built on a type of reflexive public communication between different employers and employees across geographical localities.

As we also know from previous chapters, some more leftist scholars have taken these basic ideas to suggest that we are in the midst of activism from new radical currents in the world. Autonomist writers in particular tell us that this type of communicative creativity instigates new public spheres in the work- place and between workplaces. Hardt and Negri (2009) are explicit about this point. They say that the 'industrial firm' can no longer centralise production and assimilate industrial workers into its orbit. To a certain extent, managers have now lost their hegemony in a number of organisations. Capital has respon- ded to this modification in organisational relations by extending exploitation across society as a whole. Social cooperation in the industrial firm has thereby given way to 'an increasingly autonomous labour-power and, consequently, a capital that becomes increasingly pure command' (Hardt and Negri 2009: 292). Just as capital extends itself across society in search of profits and to exclude old representatives of labour in the guise of trade unions, so it is the case that labour asserts its own autonomy through productive cooperation and, as it does so through communicative publics, affirms its oppositional identity to capital (Hardt and Negri 2009: 292–93).

From a Marxist viewpoint, however, one can argue that most everyday user activity on digital media networks and on social media sites such as Facebook is associated with unproductive labour. Naturally, this 'free labour' might increase the use-value of particular types of concrete labour. It is fairly simple to appreciate how one person who educates themselves at home about how to operate different types of digital media might prove useful to an employer later on. However, this does not mean that this person produces surplus value. The new knowledge they gain at home is a potential use-value for an employer and it is a different question as to whether this will result in the person becoming productive labour and thus going on to produce surplus value (Carchedi 2011: 224). Carchedi is correct to further observe that the immediate process of production lies on an increasing deskilling of work and a tendency towards crisis, not the progressive accumulation of knowledge skills and global co-operation, which Hardt and Negri seem to suggest is the direction that capitalism is heading towards.

This final substantive chapter explores this issue in more depth by outlining how capitalism operates along a contradictory path in the workplace by sustaining deskilling, Taylorist and lean management techniques as well as equipping workers with new communicative capacities. It shows that the contradictions of neoliberalism are refracted into the contemporary workplace organisations in different opposing ways, ensuring in the process that continuities of old work procedures and transformations into new work regimes are noticeable. These contradictions and the strategic dilemmas they usher in also provide dialogic spaces for workers to creatively generate public spheres in and against some themes of neoliberalism. We start, first, by outlining some common themes made by informational theorists about creative workplaces and digital public spheres. From here, an alternative way to explore these public spheres will start to be mapped out.

Digital public spheres in creative workplaces

For Florida, creativity shuns industrial bureaucratic organisational traits in favour of the belief that economic growth depends on 'good ideas'; or, rather, economic value originates in the creative ideas that people hold (Florida 2002: 36–37). Creative workplace clusters rely on networks forming ties between different groups so that creativity can flow through different networks and aid the 'rapid absorption of new ideas and are thus critical to the creative process' (Florida 2002: 277). A 'hive mind' has greater opportunities to flourish under these circumstances. Activity among different individuals, groups and communities is coordinated through networks across space and time. Sharing information and knowledge among 'nodes' in the network is encouraged, and these also serve to codify protocols of communal coordination. Emergent patterns of behaviour arise from these networks. Digital networks therefore make it possible for users to employ a collaborative communicative logic and draw resources from communities to design and develop content for a digital product that they can use at the same time (Bruns 2008: 19). Value chains are no longer beholden to distinctions between production, distribution and consumption, but are instead built on an 'endless string of users acting incrementally as content producers by gradually extending and improving the information present in the information commons' (Bruns 2008: 21).

An informational 'cultural economy' is thus comprised by the ability of capital to mobilise ordinary everyday life, images, objects and texts into 'simple everyday transactions which facilitate the relations of ruling of capital and mediate complex chains of commodification and communication' (Kemple 2013: 24). Social media provides the typical illustration of these processes, especially since 'users' willingly upload their personal information, tastes, leisure pursuits and so forth, which companies such as Facebook can then harvest and sell on to other companies. This economy is thus best pictured as creating a dynamic between cultural and economic activities, between the situated culture of ordinary users and the economic activities of businesses. Social media companies in particular 'provoke' ordinary users to become active in uploading content on to particular websites, to establish networks of communication with one another, to develop software, to engage in discussion with one another and so on. This in turn prompts social media companies to alter their practices, to engage with users and encourage their activity, in order that their companies gain added value (Potts *et al.* 2008: 271). As such, Potts *et al.* believe that social media offers up truly revolutionary potentials for ordinary people.

> For the first time, it is possible to imagine a 'network of networks' that enables people everywhere to participate not only in self-expression and entertainment, but in new ways of producing knowledge, which itself is scaling up from 'lab and library' situatedness to population-wide distributed networks.
>
> (Potts *et al.* 2008: 472)

Co-creation can therefore be empowering for ordinary people to the extent that they open up a space for ordinary people to have a democratic input into capitalist production. Indeed, they give consumers a voice in the public sphere about capitalist production.

But, as O'Connor (2009: 399) observes, what is more important to note on this subject-matter from a critical perspective is not only the extent to which creative (digital) companies draw on 'free labour' of consumers to co-create an object, but the degree to which these activities are commodified and subject to processes of capitalist valorisation. Certainly, some critical theorists, including some Marxists, claim that capitalists in fact exploit people who engage in co-creation on new media sites insofar that people's 'free labour' on these sites – the time they put into uploading content on them for instance – generates surplus value for capital. Fuchs (2008) makes this claim by insisting that as capitalism grows the organic composition of capital also rises. In other words, constant capital (investments in technology) increases relative to variable capital (investments in living labour). Such underinvestment in living labour is one of the main reasons that capitalists increasingly rely on the input of 'free labour', while the rise in constant capital implies that capitalists are ever more dependent on the intellectual capabilities of machines and technology in order to secure profits. For this reason, he argues that we now live in 'a new capitalist mode of development: informational capitalism/knowledge capitalism' (Fuchs 2008: 175). Accordingly, for Fuchs (2010: 188–89), exploitation currently reaches into all corners of society and includes both paid *and* unpaid labour, such as the 'free labour' of users that create 'common' knowledge on social media sites.

At this point, it is worthwhile to outline why this perspective is misplaced. As we have already noted, Fuchs wants to claim that 'free labour' is at the same time 'productive labour' because in his opinion it produces surplus value (Fuchs 2011: 287). This, however, is a fundamental misconception of what Marx means by both productive capital and productive labour. As we saw in Chapter 4, Marx says that the following circuit comprises productive capital:

$$P \dots C^1 - M^1 - C \ (LP + MP) \dots P.$$

(Marx 1992: 144)

Production starts by a capitalist creating commodities to produce surplus value. To achieve this outcome a capitalist must also purchase labour-power and the means of production. The production of surplus value then transpires, and this allows the capitalist to buy more labour-power and means of production, and so forth. In this formula, therefore, only productive capital and productive labour generates surplus value. It follows that ordinary users who go on social media sites do not create surplus value. Indeed, most of these users do not even directly sell the information content they upload in a marketplace. According to Reveley (2013: 517), this information content is commodified only because social media companies 'hive off that data and then sell it to other capitalist firms for advertising purposes'. Naturally, digital media provides capital with new profitable avenues, but it is equally true to say that 'these phenomena are the social *conditions* for production and *not* immediate *production*' (Carchedi 2011: 234; original emphasis).

We need to be clear about what is being argued here. Certainly, Sayer and Walker (1992: 74) are correct in one respect when they argue that Marxists are mistaken to suggest that indirect labour is not productive. Managerial labour and knowledge labour can also be productive and serve to generate surplus value. Marx, though, also agrees with this point. As well as manual labour, Marx observes that other types of productive labour might include employees who work with their intellectual capacities or as supervisors. For example, he lists being a 'manager', 'engineer' or 'technologist' as included in productive labour if they exist in a particular labour process in which their work directly contributes to the valorisation of capital and generation of surplus value. In other words, productive labour for Marx comprises workers who work both 'with their hands, others with their heads' (Marx 1988: 1040).

Actual productive workplaces therefore often require that a whole variety of labouring occupations be in place to ensure the production of surplus value. Carchedi, for example, discusses a range of services in order to focus on the productive/unproductive divide in a little more detail. He says that whether or not a service counts as productive labour depends on the extent to which its concrete labour is employed by capital to transform existing use-values into new use-values. For example, Carchedi (2011: 190) argues that public utilities, typical examples being the extraction of gas or production of electricity from coal, represent productive labour under a capitalist labour process in the sense they are the objective transformation of use-values and generation of surplus value. After all, these utilities help to reproduce the means of production and generate outputs in the form of money to be reinvested in production. For surplus value to be realised, however, these goods also have to be transported to users. Therefore, transportation is also productive labour in this instance, as is the labour that transmits knowledge about these objects to users, for example somebody sending an email to notify a user about these objects. Social services, as in the labour performed in health care, seeks to preserve the use-value of labour-power, and so is not strictly productive labour. Financial services distribute value and they thus lie in the unproductive sphere, while the army destroys use-value. There are also police powers and other agents of surveillance that prevent the destruction of use-values (Carchedi 2011: 191; see also Duménil and Lévy 2011; Moseley 1988).

Still, the important point to remember is that only productive capital and productive labour *consistently* create surplus value. Those users who go on social media sites are not productive labour in this sense of the term.[1] These observations also underline the further crucial point that a whole host of different types of labour can be noted in a single labour process; some are productive, some are unproductive. Certainly, as Clarke (1988) rightly stresses, we need to place the so-called demise of Fordist industrialism within a class-based context in which the neoliberal state seeks to restrict wages and expenditure within the limits of profitability. He adds, however, that neoliberalism is not an attack on the working class as a whole. Instead, it relies on the fragmentation of the working class by selectively appealing to some working class groups at the expense of others in order to restructure industrial relations and intensify labour. Different types of labour thereby operate under contradictory pressures and within various social contexts. The next section develops these insights by looking at these contradictory processes in the context of workplace digital publics.

Contradictions of creative workplace publics

Frequently, so-called lean production has been seen positively as a means to remove waste in the production process, providing more meaningful work for employees, and by management listening to the voices of workers. At the same time, these workplaces are said to build 'just in time' systems of production based on the idea that a production line receives parts when they are required and no sooner, and workers at one point of the line can instruct workers at another point to produce parts that are required. These techniques along with small batch construction enable management to switch production as required (Bradley *et al.* 2000: 36); but, as has also been noted by others, there are many negative aspects to these particular workplaces. For example, management expects total commitment from their workers and this implies working over a normal eight-hour shift. This in turn is associated with high productivity and performance targets, which again intensify the working environment. As a result, 'the sheer repetitiveness of the fragmented jobs, combined with the intense pace and long working hours, lead to significant health risks, above all cumulative trauma disorders (CTD) or repetitive strain injuries (RST)' (Berggren 1993: 176).

Tomaney (1994) likewise suggests that what informational theorists often identify as new production techniques sometimes actually imply the expansion of labour-intensive practices more attuned with mass development techniques. For example, many knowledge-based organisations simplify tasks, which lead not to high-tech skills but to the fragmentation of routinised practices. Digital technology has also enabled traditional management structures to exert and extend control over the production flow. Workers, therefore, do not gain greater control over their work practices. In fact, the opposite can be the case when digital technologies are introduced in the organisational settings. Many technological changes, for instance, are concerned simply with eradicating waiting time from the production processes. In their study of the Nissan car plant in Sunderland in the north-east of England during the late 1980s and early 1990s, Garrahan and Stewart found that this intensified and competitive working environment pushed many workers to internalise a 'management-by-stress' ethos. Autonomy bequeathed by management brought workers together to solve problems by themselves, while making them directly responsible for any problems thrown up by decisions they made. Garrahan and Stewart observed at the time that this created a rather schizoid mentality among workers. '(T)he individualism and solidarism of the "Nissan Way", refracted as they are through the canons of corporate identity, cannot exclude the consciousness of fear and personal turmoil that extends from the experience of the physical harshness of line work' (Garrahan and Stewart 1992: 118; Stewart 1998: 218).

We should also remember that there is an inherent tendency for capital to develop unevenly. Bradley *et al.* (2000: 38) note that only a handful of large multinational companies have managed to fully implement just in time strategies. Most firms select a few of these strategies and combine them with existing business and organisational approaches. Given this, it therefore should not surprise us that the move towards informational and knowledge-based employment and work practices have themselves been fragmented, contradictory and uneven. Indeed, as Vidal (2011) recognises, what comes after industrialism is less a relatively coherent informational socio-economic paradigm, but more a variety of labour processes and employment relations depending on the different spatial scales – local, regional, and national – one is exploring. For example, a 'new' informational workplace might comprise a number of labour processes, from high-tech sophisticated teamwork to low cost contract work subject to high-level managerial dominance, to multiskilled teamwork but with standardised work routines, to non-standardised routines but with fewer skills required to perform certain tasks (Vidal 2011: 281–82).

Some service occupations still enjoy a relatively robust union presence that ensures respectable employment conditions are maintained, while other new economy workplaces might be characterised by no union representation, which in turn leads to a higher degree of market-based employment relations. If the latter is the case then the new informational economy helps to increase precarious employment in some sectors based on factors such as low, weak or zero union representation in specific workplaces, little control over the labour process, uncertainty on continuing employment, a degree of regulatory protection and a basic income (Clement *et al.* 2010: 58). Knowledge workers consequently experience divergent outcomes in relation to technological change depending on their workplace and locality. In their own study of architects, drafters and engineers located in New Jersey and New York, Aronowitz and DiFazio (2010: 94) discovered these groups of workers experienced different effects of new design technology on their lives. Engineers and drafters in New Jersey faced the prospect of deskilling, while in New York nobody faced deskilling as such although drafters were to be displaced by the new technology.

These contradictory features of the informational economy are refracted into different ways in which work has been transformed in contemporary capitalism. The first point to make in this respect is that an informational economy is clearly related to a rise in service sector work. Different types of service work include that found in hospitality occupations such as bars, hotels and restaurants, while other service work can be found in the social sector and includes occupations such as education, government and health. Other service jobs are found in the producer sector and include insurance, finance and real estate, while the distribution sector includes a raft of other service jobs such as retail trade, transport and communication (Clement *et al.* 2010: 47–49).

The UK provides a particularly stark illustration of the rise of the service sector. Coates (2002) notes that in 1966 about one worker in three was employed in the manufacturing sector. By 1975, about two million people were employed in Britain's nationalised industries while, overall, 7.2 million gained employment in the public sector (Coates 2002: 159). During the 1980s and towards the end of the 1990s, employment in the private sector rose substantially. For example, employment in distribution, hotels and catering increased from 4.4 million to 5.1 million, while that in banking and finance rose from 2.4 million to 3.9 million over these years. From the 1980s, the opposite trend was noticeable in Britain's industrial sector. During the two years between 1980 and 1982, manufacturing employment decreased from 7.4 million to 5.4 million. Moreover, there was continuous underinvestment in the manufacturing base, which rose by just 12.8 percent during the 1980s. Yet, investment in the financial services rose a massive 320.3 percent (Coates 2002: 174). What such figures tell us is that the so-called new informational economy is concentrated in a narrow range of sectors that exclude comprehensive spending in manufacturing divisions. In the US, for example, this narrow base is focused on retail, securities brokerage, wholesaling, semiconductors, computer assembly and telecommunications. During the height of new economy discourse in the early 2000s, however, these sectors accounted for '76 percent of the country's productivity gain, but only for 32 percent of the US GDP' (Martin 2007: 25). Moreover, economic growth in both the US and UK during the early 2000s when the new economy was said to becoming hegemonic was actually no more significant than 1959–73 or 1983–90 (Martin 2007: 26).

In fact, while some informational theorists were heralding the dawn of a new economy in the early 1990s, government studies during the same period were actually telling us the opposite. In 1992, for example, the US Bureau of Labor Statistics estimated that those who worked in typical new economy occupations such as scientists, engineers and technicians only made up about five percent of the total workforce, while high-tech industries accounted for about a quarter of total US employment (Henwood 1995: 167–68). By 2000, the US experienced productivity increases in areas where spending on ICTs was comparatively low. Plastics, motor vehicles, food and drink and tobacco all experienced increases but without exceptional investments in ICTs (Dunn 2009: 237). Besides, while the service economy has seen an increase this is also connected with industrialism. Take the leisure industry. Sure, more occupations are now tied in with leisure activity, but at the same time, leisure pursuits are now more highly commodified and industrialised.

> On the input side, every hobby, sport, or mode of travel has become heavily laden with industrial goods: hiking boots, electronic games, power tools, and the like … On the output side, popular recreations from sports to music have become professionalized and commodified, seized upon as business ventures and raised to sublime heights of money-making … equipped with bundles of industrial goods
>
> (Sayer and Walker 1992: 87).

Perhaps, though, informational theorists are correct to argue that one innovative growth area in the new digital economy is how goods are marketed to us through and 'aesthetic' and 'cultural circuit'. In this circuit, goods are relayed to us through decentred 'immaterial' global flows of 'ideas, images, technologies and capital' (Lash and Urry 1994: 321; see also Thrift 2005). But while informational writers capture much of what is novel about capitalist economies through this viewpoint, it is also true to say that from a critical perspective some of their pronouncements on this matter are unclear. At their most extreme, this 'aesthetic' argument suggests that images and signs now dominate socio-economic relations. Yet, as Ray and Sayer (1999: 8) note, this underplays the point that many important sectors of the global economy such as 'intermediate products like oil, computer chips or bearings' operate without the need to be 'aestheticized' or subject to branding. Furthermore, by suggesting that culture is a 'circuit' there is the added danger that culture is thought to act like tangible economic objects so that culture is transformed into 'exchange values' of a symbolic nature. Problematically, however, this theoretical move not only tends to reduce culture to pseudo-economic categories, but also neglects the point that commodities have always had symbolic value attached to them in some way or another (Fine 2002: 107–8).

It should similarly be borne in mind that simply introducing technology into a workplace does not necessarily increase productivity. Just as important are the social relations and social divisions of labour already established within an organisation that mediate the technology at hand. Obviously, a firm that already utilises particular types of technology will find it easier to employ these to manufacture certain products than a firm that is using this technology for the first time (Sayer 1989). Social relations are also important in relationships between different firms. For example, one key feature of informational economies is the idea that a number of firms can quickly come together to work on a specific product. In reality, however, firms do not all work on an even playing field. Some firms will obviously be bigger and more powerful than other firms. This gives them some advantage to decide whom to join up with for a particular project or with whom to subcontract work out to in and around a specific project. Moreover, given that larger firms tend to carry more weight in interactions between different firms, smaller firms can resent this advantage enjoyed by larger firms. This can then lead to distrust emerging between the parties involved in the subcontract relationship. This is especially the case with respect to large buyers who can pick and choose which supplier they deal with in subcontracting deals (Rainnie 1991: 373).

Government and the state are at the forefront in pushing through these changes. As we have seen in other chapters, the state has been a vital mechanism in opening the way for neoliberal and financial structures and strategies to become embedded in civil society. Similarly, the state takes the lead in encouraging and forcing managers in the public sector to cut costs without affecting service provision. Governments are capable of imposing this agenda on public sector managers in various ways. For instance, public sector managers in the UK have been urged by successive governments to redefine the boundaries between different types of public sector work within the same occupation. Creating more job boundaries around specific sets of skills and grades within the same service strengthens the hand of management to then closely monitor the performance of each grade. 'Within this more pressure is being applied by managers as they seek to claw back terms of conditions and reduce union power at the level of the employer' (Seifert and Mather 2013: 459). There is good reason of course why the state wishes to push through these changes in the public sector. Knowledge-based services, which include insurance and pension funds, real estate, hardware and software consultancy, advertising, architectural design and research and development, have all been given a new lease of life through the privatisation of the public sector. Public sector outsourcing alone is worth billions in the UK (Wood 2006).

None of this is to deny that capitalism has obviously undergone changes. Indeed, those critical and Marxist theorists who explore different areas associated with the capitalist labour process argue that the way in which capitalists view the potential of labour-power to be a source of profit has indeed altered in various ways in our contemporary times. Fundamental capitalist processes associated with the capital-labour relation are of course still with us. Whether or not capital can indeed generate profits from labour-power, the control that managers must assert on their employees through the employment relation, and the resistance that labour develops in and against capital, are all vital characteristics of contemporary labour processes. As Warhurst *et al.* (2009) note, even in creative, service and knowledge-based sectors, work is nevertheless regularly organised around the standardisation of occupational practices. The classic illustration are call centres, in which workers have to learn to deal with a high volume of calls and be subject to rigorous performance targets set by management. Deskilling workers in these offices is not, though, an inevitable consequence of management procedures. Quite the reverse is the case, argue Warhurst *et al.* (2009: 102), because many who work in call centres attend training courses, embody high-level customer service skills and must develop aptitudes and competencies in discretion. Intangible skills such as 'attitude' are thereby just as important in these professions as tangible skills in and around the likes of qualifications. These skills empower workers is various ways, and open up spaces for workers to occupy lines of dissent in the workplace.

The politics of creative workplace publics

As we know from Chapter 4, Deleuze and Guattari argue that flows and networks always operate through historically specific capitalist forms. Therefore, 'staying stratified – organised, signified, subjected – is not the worst that can happen' (Deleuze and Guattari 1988: 176). It is far worse, Deleuze and Guattari continue, if one simply ignores the capitalist form or strata that enfold the conjunction of flows and continuum of intensities of social life. The whole point, then, is to recognise how these flows and intensities are caught up in specific capitalist circuits so that we might find their weak points, discover how they are assembled into specific forms and then try to 'find potential movements of deterritorialization, possible lines of flight' (Deleuze and Guattari 1988: 178).

For Deleuze and Guattari, we therefore need to recognise a social organisation and its forms for what it is, acknowledge our place within it and 'then descend from the strata to the deeper assemblage within which we are held' (Deleuze and Guattari 1988: 178). By comprehending this 'deeper assemblage', we come to realise that flows and intensities are derived from capital capturing surplus value through the exploitation of labour and the forms it assumes. As such, 'labour and surplus labour are strictly the same thing' and are 'the apparatus of capture of activity' in capitalism (Deleuze and Guattari 1988: 488). One must exist in and against capitalist forms by opening up 'new connections, creative and novel becomings that will give one new patterns and triggers of behaviour' (Protevi 2012: 258) so that one can then comprehend how forms of life are mediated through the intensities of labour (cf. Deleuze and Guattari 1988: 182). By recognising this, Deleuze and Guattari (1988: 168) say that it is then possible to strip away the phantasy that ensnares us in the circuits of industrial capital. From a critical perspective, it is thus vital, first, to place the rise of the so-called 'creative class' in its proper capitalist place. By so doing we gain a more comprehensive picture of how even 'creative' people in knowledge-based occupations are subject to alienating capitalist labour processes. From here, we can then see how creative workers can find weak points in their workplace against neoliberal hegemony.

Evidence suggests, in fact, that in the freelance world of creative IT work certain capitalistic pressures exert themselves in the labour process. It is well known that the IT sector has experienced a high degree of causalisation in the last two decades. It is not uncommon for IT workers to be self-employed or to take multiple jobs to make a living wage. Others will often do project work for different companies for a short period to earn money. Overall, then, the reality for many in the IT sector 'is the disintegration of stable careers and discontinuous employment' (Bergvall-Kåreborn and Howcroft 2013: 966). Crowdsourcing provides a concrete illustration of this latter point. Emerging in the public sphere as a name in 2006 from an article written in *Wired* magazine, crowdsourcing aims to draw on the collective acumen of a multitude of people in order to solve a problem. Many small, medium and multinational companies use crowdsourcing as a means to open up their products to IT workers to develop and improve existing products and profit from so doing. While there are obvious benefits for all involved in this particular type of crowdsourcing, it can also be viewed as a means for employers to exploit cheap, flexible and highly skilled IT workers in causal and precarious markets (Holtgrewe 2014: 17; see also Brabham 2012).

Other evidence suggests that those who work in the creative industries also experience the contradictory effects of neoliberal financialised capitalism in a manner that is remarkably similar to many who work in other professions. Creative workers are thus no less susceptible to living precarious working lives than those of 'non-creative' workers. It is now well established that some creative workers are laid off once a particular work project has been completed or when freelancing work becomes more competitive. In these circumstances, gaining a permanent work contract can be difficult. For example, 'creative industry workers in the Paris Region stand less chance of acquiring a permanent contract (60% to the 80% regional average)' (Vivant 2013: 59). Others have to engage in multi-tasking to make themselves more employable, but different skills can take a considerable amount of time to develop properly and indeed take time away from developing creative ideas in the first place. Moreover, the

2008 crisis has taken its toll on some creative sectors. Research indicates that while some employed in creative industries have fared better since 2008 than those employed in non-creative sectors it is also true to say that others working in creative sectors have not managed so well. One study of mid-sized US cities of between 250,000 to 750,000 in population found that those employed in the creative sector were just as likely to experience a decline in their communities as those belonging to non-creative occupations (Donald *et al.* 2013: 15).

Intensification of work practices is also related to financialisation and knowledge-based occupations. Case studies are useful in trying to gain greater insights on these processes. One notable study in this respect is Cushen (2013) and Cushen Thompson's (2012) in-depth six month ethnography conducted in 2007 at 'Avatar Ireland' (an alias), an Irish subsidiary of a publicly listed multinational group called Avatar Group (an alias). A hugely successful organisation, Avatar provides high-tech, knowledge-based and high quality products and services. Cushen and Thompson found that Avatar's management was intent on developing HR practices through 'best practice' normative structures. Much of the dialogue around 'best practice' was embodied in the Avatar brand, known as 'Brand Essence', which was itself based on the sort of 'passionate', 'innovative' and 'reliable' cultural themes. Through Brand Essence employees are supposed to personify a further set of workplace personality traits that included demonstrating a degree of 'empathy' in the workplace along with being the 'best in class, challenging, inspiring' and engaging in 'creativity and optimism' (Cushen and Thompson 2012: 83).

As Cushen (2013) further observes, this brand is embodied in a number of external financial pressures that come to be internalised within Avatar. To begin with, Avatar Group is responsible for the overall financial performance on behalf of financial investors. The Group thus seeks 'to deliver premium price, premium quality, high technology products and services and achieve global economies of scale' (Cushen 2013: 319). To achieve these outputs they endeavour to construct a narrative about the company in order to shape the perceptions of financial markets towards their brand. Operational expenditure (OPEX) is one such narrative and this includes information about ongoing expenses of the business such as salaries, benefits and training. Capital expenditure (CAPEX) includes a narrative about funding new developments and projects in the Group. As Cushen notes, markets often react positively to cuts in OPEX such as layoffs as well as increases in CAPEX. In 2006, however, investors staged a protest at an Avatar Group AGM due to low returns on CAPEX expenditure. The Group's board reacted and, among other things, reduced both CAPEX and OPEX budgets for Avatar Ireland and set them various stringent targets. In particular, 'OPEX reduction targets came largely from Group via benchmarking consultants. Each department in Avatar Ireland was allocated a finance "business partner" who managed the department's progress against budgets' (Cushen 2013: 321). However, managers only ever presented their own carefully constructed of Avatar's workplace through Brand Essence and thereby presented a management-based (or, to use Bakhtin's term, monologic) narrative. Brand Essence did not recognise the dialogic utterances of Avatar's knowledge workers, especially their dialogue about the negative themes contained in the informational genres adopted by Avatar's managers.

Cushen and Thompson soon discovered some of these negative themes when they interviewed actual knowledge workers at Avatar. They found an almost universal rejection of the culture embodied in Essence Brand by the workers as well as criticisms directed towards the financial strategies. While managers tried to rationalise this rejection through further monologic dialogue – some managers claimed that the brand message was not for example being filtered down effectively through various lines of command or that some lower level employees did not have the requisite intelligence to understand the changes – knowledge workers themselves focused in on specific meanings of the brand. They then opened these up to their own subversive heteroglossic dialogue (on the meaning of 'heteroglossia', see Chapter 4). In one important respect, they connected such dialogue up to some of the contradictions evident in a wider neoliberal restructuring of work practices. The highly skilled knowledge workers did not reject the capitalist profit motive as such, but they expressed anger towards the monologic narrative embedded in Brand Essence, which they felt took no realistic account of external financial constraints Avatar was under to provide shareholder value. Some employees felt that Brand Essence was in fact an attack on their professional identity as skilled knowledge workers. As an engineer observed:

> For professionals like me or relatively intelligent people it really is insulting ... [...] ... massively negative, it's like 'where's my school uniform?' when I'm getting up in the morning. I'm a professional, I've been to college and I've qualified and there's people even more qualified than me and they're suffering this.
>
> (cited in Cushen and Thompson 2012: 87)

Workers thus connected the monologic utterances embodied in Brand Essence with broader external changes to the working environment. Some knowledge workers recognised, for instance, that the external financial constraints on the company brought with it an insecure working environment, which again contradicted the positive monologic cultural rhetoric being articulated by management. Another engineer observed:

> It's very hard to swallow, extremely hard, they're telling you one day how important you are to them and the next day they're making more redundant ... [...] ... It's just hypocrisy after hypocrisy; they don't eat their own dog food basically.
>
> (cited in Cushen and Thompson 2012: 88)

The heteroglossic utterance, 'it's just hypocrisy after hypocrisy', testifies to the conflict at the heart of the employment contract in this organisation and the micro-politics of how exploitative practices occur therein. Other knowledge workers recognised that cost cutting and targets were part of a wider strategy of improving the share price of Avatar Ireland.

While specific contradictions came to be embodied in knowledge-based work practices at Avatar, these were not merely fortuitous but refracted broader contradictions evident in the creator sector itself. Indeed, these contradictions are also reproduced in community publics as well. To begin to understand this point, it is important to appreciate that far from dismissing inequalities in contemporary societies, those who espouse the virtues of the creative class also recognise some of its vices. Social inequality is acknowledged by Florida as being a drain on circulating the merits of creativity across American society. He derides the increasing social divides and widening income gaps in America between the creative class and working and service classes. Divisions along the lines of social class 'will eventually limit our long-run economic growth and development' and reinforce 'a monstrous waste of human capabilities' (Florida 2002: 321). It is thus incumbent upon the creative class to show a way forward, to 'offer those in the other classes a tangible vision of ways to improve their own positions, either by becoming part of the Creative Economy or by coexisting with it' (Florida 2002: 321). Even so, there is a truism to Peck's complaint that for all of his cries against increasing social divisions Florida's own 'vision' is mediated through a neoliberal prism. According to Florida, for example, creative class values include 'individuality' and not conforming to 'organizational or institutional directives', 'meritocracy' based purely on 'abilities and efforts', and 'diversity and openness' founded on the idea that people from different social backgrounds will be welcome in a creative environment and learn from one another (Florida 2002: 77–79). All of these values, however, can quite easily be seen as being key neoliberal qualities, especially since they favour assets associated with self-interest rather than qualities associated with the likes of structurally inscribed class constraints.

For Peck, Florida's diagnosis for society is consequently one that nurtures and rewards creativity rather than one that compensates the 'creative have-nots' (Peck 2010: 217). For example, Florida argues that cities need to pre-empt creativity by investing in potentials for new thriving creative spaces in urban spaces. Problematically, though, such investments are in reality often aligned with processes of gentrification and groups of middle-class gentrifiers, 'whose *lack* of commitment to place and whose weak community ties is perversely celebrated' (Peck 2010: 219; original emphasis). Normal indicators of robust investment in building, redeveloping and sustaining community capacity through the likes of job creation are put aside under these circumstances and energy is instead devoted to preempting the changing creative tastes of the creative class. Talk about fostering a creative class and creative jobs in particular cities is thus directed by somewhat universal liberal notions that target a particular privileged audience at the expense of a diverse mixed population in specific cities (Pratt 2011: 127).

Even experts that show a degree of sympathy towards those from working class areas can nevertheless be caught up in the contradictions of neoliberalism. City planners, for example, will endeavour to overcome alienating effects of cities on particular groups of residents by thinking about how changes to city landscapes might redistribute power and resources more evenly across class boundaries. At the same time, planners see their remit as simply posing technical questions around land use decisions. Under this guise, planners become caught up in ideological programmes associated with the likes of creativity and articulate this ideology to distinctive communities (Eisenschitz 2008: 134). Gentrification becomes an unavoidable element of this class-based politics, especially if it intentionally or unintentionally serves to displace working class members from a locality so that middle class residents can then occupy those spaces (Slater 2008: 212–13).

Conclusion

Neoliberals seek to depoliticise democracy in the realm of the economy, believing instead that economic markets guarantee social rights by themselves without the need for the state. They thus attempt to take many economic decision-making powers away from the state and give them instead to non-state regulatory bodies at a global level such as the IMF and World Bank, or grant such powers to local and regional non-state organisations such as public–private partnerships and quangos. These institutions are then thought to revive the democratic capabilities inherent in civil society. But the belief in the sanctity of markets contradicts the reality of how depoliticised markets increase global and local poverty through uneven development. Free markets certainly grow and prosper but without real democratic input from ordinary people. 'As such, the promotion of a development agenda focused solely on market-friendly reforms will not promote the goal of free market democracy. What current reform suggestions are likely to achieve is the unintended consequence of markets without democracy' (Glinavos 2008: 1097). Furthermore, those with economic power in society will use their wealth to influence political decision-making. Neoliberalism thus opens new ways for 'free markets' to become embroiled in politics and vice versa (Bonefeld 2012; Crouch 2011).

This dialectic of politicisation and depoliticisation is refracted into the contemporary knowledge-based workplace. To understand this it is important, first, to remember that workers can gain some satisfaction from their 'creative' working conditions. Many workers manage to carve out a space of work autonomy from management through which they can then maintain their own beliefs about work quality (see also Vidal 2007). In one respect, however, this is where the contradiction of knowledge work presents itself in one of its starkest forms and generates some of the most intense critical dialogue among employees. Cushen and Thompson discovered, for example, that trying to balance negative effects of management narratives with a sense of work autonomy and quality built up tensions at Avatar Ireland. As a result, one knowledge worker stated: 'I really like the work ... [but] ... I can't stop thinking about how negative I feel about certain things in work ... I am looking for a new job in January that's how bad this company is' (cited in Cushen and Thompson 2012: 88). For this employee, then, a way to overcome the contradictions experienced was to withdraw from the organisation itself.

Specific contradictions embedded in socio-economic relations are thus refracted in unique ways into knowledge-based public spheres at work. As the chapter has shown, sometimes these contradictions help to create dialogic events that then go on to politicise knowledge workers. Mulholland's qualitative study of a call centre in Ireland called PhoneCo (alias), which employed 300 workers, is a case in point. Mulholland (2004) found that telesales workers were adept at forming networks of dissent with one another against certain management narratives. Notably, management was intent on ensuring that telesales workers kept to a pre-established sales 'script' when interacting with customers on the phone. Any attempt to go off the 'script', for example by adding one's own personality and style into sales speak, was punishable through fines. Moreover, the 'script' was embedded in a specific type of intensification at PhoneCo. Each telesales worker was told to make a call every four to five minutes with the expectation that 80 percent would be transformed into sales. Technology empowered management to monitor the performance of telesales workers and thus subject them to these sales targets (Mulholland 2004: 714).

Some telesales workers, however, expressed degrees of hostility towards the wage structure at PhoneCo, with particular anger and resentment directed at management's failed promise to provide higher wage rates. This was transformed into a politicised sense of injustice and unfairness that, moreover, encouraged some workers to establish a sense of solidarity between one another. For example, workers would not tell management if other workers had falsely claimed to make a sale. Indeed, workers developed their own utterance to describe this practice of 'cheating' at sales, which they termed *slammin'*. One worker justified *slammin'* by arguing that it offered up some form of opposition to the perceived workplace mantra of 'flogging myself for nothing' (cited in Mulholland 2004: 714). Like Cushen and Thompson along with numerous similar case studies, then, Mulholland manages to capture a more complex picture of knowledge-based work. She shows how such work harbours informal collective modes and types of dissent and resistance to management prerogatives. These words created different cultural themes at PhoneCo to those envisaged by management. Specific utterances helped to produce in a small but significant way cultural moments of dissent and opposition. More broadly, these studies demonstrate that discursive and semiotic hegemony is both contradictory and never completely stable. This relatively simple point takes us back to where the book started, which is back to cultural political economy and the contested nature of its hegemonic potential. The next chapter makes some final brief observations about this theme.

Note

1 Similarly, as Ruccio (2003) explains, a multinational corporation might subcontract out some of its production processes to a developing country – the so-called 'sweatshop production' phenomenon of contemporary globalisation. But if the multinational in question does not directly appropriate surplus value from the local firm in the developing country, then the multinational cannot be accused of exploiting the local firm. 'The fact that the purchaser is a capitalist enterprise does not, in and of itself, tell us the class character of the production that takes place on the other end' (Ruccio 2003: 88).

8 Conclusion

Contradictions of cultural political economy

Neoliberals argue that the marketplace is a sphere in which equal individuals exchange goods with one another through perfect information on issues such as the price of goods on offer. Far from this neoliberal utopia, the reality is noticeably different. In real markets, perfect information is hard to come by, not least because capitalism is necessarily structured by various inequalities at various levels of abstraction. Under such conditions, as Crouch (2011: 43) notes, information will inevitably have a price attached to it, especially since those who gain a monopoly on resources will aim to increase their revenue and profit from them. Information therefore becomes a major transaction cost. Fully informed opinions about market transactions come with a price tag attached to them, ensuring that the wealthier one is the more informed one can be in making economic decisions. Neoliberalism thus increases inequalities in and around sources of information, rather than reducing them.

In this final chapter, we will extend and develop some of these insights to make some concluding observations about cultural political economy. In particular, it will be suggested that a cultural political economy approach must always ensure that it relates the ideological discourses of society to the actual contradictory reality of how capitalism operates as a system. After all, the crisis-tendencies of capitalism means that capital is reproduced through uneven socio-economic development at national, regional and global levels. In our financialised age, these contradictions are not contingent outcomes but are part of the fabric of the neoliberal state project. As Harvey (2005: 70–71) observes, the neoliberal state contains systematic biases within its very foundations. It must create, first, a 'good' business investment climate for capitalists and it does this by treating labour and the environment as mere commodities. At the same time, and second, the neoliberal state favours financial systems and financial institutions over and above institutions promoting welfare and social democracy. But how does this viewpoint help us to better understand the usefulness of a cultural political economy perspective? We now turn to this question.

Neoliberalism, finance and knowledge-based economies

Some argue that critical theories of neoliberalism establish ideal-typical models, which fail to take account of the complexities of societies. Wacquant

(2012) in particular finds fault with what he considers to be some one-sided views of neoliberalism. He says that Marxists regard neoliberalism as a strictly economic macro project, while Foucauldians regard neoliberalism as a concrete social project comprised by a 'conglomeration of calculative notions, strategies and technologies aimed at fashioning populations and people' (Wacquant 2012: 69; see also Barnett *et al.* 2008). Unlike these two approaches, Wacquant prefers to view neoliberalism as a state project that includes fiscal constraints on welfare policy alongside an increase in penal policies aiming to curb disorders generated by welfare reform. In a reply to Wacquent, Jessop (2012) also reminds us that neoliberalism has assumed different guises during specific periods in time and in specific countries. Hence, neoliberalism has not remained an unchanging and static phenomenon as is perhaps suggested by Wacquant's definition.

In a thought-provoking article, however, Thompson and Harley (2012) criticise Jessop's contribution to debates around neoliberalism and cultural political economy. They begin their argument by suggesting that two prominent discourses have been deployed to explain recent transformations in the global economy. The first is labelled as a knowledge-based economy (KBE) discourse and is believed to have emerged in the early 1990s. In this discourse, capital is said to no longer play a decisive role in economic transactions. Information instead assumes this function especially in respect to 'high value-added activities, specialized knowledge and services' (Thompson and Harley 2012: 1370). Thompson and Harley claim that a variety of academics became ensnared in this discourse, and not just the usual suspects such as Castells. Thompson and Harley also contend that critical and Marxist scholars such as Jessop similarly fell for the allure of the KBE discourse. According to Thompson and Harley, however, KBE discourse was mostly just that, namely a discourse with little actual material support and evidence for its main assertions even if many academics support it. Thompson and Harley do, however, find that another discourse contains a more convincing explanation of recent changes in the global economy. A shareholder value (SV) discourse arose in the US during the 1970s and was primarily based around a struggle between managers and investors for the control of companies. Soon a dominant discourse took hold across capitalist economies that stated that firms should be judged on value delivered to shareholders. This discourse was in turn supported by a move towards neoliberal policies and the marketisation of society (Thompson and Harley 2012: 1372).

For Thompson and Harley, SV discourse makes better sense of changes in the global economy because it has has has more significant material effects on society than the KBE discourse. Most notably, they suggest that the KBE discourse failed to register real underlying transformations that have occurred to the global economy, particularly those changes associated with the financialisation of economic transactions. Highly risky financial mechanisms such as collateralised debt obligations existed under the surface of normal financial practices to such an extent that many of those working in the banking sector knew nothing of their toxic nature until the 2008 financial crisis. Those academics such as Jessop who employed the KBE discourse likewise overlooked the importance of these processes until the 2008 crisis erupted. Certainly, Thompson and Harley are aware that KBE discourse has had some real effects in society, particularly around supply-side policies and in knowledge intensive sectors such as the biotechnology and pharmaceutical industry. Yet, SV perspectives provide a more powerful and constraining discourse for them because ultimately it represents 'a major constraint on innovative enterprise, draining companies of the necessary financial and human resources' (Thompson and Harley 2012: 1376).

To what extent, however, is it correct that somebody like Jessop can be readily assimilated to the KBE discourse? In my opinion, Thompson is too harsh to argue that Jessop is some sort of organic intellectual for the KBE discourse. In fact, Jessop carefully relates the *discourse* about KBE to the underlying *contradictory reality* that underpins this discourse. In this respect, Jessop's observations are quite different to the arguments advanced by other leading theorists of KBE discourse such as those of Castells. To expand on this point in more detail the next section firstly sets out some criticisms of cultural political economy perspective that is similar to Jessop's approach in order to say why these criticisms are misplaced.

Cultural political economy, contradictions and discourse

Some Marxist critics note that those who pursue a cultural political economy approach often do so by incorporating a discourse analysis that draws too heavily on abstract linguistic analytical conventions. These linguistic approaches therefore invariably lack a contextual and historical perspective. It is within this critical framework that Jones and Collins (2006) admonish Fairclough's attempt to employ a cultural political economy analysis to examine the language of neoliberalism. Fairclough's work is interesting to the extent that he has written on these issues with Jessop (see for example Fairclough, Jessop and Sayer 2004). Nevertheless, Jones and Collins believe that Fairclough's excursions through neoliberal ideology are made primarily at a textual level in which he endeavours to apply, albeit critically, abstract linguistic analysis to assess the speeches and texts of neoliberal ideologues. In practice, this means that neoliberalism is examined as being comprised of lexical and grammatical properties of sentences and texts that have a similar identity in terms of words, phrases and texts. In other words, neoliberalism for Fairclough can be read as a relatively coherent and stable linguistic discourse that can nevertheless be subject to critical scrutiny through functional linguistics.

An illustration of Fairclough's application of critical discourse analysis can be found in a piece he co-wrote with Eve Chiapello. They build on Chiapello's earlier work with Luc Boltanski. As Chapter 3 noted, in *The New Spirit of Capitalism* Boltanski and Chiapello (2003) observe that since the 1990s a 'network' discourse has grown in importance for social analysis that gains justification by its close allegiance to another discourse, termed as the 'projective city'. Highlighting the benefits for different individuals to temporarily come together to complete a specific project, this latter discourse emphasises a degree of mobility that individuals must possess in order to slide in and out of networks around the project in question (Boltanski and Chiapello 2003: 134). With Chiapello, Fairclough (2010) develops these insights by amalgamating them with critical discourse analysis. An example they examine is a management guru text that proclaims we are living in new network times. This text contains lexico-grammatical features that make categorical assertions on readers to be 'creative', 'innovative' and 'smart'. These are 'normal' and 'normative' claims typically associated with those management gurus texts that insist that only creative, innovative and smart people can succeed in new knowledge-based societies. Discursively, the management text therefore implores readers to embody these traits by becoming flexible and adaptable, open to the flux of life and open to discovering new projects with liked-minded individuals in distinctive communities (see Chiapello and Fairclough in Fairclough 2010). As a result, the discursive claims made in the text can be situated in a wider network discourse identified by Boltanski and Chiapello.

Yet for Jones and Collins, it is exactly this emphasis on the relatively coherent nature of discourse, as expressed in specific texts, that becomes a burdensome weight around the neck of critical discourse analysis. They claim that all critical discourse analysis is really doing in these sorts of linguistic endeavours is describing grammatical properties of texts and then reading one's own political bias into this description. What is missing in this analysis is an engagement with real contradictory processes outside of a text, which leaves its traces in the text being explored and vice versa. That is to say, Jones and Collins insist that language and a text are always responses to wider social and political events that play themselves out at different levels of abstraction. As they observe:

> (S)uch an analysis presupposes the requisite theoretical understanding of the relevant phenomena – surplus value, the capital-labour relation, the capitalist state, and not least, social democracy (in a country) – but exactly how the bodies of theory we may draw on to relate to newly unfolding events or conjunctures is an open question which requires difficult intellectual labour in the course of which the theories themselves may be revised or modified.
>
> (Jones and Collins 2006: 37)

Those who work within a critical cultural political economy analysis are said to bracket these contradictory properties of capitalism in their respective analyses in favour of exploring discourse as relatively coherent and stable discourses. For example, one can make the argument that Boltanski and Chiapello remain wedded to the idea that, generally speaking, dominant discourses can absorb critiques outlined by other groups in society. This is because critiques are usually too fragmented to be convincing to ordinary people. For instance, one critique of neoliberal visions of networks suggests that capitalism actually stifles creativity and freedom, while another critique believes that capitalism promotes a destructive selfish self-interest among individuals (Boltanski and Chiapello 2003: 42). But, continue Boltanski and Chiapello, because these critiques remain separate from one another they fail to reach their full critical potential and, thus, remain unconvincing to ordinary people. From a Marxist viewpoint, however, Boltanski and Chiapello's observations could be seen to problematically emphasise the consistency of a discursive framework at the expense of the inherent contradictory nature of how discourses actually operate. Indeed, such is the coherent and consistent potency of these discourses that they are seen to pave over contradictions in the 'real' world in order to represent the world as just plain common sense. On balance, Boltanski and Chiapello argue that critiques open themselves up to being ideologically 'neutralised' by the spirit of capitalism, to being 'codified' by the spirit's discourses, so that while the practical dimension of critique might still be in play, its ideological dimension is effectively disarmed (Boltanski and Chiapello 2003: 41).

Still, it also needs to be said that most of those who work within a cultural political economy perspective do not merely believe that people are ideological dupes who slavishly follow semiotic discourses. Boltanski and Chiapello also skilfully show how some discourses justify capitalism by helping to establish and maintain distinctive 'spirits' that reconcile people's practical experience of exploitation and inequality with a means to gain their consent to these in capitalism. In this respect, each spirit sets out 'not only advantages which participation in capitalist processes might afford on an individual basis, but also the collective benefits, defined in terms of the common good, which it contributes to producing for everyone' (Boltanski and Chiapello 2003: 8). Boltanski and Chiapello are equally clear in their judgement that these discourses are not simply accepted by ordinary people. Indeed, they realise that at the level of real practice located in concrete historical contexts people are often 'not content with a given social condition, and think that human beings must seek to improve the society they live in' (Boltanski and Chiapello 2003: 41). For Boltanski and Chiapello, ordinary people are endowed with critical capacities and faculties that enable them to question and criticise prevailing ideological justifications of capitalism. It is in part for this reason that those in control try to gain hegemony over those they seek to govern. In particular, capitalism must offer people explanations as to why they should accept their lot under capitalism; one way this occurs is when a discourse outlines how it encapsulates a type of justice, fairness and common good for all.

Jessop makes similar observations. He maintains that discourses are integrally bound to specific contradictions, ensuring that discourses in and around knowledge-based narratives are themselves contradictory. Elsewhere, Jessop (2000) claims that not only is knowledge a fundamental contradictory property of the most abstract mechanisms of capitalism (e.g. the separation of intellectual from manual labour characteristic of an economy based on wage-labour), but that these mechanisms have assumed new contradictory forms in our contemporary age. Digital technology is a case in point, which creates a contradiction between common knowledge that is freely shared through ICTs against corporations seeking to enclose knowledge by strengthening their intellectual property rights over ICTs. As we know from other chapters, organisations are encouraged these days to draw on extra-economic resources such as communities of learning, social capital and trust in order to maintain a high skilled economy. Yet, as Jessop notes, the neoliberal marketisation of society pushes companies in the opposite direction of engaging in short-term speculative activity that rejects the sharing of knowledge (Jessop 2000: 65–70). Given these materialist concerns to highlight the underlying contradictory structures of the current capitalist formation, it seems hardly fair of Thompson and Harley to place Jessop together with non-realist thinkers of the KBE discourse. It is more reasonable to acknowledge that Jessop's work reaches quite different materialist conclusions to those presented by the likes of Castells and Lash and Urry.

One of the aims of this book has been to contribute towards a Marxist cultural political perspective in respect to digital publics. To this end, the book has incorporated insights from both labour process theorists such as Thompson and Harley and other Marxist perspectives, such as that provided by Jessop. In addition, this book has employed theoretical insights from the likes of Bakhtin, Deleuze and Guattari and Gramsci. These figures all suggest that hegemonic discourses are rarely, if ever, self-enclosed entities. Instead, a discourse will exist in a dialogic relationship with other discourses because they live and breathe in real social relations marked by historically specific contradictions. Discourses always internalise real contradictions and their associated dilemmas, themes and utterances, and it is these social mediations that in turn make discourses contradictory, unstable and open to interpretation through other discourses (see also Boje 2008).

Discourses are therefore not self-contained entities, but rather subsist in part through other discourses and through other extra-discursive realities. To think otherwise is to stray close to what Bakhtin (1981) has argued is a monologic reading of discourse. Under a monologic perspective, discourse is said to be comprised by relatively stable combinations of meanings that subsist through codes, signs and words, which can then be transferred from one context to another without loss of meaning. Active interpretations of discourse based on how language refracts the messiness of real life is thus replaced in a monologic perspective by a passive understanding of ideal-typical language forms (see also Linell 2009: 36).

This book has rejected a monologic approach in favour of a dialogic one. Rather than two discourses – the KBE and SV discourses – existing as distinct competing entities, it is therefore probably truer to say that many of those who insisted we had arrived at a networked information society were at the same time suggesting that global finance was an integral part of this transition. In fact, even academic theorists (e.g. Castells 2000: 102–6; Lash and Urry 1994: 285–92) and business and management theorists (e.g. Drucker 1971: 108–15; Ohmae 1994: 137–71) have argued that transformations in global finance have been part of a move towards a networked information society and knowledge-based economy. In other words, they have placed both KBE and SV discourses in a dialogue with one another even if this has been achieved through a monologic framework. They can then selectively take certain themes from both to construct particular narratives about the global economy. In making these critical points, this book has sought to bring to the fore the dialogic nature of these discourses by situating them more readily in the ongoing contradictions of contemporary capitalism as well as pointing to gaps in these processes and practices for an ongoing politics of dissent to emerge in and against neoliberal ideology.

Bibliography

Albritton, R. (2007) *Economics Transformed*, London: Pluto.

Anderson, K.M., Henriksen, H.Z., Medaglia, R., Danziger, J.N., Sannarnes, M.K. and Enemaerke, M. (2010) 'Fads and Facts of E-Government: A Review of Impacts of E-Government (2003–9)', *International Journal of Public Administration* 33(11): 564–79.

Anthony, P. (1994) *Managing Culture*, Milton Keynes: Open University Press.

Aronowitz, S. and DiFazio, W. (2010) *The Jobless Future*, second edition, Minneapolis: University of Minnesota Press.

Arvidsson, A. (2013) 'The Potential of Consumer Publics', *ephemera* 13(2): 367–91.

Arvidsson, A. and Colleoni, E. (2012) 'Value in Informational Capitalism and on the Internet', *The Information Society* 28(3): 135–50.

Bakhtin, M. (1981) *The Dialogic Imagination*, trans. by C. Emerson and M. Holquist, Austin: University of Texas Press.

——(1984) *Problems of Dostoevsky's Poetics*, trans. by C. Emerson and M. Holquist, Austin: University of Texas Press.

Bakhtin, M.M. and P.N. Medvedev (1991) *The Formal Method in Literary Scholarship*, trans. by A. J. Wehrle, Baltimore: John Hopkins University Press.

Ball, P. (2004) *Critical Mass*, London: Arrow Books.

Barnes, B. (1995) *The Elements of Social Theory*, London: UCL Press.

Barnett, C., Clarke, N., Cloke, P. and Malpass, A. (2008) 'The Elusive Subjects of Neo-Liberalism: Beyond the Analytics of Governmentality', *Cultural Studies* 22(5): 624–53.

Baudrillard, J. (1993) *Symbolic Exchange and Death*, trans. I.H. Grant, London: Sage.

Bauman, Z. (2000) *Liquid Modernity*, Cambridge: Polity.

Beck, U. (1992) *Risk Society*, London: Sage.

Bell, D. (1999) *The Coming of Post-Industrial Society*, New York: Basic Books.

Berardi, F. (2009) *The Soul at Work*, trans. F. Cadel and G. Mecchia, Los Angeles: Semiotext(e).

Berggren, C. (1993) 'Lean Production – The End of History?' *Work, Employment and Society* 7(2): 163–88.

Bergvall-Kåreborn, B. and Howcroft, D. (2013) '"The Future's Bright, the Future's Mobile": A Study of Apple and Google Mobile Application Developers', *Work, Employment and Society* 27(6): 964–81.

Berry, M. (2013) 'The "Today" Programme and the Banking Crisis', *Journalism* 14(2): 253–70.

Bhaskar, R. (1993) *Dialectic: The Pulse of Freedom*, London: Verso.

Blackburn, R. (2008) 'The Subprime Crisis', *New Left Review* 50(March–April): 63–106.

Boje, D.M. (2008) *Storytelling Organizations*, London: Sage.

Boltanski, L. and Chiapello, E. (2003) *The New Spirit of Capitalism*, London: Verso.

Boltanski, L. and Thévenot, L. (2006) *On Justification*, trans. C. Porter, Princeton: Princeton University Press.

Bonefeld, W. (2009) 'Emancipatory Praxis and Conceptuality in Adorno' in J. Holloway, F. Matamoros and S. Tischler (eds) *Negativity and Revolution*, London: Pluto: 122–47.

Bonefeld, W. (2012) 'Freedom and the Strong State: On German Ordoliberalism', *New Political Economy* 17(5): 633–56.

Bogue, R. (2003) *Deleuze on Literature*, London: Routledge.

Boreham, P., Parker, R., Thompson, P. and Hall, R. (2008) *New Technology @ Work*, London: Routledge.

Bowring, F. (2004) 'From the Mass Worker to the Multitude: A Theoretical Contextualisation of Hardt and Negri's *Empire*', *Capital and Class* 83(Summer): 101–32.

Brabham, D.C. (2012) 'The Myth of Amateur Crowds: A Critical Discourse Analysis of Crowdsourcing Coverage', *Information, Communication and Society* 15(3): 394–410.

Bracking, S. (2009) *Money and Power*, London: Pluto.

Bradley, H., Erickson, M., Stephenson, C. and Williams, S. (2000) *Myths at Work*, Cambridge: Polity.

Bristow, G. (2010) 'Resilient Regions: Re-'place'ing Regional Competitiveness', *Cambridge Journal of Regions, Economy and Society* 3(1): 153–67.

Bruns, A. (2008) *Blogs, Wikipedia, Second Life and Beyond*, New York: Peter Lang.

Bryan, R., Martin, R., Montgomerie, J. and Williams, K. (2012) 'An Important Failure: Knowledge Limits and the Financial Crisis', *Economy and Society* 41(3): 299–315.

Bruff, I. (2014) 'The Rise of Authoritarian Neoliberalism', *Rethinking Marxism* 26(1): 113-129.

Buchanan, M. (2002) *Nexus*, London: W.W. Norton and Co.

Burnham, P. (2002) 'Class Struggle, States and Global Circuits of Capital' in M. Rupert and H. Smith (eds) *Historical Materialism and Globalization*, London: Routledge: 113–28.

Burnham, P. (2006) 'Marxism, the State and British Politics', *British Politics* 1: 67–83.

Burton-Jones, A. (1999) *Knowledge Capitalism*, Oxford: Oxford University Press.

Butler, J., Laclau, E. and Žižek, S. (2000) *Contingency, Hegemony, Universality*, London: Verso.

Büscher, M. and Urry, J. (2009) 'Mobile Methods and the Empirical', *European Journal of Social Theory* 12(1): 99–116.

Byrne. D. (1998) *Complexity Theory and the Social Sciences*, London: Routledge.

Çalişkan, K. and Callon, M. (2010) 'Economization, Part 2: A Research Programme for the Study of Markets', *Economy and Society* 39(1): 1–32.

Callinicos, A. (1985) 'Anthony Giddens: A Contemporary Critique', *Theory and Society* 14(2): 133–66.

Callon, M. (2007) 'An Essay on the Growing Contribution of Economic Markets to the Proliferation of the Social', *Theory, Culture and Society* 24(7–8): 139–63.

Callon, M., Méadel, C. and Rabeharisoa, V. (2005) 'The Economy of Qualities' in A. Barry and D. Slater (eds) *The Technological Economy*, London: Routledge: 28–50.

Capra, F. (1996) *The Web of Life*, New York: Anchor Books.

Capra, F. (2002) *The Hidden Connections*, London: HarperCollins.

Carchedi, G. (2011) *Behind the Crisis*, Leiden: Brill.

Castells, M. (2000) *The Rise of the Network Society*, second edition, Oxford: Blackwell.

Castells, M. (2010) *Communication Power*, Oxford: Oxford University Press.

Castells, M. (2011) 'The Crisis of Global Capitalism: Towards a New Economic Culture?' in C. Calhoun and G. Derluguian (eds) *The Roots of the Global Financial Meltdown*, New York: New York University Press: 185–210.

Castells, M., Caraça, J. and Cardoso, G. (2012) 'The Cultures of the Economic Crisis: An Introduction' in M. Castells, J. Caraça and G. Cardoso (eds) *Aftermath: The Cultures of the Economic Crisis*, Oxford: Oxford University Press: 1–14.

Chadwick, A. (2009) 'Web 2.0: New Challenges for the Study of E-Democracy in an Era of Informational Exuberance', *I/S: A Journal of Law and Policy for the Information Society* 5(1): 11–41.

Charles, A. (2012) *Interactivity*, Oxford: Peter Lang.

Cilliers, P. (1998) *Complexity and Postmodernism*, London: Routledge.

Clarke, S. (1988) *Keynesianism, Monetarism and the Crisis of the State*, Aldershot and Gower, Vermont: Edward Elgar.

Clarke, S. (1990–91) 'The Marxist Theory of Crisis', *Science and Society* 54(4): 442–67.

Clarke, S. (1991) *Marx, Marginalism and Modern Sociology*, London: Macmillan.

Clarke, S. (2005) 'The Neoliberal Theory of Society' in A. Saad-Filho and D. Johnston (eds) *Neoliberalism: A Critical Reader*, London: Pluto: 50–59.

Clarke, J. (2010) 'After Neo-Liberalism? Markets, State and the Reinvention of Public Welfare', *Cultural Studies* 24(3): 375–94.

Cleaver, H. (1979) *Reading* Capital *Politically*, Brighton: Sussex.

Clement, W., Mathieu, S., Prus, S. and Uckardesler, E. (2010) 'Restructuring Work and Labour Markets in the New Economy' in N.J. Pupo and M.P. Thomas (eds) *Interrogating the New Economy*, Toronto: University of Toronto Press: 43–64.

Coates, D. (2002) 'The New Political Economy of Postwar Britain' in C. Hay (ed.) *British Politics Today*, Cambridge: Polity: 157–84.

Coleman, S. (2004) 'Connecting Parliament to the Public via the Internet: Two Case Studies of Online Consultations', *Information, Communication and Society* 7(1): 1–22.

Collins, D. (2000) *Management Fads and Buzzwords*, London: Routledge.

Comor, E.A. (2008) *Consumption and the Globalization Project*, London: Routledge.

Crouch, C. (2011) *The Strange Non-Death of Neoliberalism*, Cambridge: Polity.

Cumbers, A. (2012) *Reclaiming Public Ownership*, London: Zed.

Cushen, J. (2013) 'Financialization in the Workplace: Hegemonic Narratives, Performative Interventions and the Angry Knowledge Worker', *Accounting Organisations and Society* 38(4): 314–31.

Cushen, J. and Thompson, P. (2012) 'Doing the Right Thing? HRM and the Angry Knowledge Worker', *New Technology, Work and Employment* 27(2): 79–92.

Dahlgren, P. (2009) *Media and Political Engagement*, Cambridge: Cambridge University Press.

Das, S. (2010) *Traders, Guns and Money*, revised edition, London: Financial Times Prentice Hall.

Davis, S. and Meyer, C. (1998) *Blur: The Speed of Change in the Connected Economy*, New York: Warner Books.

Dienst, R. (2011) *The Bonds of Debt*, London: Verso.

De Angelis, M. (2004) 'Separating the Doing and the Deed: Capital and the Continuous Character of Enclosures', *Historical Materialism* 12(2): 57–87.

Dean, J. (2005) 'Communicative Capitalism: Circulation and the Foreclosure of Politics', *Cultural Politics* 1(1): 51–74.

DeLanda, M. (2006) *A New Philosophy of Society*, London: Continuum.

Deleuze, Gilles (2005) *Francis Bacon*, trans. Daniel W. Smith, London: Continuum.

Deleuze, G. and Guattari, F. (1984) *Anti-Oedipus: Capitalism and Schizophrenia*, trans. R. Hurley, M. Seem and H. R. Lane, London: Athlone Press.

Deleuze, G. and Guattari, F. (1988) *A Thousand Plateaus*, trans. B. Massumi, London: Althone Press.

Devitt, K. and Roker, D. (2009) 'The Role of Mobile Phones in Family Communication', *Children and Society* 23(3): 189–202.

Doogan, K. (2009) *New Capitalism?* Cambridge: Polity.

Donald, B., Gertler, M.S. and Tyler, P. (2013) 'Creative after the Crash', *Cambridge Journal of Regions, Economy and Society* 6(1): 3–21

Drache, D. (2008) *Defiant Publics*, Cambridge: Polity Press.

Drucker, P. (1970) *Technology, Management and Society*, London: Heinemann.

Drucker, P. (1971) *The Age of Discontinuity*, London: Pan Books.

Drucker, P. (1993a) *The Practice of Management*, New York: HarperCollins.

Drucker, P. (1993b) *Post-Capitalist Society*, Harper Business: New York.

du Gay, P. (ed.) (1997) *Production of Cultures, Cultures of Production*, London: Sage.

Duménil, G. and Lévy, D. (2011) *The Crisis of Neoliberalism*, Cambridge: Harvard University Press.

Dunn, B. (2009) *Global Political Economy*, London: Pluto.

Dyer-Witheford, N. (1999) *Cyber-Marx: Cycles and Circuits of Struggle in High-Technology Capitalism*, Urbana and Chicago: University of Illinois Press.

Eisenschitz, A. (2008) 'Town Planning, Planning Theory and Social Reform', *International Planning Studies* 13(2): 133–49.

Elliot, L. and Atkinson, D. (2012) *Going South*, London: Palgrave.

Engelbrecht, H-J. (2009) 'Pathological Knowledge-Based Economies: Towards a Knowledge-Based Economy Perspective on the Current Crisis', *Prometheus* 27(4): 403–14.

English Housing Survey (2013) 'Headline Report 2011–12', *Department for Communitiesand Local Government* at: https://www.gov.uk/government/uploads/system/uploads/attachment_data/file/211288/EHS_Headline_Report_2011–12.pdf (accessed 27 August 2013).

Evans-Cowley, J. S. and Hollander, J. (2010) 'The New Generation of Public Participation: Internet-based Participation Tools', *Planning Practice and Research* 25(3): 397–408.

Fairclough, N. (2010) *Critical Discourse Analysis*, Longman: Harlow.

Fairclough, N., Jessop, B. and Sayer, A. (2004) 'Critical Realism and Semiosis' in J. Joseph and J.M. Roberts (eds) *Realism, Discourse and Deconstruction*, London: Routledge: 23–42.

Farman, J. (2012) *Mobile Interface Theory*, London: Routledge.

Featherstone, M. (1990) *Consumer Society and Postmodernism*, London: Sage.

Fenton, N. (2012) 'The Internet and Social Networking' in J. Curran, N. Fenton and D. Freedman, *Misunderstanding the Internet*, London: Routledge: 123–48.

Fitzgerald, L.A. and Eijnatten, F.M. (2002) 'Reflections: Chaos in Organizational Change', *Journal of Organizational Change Management* 15(4): 402–11.

Fitzgerald, S.W. (2012) *Corporations and Cultural Industries*, Plymouth: Lexington Books.

Fine, B. (2002) *The World of Consumption*, second edition, London: Routledge.

Fine, B. (2005) 'From Actor-Network to Political Economy', *Capitalism, Nature, Socialism* 16(4): 91–108.

Florida, R. (2002) *The Rise of the Creative Class*, New York: Basic Books.

Florida, R. (2010) *The Great Reset*, New York: Harper.

Folkman, P., Froud, J., Johal, S. and Williams, K. (2007) 'Working for Themselves? Capital Market Intermediaries and Present Day Capitalism', *Business History* 49(4): 552–72.

Foster, C.D. (1992) *Privatization, Public Ownership and the Regulation of Natural Monopoly*, Oxford: Blackwell.

Foster, J.B. and Magdoff, F. (2009) *The Great Financial Crisis*, New York: Monthly Review Press.

Frankel, B. (1987) *The Post-Industrial Utopians*, Cambridge: Polity.

Froud, J., Sukhdev, J. and Williams, K. (2002) 'Financialisation and the Coupon Pool', *Capital and Class* 78(Autumn): 119–51.

Fuchs, C. (2008) *Internet and Society*, London: Routledge.

Fuchs, C. (2010) 'Labor in Informational Capitalism and on the Internet', *The Information Society* 26(3): 179–96.

Fuchs, C. (2011) *Foundations of Critical Media Studies*, London: Routledge.

Gamble, P.R. and Blackwell, J. (2001) *Knowledge Management*, London: Kogan Page.

Garrahan and Stewart (1992) *The Nissan Enigma*, London: Mansell.

Geser, H. (2006) 'Is the Cell Phone Undermining the Social Order? Understanding Mobile Technology from a Sociological Perspective', *Knowledge, Technology and Policy* 19(1): 8–18.

George, S. (2000) 'A Short History of Neoliberalism: Twenty Years of Elite Economics and Emerging Opportunities for Structural Change' in W. Bello, N. Bullard and K. Malhotra (eds) *Global Finance*, London: Zed: 27–35.

Giddens, A. (1984) *The Constitution of Society*, Cambridge: Polity.

Giddens, A. (1990) *Consequences of Modernity*, Cambridge: Polity.

Giddens, A. (1991) *Modernity and Self-Identity*, Cambridge: Polity.

Giddens, A. (1995) *A Contemporary Critique of Historical Materialism*, second edition, Basingstoke, Hants: Palgrave.

Gleick, J. (1997) *Chaos: Making a New Science*, London: Vintage.

Glinavos, I. (2008) 'Neoliberal Law: Unintended Consequences of Market-Friendly Law Reforms', *Third World Quarterly* 29(6): 1087–99.

Glyn, A. (2006) *Capitalism Unleashed*, Oxford: Oxford University Press.

Godin, B. (2006) 'The Knowledge-Based Economy: Conceptual Framework or Buzzword?' *Journal of Technology Transfer* 31(1): 17–30.

Gramsci, A. (1986) *Selections from Prison Notebooks*, ed. Q. Hoare and G. Nowell-Smith, London: Lawrence and Wishart.

Granovetter, M. (1973) 'The Strength of Weak Ties', *American Journal of Sociology* 78(6): 1360–80.

Green, E.N. (2010) *Anywhere*, New York: McGraw-Hill.

Green, N. and Haddon, L. (2009) *Mobile Communications*, Oxford: Berg.

Hague, B.N. and Loader, B.A. (1999) 'Digital Democracy: An Introduction' in B.N. Hague and B.D. Loader (eds) *Digital Democracy*, London: Routledge: 3–22.

Hall, S. (1988) *The Hard Road to Renewal*, London: Verso.

Hall, S. (2009) 'Financialised Elites and the Changing Nature of Finance Capitalism: Investment Bankers in London's Financial District', *Competition and Change* 13(2): 173–89.

Hannam, K., Sheller, M. and Urry, J. (2006) 'Editorial: Mobilities, Immobilities and Moorings', *Mobilities* 1(1): 1–22.

Hardt, M. and Negri, A. (2000) *Empire*, Cambridge: Harvard University Press.

Hardt, M. and Negri, A. (2004) *Multitude*, New York: Penguin.

Hardt, M. and Negri, A. (2009) *Commonwealth*, Cambridge: Harvard University Press.

Hart-Landsberg, M. (2013) *Capitalist Globalization*, New York: Monthly Review Press.

Harrison, M. and Reeve, K. (2002) 'Social Welfare Movements and Collective Action: Lessons from Two UK Housing Cases', *Housing Studies* 17(5): 755–71.

Harvey, D. (2005) *Neoliberalism: A Brief History*, Oxford: Oxford University Press.

Harvey, D. (2013) *A Companion to Marx's* Capital, Volume 2, London: Verso.

Hatt, K. (2009) 'Considering Complexity: Toward a Strategy for Non-Linear Analysis', *Canadian Journal of Sociology* 34(2): 313–47.

Hay, C. (1992) 'Housing Policy in Transition: From the Post-War Settlement towards a "Thatcherite" Hegemony', *Capital and Class*, 46(Spring): 27–64.

Hayes, N.K. (1991) 'Introduction: Complex Dynamics in Literature and Science' in N.K. Hayes (ed.) *Chaos and Order*, Chicago: University of Chicago Press: 1–33.

Henwood, D. (1995) 'Info Fetishism' in J. Brooks and I. Boal (eds) *Resisting the Virtual Life*, San Francisco: City Lights: 163–72.

Henwood, D. (2003) *After the New Economy*, New York: The New Press.

Holloway, J. and Picciotto, S. (eds) (1978) *State and Capital*, London: Edward Arnold.

Holtgrewe, U. (2014) 'New New Technologies: The Future and the Present of Work in Information and Communication Technology', *New Technology, Work and Employment* 29(1): 9–24.

Hope, W. (2010) 'Time, Communication, and Financial Collapse', *International Journal of Communication* 4: 649–69.

Huczynski, A. (2006) *Management Gurus*, revised edition, London: Routledge.

Inglehart, R. (1971) 'The Silent Revolution in Europe', *The American Political Science Review* 65(4): 991–1017.

Jessop, B. (1982) *The Capitalist State*, Oxford: Martin Robertson.

Jessop, B. (1990) *State Theory*, Cambridge: Polity.

Jessop, B. (2000) 'The State and the Contradictions of the Knowledge-Driven Economy' in J. Bryson, P. W. Daniels, N. Henry and J. Pollard (eds) *Knowledge, Space, Economy*, London: Routledge: 63–78.

Jessop, B. (2004) 'Critical Semiotic Analysis and Cultural Political Economy', *Critical Discourse Analysis* 1(2): 159–74.

Jessop, B. (2005) 'Cultural Political Economy, the Knowledge-Based Economy, and the State' in A. Barry and D. Slater (eds) *The Technological Economy*, London: Routledge: 144–66.

Jessop, B. (2010) 'From Hegemony to Crisis? The Continuing Ecological Dominance of Neoliberalism' in K. Birch and V. Mykhnenko (eds) *The Rise and Fall of Neoliberalism*, London: Zed: 171–87.

Jessop, B. (2012) 'A Cultural Political Economy of Competitiveness: And its Implications for Higher Education' in D.W. Livingstone and D. Guile (eds) *The Knowledge Economy and Lifelong Learning*, Rotterdam: Sense Publications: 57–83.

Jessop, B., Bonnett, K., Bromley, S. and Ling, T. (1988) *Thatcherism: A Tale of Two Nations*, Cambridge: Polity.

Jessop, J. (2002) *The Future of the Capitalist State*, Cambridge: Polity.

Johnson, N. (2007) *Two's Company, Three is Complexity*, London: Oneworld.

Jones, M. (2008) 'Recovering a Sense of Political Economy', *Political Geography* 27(4): 377–99.

Jones, P. E. and Collins, C. (2006) 'Political Analysis versus Critical Discourse Analysis in the Treatment of Ideology: Some Implications for the Study of Communications', *Atlantic Journal of Communication* 14(1 and 2): 28–50.

Kaletsky, A. (2010) *Capitalism 4.0*, London: Bloomsbury.

Kapferer, J-N. (2000) *Strategic Brand Management*, second edition, London: Kogan Page Ltd.

Katz, J. and Sugiyama (2006) 'Mobile Phones as Fashion Statements: Evidence from Student Surveys in the US and Japan', *New Media and Society* 8(2): 321–37.

Kay, J.B. and Salter, L. (2013) 'Framing the Cuts: An Analysis of the BBC's Discursive Framing of the ConDem Cuts Agenda', *Journalism*, early view: 1–19.

Kemple, T. (2013) 'The Eye/I of Capital: Classical Theoretical Perspectives on the Spectral Economies of Late Capitalism' in T. Dufresne and C. Sacchetti (eds) *The Economy as Cultural System*, London: Bloomsbury.

Kiely, R (2005) *Empire in the Age of Globalisation*, London: Pluto.

Kirsch, S. and Mitchell, D. (2004) 'The Nature of Things: Dead Labor, Nonhuman Actors, and the Persistence of Marxism', *Antipode* 36(4): 687–705.

Krippner, G.R. (2011) *Capitalizing on Crisis*, Cambridge: Harvard University Press.

Kregel, J. (2008) 'Minsky's Cushions of Safety: Systemic Risk and the Crisis in the US Subprime Mortgage Market', *The Levy Economics Institute of Bard College: Public Policy Brief* no. 93: 1–29.

Kumar, K. (1978) *Prophecy and Progress: The Sociology of Industrial and Post-Industrial*, London, Allen Lane: The Penguin Press.

Lacohée, H., Wakeford, N. and Pearson, I. (2003) 'A Social History of the Mobile Telephone with a View to its Future', *BT Technology Journal* 21(3): 203–11.

Laguerre, M.S. (2004) 'Virtual Time: The Processuality of the Cyberweek', *Information, Communication and Society* 7(2): 223–47.

Lange, P.G. (2007) 'Publicly Private and Privately Public: Social Networking on YouTube', *Journal of Computer-Mediated Communication* 13(1): 361–80.

Langley, P. (2008) *The Everyday Life of Global Finance*, Oxford: Oxford University Press.

Langley, P. (2013) 'Equipping Entrepreneurs: Consuming Credit and Credit Scores', *Consumption, Markets and Culture* early view: 1–20.

Lapavitsas, C. (2013) *Profiting without Producing*, London: Verso.

Lapavitsas, C. and Dos Santos, P.L. (2008) 'Globalization and Contemporary Banking: On the Impact of New Technology', *Contributions to Political Economy* 27(1): 31–56.

Larrain, J. (1983) *Marxism and Ideology*, London: Macmillan.

Lash, S. (2002) *Critique of Information*, London: Sage.

Lash, S. (2007) 'Power after Hegemony: Cultural Studies in Mutation', *Theory, Culture and Society* 24(3): 55–78.

Lash, S. (2011) *Intensive Culture*, London: Sage.

Lash, S. and Urry, J. (1987) *The End of Organised Capitalism*, Cambridge: Polity.

Lash, S. and Urry, J. (1994) *Economies of Signs and Space*, London: Sage.

Latour, B. (2005) *Reassembling the Social*, Oxford: Oxford University Press.

Law, J. (1991) 'Power, Discretion and Strategy' in J. Law (ed.) *A Sociology of Monsters*, London: Routledge: 165–91.

Law, J. (1999) 'After ANT: Complexity, Naming and Topology' in J. Law and J. Hassard (eds) *Actor Network Theory and After*, Oxford: Blackwell: 1–15.

Lazonick, W. and O'Sullivan, M (2000) 'Maximizing Shareholder Value: A New Ideology for Corporate Governance', *Economy and Society* 29(1): 13–35.

Lazzarato, M. (2012) *The Making of the Indebted Man*, Los Angeles, CA: Semiotext(e).

Lee, D-H. (2009) 'Mobile Snapshots and Private/Public Boundaries', *Knowledge, Technology and Policy* 22(3): 161–71.

Lee, M. (2012) 'Time and the Political Economy of Financial Television', *Journal of Communication Inquiry* 36(4): 322–39.

Leys, C. (1989) *Politics in Britain*, revised edition, London: Verso.

Leys, C. (2001) *Market-Driven Politics*, London: Verso.

Lindsay, C., McQuaid, R.W. and Dutton, M. (2008) 'Inter-Agency Cooperation and New Approaches to Employability', *Social Policy and Administration* 42(7): 715–32.

Linell, P. (2009) *Rethinking Language, Mind, and World Dialogically*, Charlotte: Information Age Publishing.

Lowe, S.G, Searle, B.A. and Smith, S.J. (2011) 'From Housing Wealth to Mortgage Debt: The Emergence of Britain's Asset-Shaped Welfare State', *Social Policy and Society* 11(1): 105–16.

Macartney, H. (2011) 'Finance Unravelled: A Historical Materialist Analysis of EU Public Policy', *Competition and Change* 15(1): 48–70.

MacKenzie, D. (2007a) 'Is Economics Performative? Option Theory and the Construction of Derivatives Markets' in D. Mackenzie, F. Muniesa and L. Siu (eds) *Do Economists Make Markets?* Princeton: Princeton University Press: 54–86.

MacKenzie, D. (2007b) 'The Material Production of Virtuality: Innovation, Cultural Geography and Facticity in Derivatives Markets', *Economy and Society* 36(3): 355–76.

MacKenzie, D. (2011) 'The Credit Crisis as a Problem in the Sociology of Knowledge', *American Journal of Sociology* 116(6): 1778–1841.

McKeown, P. (2009) *Information Technology and the Networked Economy*, second edition, Boston: Thomson Course Technology Publishing.

'Manifesto for New Times' (1989) in S. Hall and M. Jacques (eds) *New Times*, London: Lawrence and Wishart: 23–37.

Mansell, R. (2012) *Imagining the Internet*, Oxford: Oxford University Press.

Manson, S. M. (2001) 'Simplifying Complexity: A Review of Complexity Theory', *Geoforum* 32: 405–13.

Manzi, T. (2007) 'Cultural Theory and the Dynamics of Organizational Change: The Response of Housing Associations in London to the *Housing Act 1988*', *Housing, Theory and Society* 24(4): 251–71.

Marazzi, C. (2010) 'The Violence of Financial Capitalism' in A. Fumagalli and M. Mezzadra (eds) *Crisis in the Global Economy*, Los Angeles, CA: Semiotext(e): 17–60.

Marazzi, C. (2011) *Capital and Affects*, trans. G. Mecchia, Los Angeles: Semiotext(e).

Martin, R. (2002) *The Financialization of Daily Life*, Philadelphia: Temple University Press.

Martin, R. (2007) 'Making Sense of the New Economy? Realities, Myths and Geographies' in P. Daniels, A. Leyshon, M. Bradshaw and J. Beaverstock (eds) *Geographies of the New Economy*, London: Routledge: 15–48.

Marx, K. (1973) *Grundrisse*, London: Pelican.

Marx, K. (1988) *Capital*, vol. 1, London: Penguin.

Marx, K. (1992) *Capital*, vol 2, London: Penguin.

Micklethwaite, J. and Wooldridge, A. (1997) *The Witch Doctors*, London: Mandarin.

Milbourne, L. and Cushman, M. (2012) 'From the Third Sector to the Big Society: How Changing UK Government Policies have Eroded Third Sector Trust', *Voluntas* 24(2): 485–508

Miller, V. (2011) *Understanding Digital Culture*, London: Sage.

Mirowski, P. (2013) *Never Let a Serious Crisis Go to Waste*, London: Verso.

Mitchell, M. (2009) *Complexity*, Oxford: Oxford University Press.

Mittelman, J.H. (2004) 'Ideologies and the Globalization Agenda' in M. B. Steger (ed.) *Rethinking Globalism*, New York: Rowan and Littlefield: 15–26.

Montgomerie, J. (2006) 'Financialisation of the American Credit Card Industry', *Competition and Change* 10(3): 301–19.

Montgomerie, J. (2008) 'Bridging the Critical Divide: Global Finance, Financialisation and Contemporary Capitalism', *Contemporary Politics* 14(3): 233–52.

Montgomerie, J. (2009) 'The Pursuit of (Past) Happiness? Middle-Class Indebtedness and American Financialisation', *New Political Economy* 14(1): 1–24.

Mosco, V. (2004) *The Digital Sublime*, Cambridge: The MIT Press.

Moseley, F. (1988) 'The Increase of Unproductive Labor in the Postwar U.S. Economy', *Review of Radical Political Economics* 20(2 and 3): 100–6.

Mulholland, K. (2004) 'Workplace Resistance in an Irish Call Centre: Slammin', Scammin', Smokin' an' Leavin'', *Work, Employment and Society* 18(4): 709–24.

Munro, R. (1999) 'Power and Discretion: Membership Work in the Time of Technology', *Organization* 6(3): 429–50.

Naisbitt, J. (1982) *Megatrends: Ten New Directions Transforming Our Lives*, London: Macdonald and Co.

Negri, A. (1989) *The Politics of Subversion*, Cambridge: Polity.

Negri, A. (1991) *Marx beyond Marx*, London: Pluto.

Negri, A. (1996) 'Twenty Theses on Marx: Interpretation of the Class Situation Today' in S. Makdisi, C. Casarino and R.E. Karl (eds) *Marxism Beyond Marxism*, London: Routledge: 149–80.

Negroponte, N. (1995) *Being Digital*, London: Coronet.

Nesvetailova, A. (2005) 'United in Debt: Towards a Global Crisis of Debt-Driven Finance?' *Science and Society* 69(3): 396–419.

Neubauer,R. (2011) 'Neoliberalism in the Information Age, or Vice Versa? Global Citizenship, Technology, and Hegemonic Ideology', *tripleC* 9(2): 195–230.

Newman, J. and Clarke, J. (2009) *Publics, Politics and Power*, London: Sage.

Nora, S. and Minc, A. (1980) *The Computerization of Society*, Cambridge: The MIT Press.

Oakland, J.S. (1989) *Total Quality Management*, Oxford: Butterworth-Heinemann.

O'Connor, J. (2009) 'Creative Industries: A New Direction?' *International Journal of Cultural Policy* 15(4): 387–402.

Ohmae, K. (1994) *The Borderless World*, London: Harper Collins.

Office for National Statistics [ONS] (2013) 'A Century of Home Ownership and Renting in England and Wales', April, at: http://www.ons.gov.uk/ons/rel/census/2011-census-analysis/a-century-of-home-ownership-and-renting-in-england-and-wales/short-story-on-housing.html (accessed 27 August 2013).

Orhangazi, Ö. (2008) 'Financialisation and Capital Accumulation in the Non-financial Corporate Sector: A Theoretical and Empirical Investigation on the US Economy: 1973–2003', *Cambridge Journal of Economics*, 32(6): 863–86.

O'Sullivan, D. (2004) 'Complexity Science and Human Geography', *Transactions of the Institute of British Geographers* 29: 282–95.

Papows, J. (1999) *Enterprise.com*, London: Nicholas Brealey Publishing.

Parker, M. (2000) *Against Management*, Cambridge: Polity.

Pascale, R., Millemann, M. and Gioja, L. (2000) *Surfing the Edge of Chaos*, New York: Three Rivers.

Peck, J. (2010) *Constructions of Neoliberal Reason*, Oxford: Oxford University Press.

Perez, C. (2009) 'The Double Bubble at the Turn of the Century: Technological Roots and Structural Implications', *Cambridge Journal of Economics* 33(4): 779–805.

Peters, T. (1987) *Thriving on Chaos*, London: Book Club Associates.

Peters, T. J. and Waterman, R. H. (1982) *In Search of Excellence*, New York: Harper and Row.

Pollin, R. (2003) *Contours of Descent*, London: Verso.

Potts, J., Hartley, J., Banks, J., Burgess, J., Cobcroft, R., Cunningham, S. and Montgomery, L. (2008) 'Consumer Co-creation and Situated Creativity', *Industry and Innovation*, 15(5): 459–74.

Poulantzas, N. (2000) *State, Power, Socialism*, new edition, trans. P. Camiller, London: Verso.

Pratt, A.C. (2011) 'The Cultural Contradictions of the Creative City', *City, Culture and Society* 2(3): 123–30.

Prigogine, I. and Stengers, I. (1984) *Order out of Chaos*, London: Flamingo.

Protevi, J. (2012) 'Deleuze and Life' in H. Somers-Hall and D. W Smith (eds.) *The Cambridge Companion to Deleuze*, Cambridge: Cambridge University Press: 239–64.

Pryke, M. and du Gay, P. (2007) 'Take an Issue: Cultural Economy and Finance', *Economy and Society* 36(1): 339–54.

Rainnie, A. (1991) 'Just-in-Time, Sub-Contracting and the Small Firm', *Work, Employment and Society* 5(3): 353–75.

Ray, L. and Sayer, A. (1999) 'Introduction' in L. Ray and A. Sayer (ed.) *Culture and the Economy After the Cultural Turn*, London: Sage: 1–24.

Reed, A. (2003) *Capitalism is Dead: Peoplism Rules*, Berkshire, Maidenhead: McGraw-Hill Professional.

Rettie, R. (2009) 'Mobile Phone Communication: Extending Goffman to Mediated Interaction', *Sociology* 43(2): 421–38.

Reveley, J. (2013) 'The Exploitative Web: Misuses of Marx in Critical Social Media Studies', *Science and Society* 77(4): 512–35.

Ridderstråle, J. and Nordström, K. (2008) *Funky Business Forever*, third edition, London: Prentice Hall and Financial Times.

Rifkin, J. (1995) *The End of Work*, G.P. Putnam and Sons: New York.

Roberts, J.M. (2014) *New Media and Public Activism*, Bristol: Policy Press.

Roberts, J.M. and Joseph, J. (2014) 'Beyond Flows, Fluids and Networks: Social Theory and the Fetishism of the Global Economy', *New Political Economy*, early view.

Ruccio, D. (2003) 'Globalization and Imperialism', *Rethinking Marxism* 15(1): 75–94.

Samuel, R. and Thompson, P. (eds) (1990) *The Myths We Live By*, London: Routledge.

Sayer, A. (1989) 'Postfordism in Question', *International Journal of Urban and Regional Research* 13(4): 666–95.

Sayer, A. and Walker, R. (1992) *The New Social Economy*, Oxford: Blackwell.

Scase, R. (2007) *Global Remix*, London: Kogan Page.

Schroeder, R. (2010) 'Mobile Phones and the Inexorable Advance of Multimodal Connectedness', *New Media and Society* 12(1): 75–90.

Scott, B. (2013) *The Heretic's Guide to Global Finance*, London: Pluto.

Sheller, M. and Urry, J. (2003) 'Mobile Transformations of "Public" and "Private" life', *Theory, Culture and Society* 20(3): 107–25.

Shelter (2013) 'Shelter Reveals Unaffordable Housing Costs', February, at: http://england.shelter.org.uk/news/february_2013/shelter_reveals_unaffordable_housing_costs (accessed 27 August 2013).

Seifert, R. and Mather, K. (2013) 'Neo-Liberalism at Work: A Case Study of the Reform of the Emergency Services in the UK', *Review of Radical Political Economics* 45(4): 456–62.

Slater, T. (2008) '"A Literal Necessity to be Re-Placed": A Rejoinder to the Gentrification Debate', *International Journal of Urban and Regional Research* 32(1): 212–23.

Sloop, J. M. and Gunn, J. (2010) 'Status Control: An Admonition Concerning the Publicized Privacy of Social Networking', *The Communication Review* 13(4): 289–308.

Smith, N. (2010) *Uneven Development*, third edition, London: Verso.

Smith, S.J. and Searle, B.A. (2008) 'Dematerialising Money? Observations on the Flow of Wealth from Housing to Other Things', *Housing Studies* 23(1): 21–43.

Soederberg, S. (2013) 'The US Debtfare State and the Credit Card Industry: Forging Spaces of Dispossession', *Antipode* 45(2): 493–512.

Somers, M.R. (1993) 'Citizenship and the Place of the Public Sphere: Law, Community, and Political Culture in the Transition to Democracy', *American Sociological Review* 58(5): 587–620.

Sotiropoulos, D.P., Milios, J., and Lapatsioras, S. (2013) *A Political Economy of Contemporary Capitalism and its Crisis*, London: Routledge.

Stacey, R.D. (2010) *Complexity and Organizational Reality*, London: Routledge.

Stiegler, B. (2010) *For a New Critique of Political Economy*, Cambridge: Polity.

Stewart, P. (1998) 'Out of Chaos Comes Order: From Japanization to Lean Production: A Critical Commentary', *Employee Relations* 20(3): 213–23.

Sum, N-L (2009) 'The Production of Hegemonic Policy Discourses: "Competitiveness" as a Knowledge Brand and its (Re-)Contextualizations', *Critical Policy Studies* 3(2): 184–203.

Sum, N-L. (2013) 'A Cultural Political Economy: (Trans)national Imaginaries of "BRIC" and Subaltern Groups in China', *Economy and Society* 42(4): 543–70.

Szerszynski, B. and Urry, J. (2006) 'Visuality, Mobility and the Cosmopolitan: Inhabiting the World from Afar', *The British Journal of Sociology* 57(1): 113–31.

Tabb, W.K. (2005) 'Capital, Class and the State in the Global Political Economy', *Globalizations*, 2(1): 47–60.

Tapscott, D. and Williams, A.D. (2008) *Wikinomics*, revised edition, London: Atlantic Books.

Terranova, T. (2004) *Network Culture*, London: Pluto.

Terranova, T. (2010) 'New Economy, Financialization and Social Production in the Web 2.0' in A. Fumagalli and M. Mezzadra (eds) *Crisis in the Global Economy*, Los Angeles, CA: Semiotext(e): 153–70.

The Guardian (2006) 'Labour's £2bn Army of Consultants', 2 September.

Thompson, P. and Harley, B. (2012) 'Beneath the Radar? A Critical Realist Analysis of "The Knowledge Economy" and "Shareholder Value" as Competing Discourses', *Organization Studies* 33(10): 1363–81.

Thrift, N. (2005) *Knowing Capitalism*, London: Sage.

Tickell, A. and Peck, J. (2003), 'Making Global Rules: Globalisation or Neoliberalisation' in J. Peck and H. Wai-chung Yeung (eds.), *Remaking the Global Economy*, London: Sage: 163–81.

Tomaney, J. (1994) 'A New Paradigm of Work Organization and Technology?' in A. Amin (ed.) *Post-Fordism: A Reader*, Oxford: Blackwell: 157–94.

Tomlinson, J. (2012) 'Thatcher, Monetarism and the Politics of Inflation' in B. Jackson and R. Saunders (eds) *Making Thatcher's Britain*, Cambridge: Cambridge University Press: 62–77.

Touraine, A. (1974) *The Post-Industrial Society*, London: Wildwood House Ltd.

Tsekeris, C. (2010) 'Chaos and Unpredictability in Social Thought: General Considerations and Perspectives', *Sociologija. Mintis ir veiksmas* 27(2): 34–47.

Urry, J. (2000) *Sociology beyond Societies*, London: Routledge.

Urry, J. (2003) *Global Complexity*, Cambridge: Polity.

Van Dijk, J.A.G.M. (2012) *The Network Society*, third edition, London: Sage.

Vidal, M. (2007) 'Lean Production, Worker Empowerment, and Job Satisfaction: A Qualitative Analysis and Critique', *Critical Sociology* 33(1–2): 247–78.

Vidal, M. (2011) 'Reworking Postfordism: Labor Process versus Employment Relations', *Sociology Compass* 5(4): 273–86.

Virno, P. (2004) *A Grammar of the Multitude*, New York: Semiotext(e).

Vivant, E. (2013) 'Creatives in the City: Urban Contradictions of the Creative City', *City, Culture and Society* 4(2): 57–63.

Volkmer, I. (2007) 'Governing the "Spatial Reach"? Spheres of Influence and Global Media Policy', *International Journal of Communication* 1: 56–73.

Voloshinov, V.N. (1973) *Marxism and the Philosophy of Language*, trans. L. Matejka and I.R. Titunik, London: Seminar Press.

Wacquant, L. (2012) 'Three Steps to a Historical Anthropology of Actually Existing Neoliberalism', *Social Anthropology* 20(1): 66–79.

Walby, S. (2009) *Globalization and Inequalities*, London: Sage.

Warhurst, C. (2008) 'The Knowledge Economy, Skills and Government Labour Market Intervention', *Policy Studies* 29(1): 71–86.

Warhurst, C., Thompson, P. and Nickson, D. (2009) 'Labor Process Theory: Putting the Materialism Back into the Meaning of Service Work' in M. Korczynski and C.L. Macdonald (eds) *Service Work: Critical Perspectives*, London: Routledge: 91–112.

Watts, D. (2004) *Six Degrees*, London: Vintage.

Webster, F. (2006) *Theories of the Information Society*, third edition, London: Routledge.

Wellman, B. (2001) 'Physical Space and Cyberspace: The Rise of Personalized Networking', *International Journal of Urban and Regional Research* 25(2): 227–52.

Witheford, N. (1994) 'Autonomist Marxism and the Information Society', *Capital and Class* 52(Spring): 85–125.

Williams, K., Cutler, T., Williams, J. and Haslam, C. (1987) 'The End of Mass Production?' *Economy and Society* 16(3): 405–39.

Wood, P. (2006) 'Urban Development and Knowledge-Intensive Business Services: Too Many Unanswered Questions?' *Growth and Change* 37(3): 335–61.

Žižek, S. (2002) *For They Know Not What They Do*, second edition, London: Verso.

Žižek, S. (2008) *Violence*, London: Profile Books.

Žižek, S. (2009) *First as Tragedy, then as Farce*, London: Verso.

Index

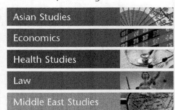